THE
OLYNTHIAC SPEECHES
OF
DEMOSTHENES

THE
OLYNTHIAC SPEECHES
OF
DEMOSTHENES

BY

J. M. MACGREGOR

Cambridge:
at the University Press
1950

CAMBRIDGE UNIVERSITY PRESS
Cambridge, New York, Melbourne, Madrid, Cape Town,
Singapore, São Paulo, Delhi, Mexico City

Cambridge University Press
The Edinburgh Building, Cambridge CB2 8RU, UK

Published in the United States of America by Cambridge University Press, New York

www.cambridge.org
Information on this title: www.cambridge.org/9781107620179

First edition 1915
First published 1915
Reprinted 1926, 1940, 1950
First paperback edition 2013

A catalogue record for this publication is available from the British Library

ISBN 978-1-107-62017-9 Paperback

PREFACE

THE present edition has been prepared at the request of the Syndics of the University Press to whom an apology for its tardy appearance is due.

In the preparation of the text I have used that of Blass as a basis; but I have divided the speeches into paragraphs to accord with my own analysis of their contents, and have everywhere pursued a much closer adherence to the MSS. In particular I have abstained from elisions and transpositions designed solely to remove hiatus or a sequence of short syllables, since in the great majority of instances these are to be found where a natural pause on the part of the speaker would avoid all difficulty in recitation. Nor have I thought it necessary to resort to prodelision (e.g. ἢ ᾽κεῖ) or crasis (τοὔργον), although it should be understood that in reading the two sounds merge into each other.

For the matter of the *Introduction* I have relied on the writings of Demosthenes and his contemporaries and on Plutarch's *Life*. I have had recourse also to the histories of Grote, Holm and Bury; to Schaefer's *Demosthenes and his time*; to Butcher's monograph, the insight and inspiration of which are scarcely to be gauged by its modest exterior; and to works of general reference such as Gilbert's *Antiquities*. Mr Pickard-Cambridge's admirably balanced volume on Demosthenes appeared when my own introduction was already written; but I have been able to consult it on some particulars in revising the proof.

In regard to the notes I have had the advantage of consulting numerous editions—in particular those of Weil, Sandys, Heslop, and Abbott and Matheson —as well as the translations of Kennedy and Pickard-Cambridge, the latter of whom has in his *Introduction* (vol. I. pp. 28-9) a brief but illuminating account of Demosthenes' chief oratorical qualities.

To my colleague Mr Caspari I am indebted for his kindness in reading the proofs of the *Introduction* and *Appendices* and sending me some criticisms thereon. My thanks are also due to the Readers of the University Press.

I have aimed at showing these speeches in their due relation to Demosthenes' whole career and at providing the student with the means for an effective understanding of them. In so far as that aim has not been achieved I alone am to blame.

J. M. M.

St John's Wood,
May 1915.

CONTENTS

INTRODUCTION   **PAGE**

THE STORY OF DEMOSTHENES: ix–xliv

    (i)   Birth, Education and Early Manhood   ix

    (ii)   The Uprising of Macedon .   .   .   xv

    (iii) From the First Philippic to the Peace .   xxi

    (iv) From the Peace to Chaeroneia .   .   xxix

    (v)   The Triumph of Macedon   .   .   xxxvi

    (vi) The Last Effort   xlii

ANALYSIS OF THE SPEECHES: xlv–l

    Olynthiac i.   xlvi

    Olynthiac ii.   xlvii

    Olynthiac iii.   xlviii

THE SOURCES OF THE TEXT   .   .   .   l–lii

TEXT   1–31

NOTES   32–89

APPENDIX A   90

    „   B   93

INDEX A   97

    „   B   99

Λαμπρὸς μὲν τῷ μεγέθει, σφοδρὸς δὲ τῷ πνεύματι, σωφρον-
έστατος δὲ τῶν ὀνομάτων καὶ τῶν ιοημάτων τὴν ἐγκράτειαν,
ποικιλώτατος δ' ἐναλλαγαῖς σχημάτων.

LUCIAN, *Encomium Demosthenis* 14.

'Ωσπερεὶ καταβροντᾷ καὶ καταφέγγει τοὺς ἀπ' αἰῶνος ῥήτορας,
καὶ θᾶττον ἄν τις κεραυνοῖς φερομένοις ἀντανοῖξαι τὰ ὄμματα δύναιτο
ἢ ἀντοφθαλμῆσαι τοῖς ἐπαλλήλοις ἐκείνου πάθεσιν.

<LONGINUS>, *de Sublimitate* 34.

INTRODUCTION

THE STORY OF DEMOSTHENES

(i) *Birth, Education and Early Manhood.*

DEMOSTHENES, the son of Demosthenes, of the deme
Paeania, situate to the south of Athens on the   Birth and
eastern slope of Mt Hymettus, was born about   Family.
the year 384 B.C. His father was a man of good standing and
considerable wealth, the owner of two factories, the one for the
manufacture of cutlery[1] and the other for that of couches. His
mother was Cleobule, daughter of a certain Gylon, who had
fled from Athens to escape death for treason and had married
a Scythian lady[2]. The elder Demosthenes died when his son
was seven years old, leaving him, together with a sister two
years younger, in the charge of three guardians, Aphobus, Onetor
and Therippides.

A thin and sickly child, the future orator was not, it is said,
subjected to the regular physical exercises of the free-born

---

[1] Hence the orator was nicknamed "the cutler" (ὁ μαχαιροποιός).

[2] This is the account of Aeschines, the opponent of Demosthenes,
who does not controvert the statement. The offence of Gylon was the
betrayal of Nymphaeum, a colony of Miletus in the Tauric Chersonese,
tributary to Athens. The fiery vehemence of Demosthenes has been
ascribed to the northern strain in his blood ; but others believe Gylon's
wife to have been the daughter of a Greek settled in the region of the
Crimea, and the sentence passed upon him to have been less severe than
one of death. *Vide* Aeschines, *Against Ctesiphon* 171-2 ; Demosthenes
Against Aphobus ii. 2-3.

Greek boy; but he himself assures us that he received the liberal training proper to one in his position[1]. His ambition

Boyish am-bition to be an orator. to become an orator was, the story runs, fired by a *cause célèbre* of the day at which he contrived to be present. Callistratus, the distinguished statesman, general and orator, was on trial for his life[2], and Demosthenes heard his paedagogus arranging with others to witness the scene in the court. He succeeded in gaining permission to accompany them, and the servants of the court, who were intimate with the paedagogus and his friends, provided them with a good position. The boy's heart was stirred by the glory attendant upon the accused's successful defence; but still more deeply impressed was he by the power of an eloquence which could thus charm hostility and dominate opposition. Abandoning all other pursuits he devoted himself

A pupil of Isaeus. to the study of oratory, taking for his teacher Isaeus[3], a master of cogent reasoning and a vigorous style, whose influence can be clearly traced in the earlier speeches of his pupil[4].

At his death the elder Demosthenes had left an estate estimated as worth more than 14 talents. With good manage-

---

[1] *de Cor.* 312, ἐμοὶ μὲν τοίνυν ὑπῆρξεν, Αἰσχίνη, παιδὶ μὲν ὄντι φοιτᾶν εἰς τὰ προσήκοντα διδασκαλεῖα. But elsewhere (*Against Aphobus*, i. 46) he complains that his guardians' peculations had deprived him of his proper advantages. Cf. Plut. *Vit. Dem.* iv.

[2] Plutarch (*Vit. Dem.* v.) states that the trial was "concerned with Oropus." Aristotle (*Rhet.* i. 7) mentions an attack by Leodamas upon Callistratus for advice which he had given. It is generally assumed that this "advice" was concerned with the affairs of Oropus; that the prosecution of Leodamas took the form of an impeachment before the people (ἐν τῷ δήμῳ); and that it occurred in 365 B.C. when Demosthenes was 19 years old.

[3] Cf. Jebb, *Attic Orators*, ii. 301 ff. It is suggested (Plut. *Vit. Dem.* v.) that Demosthenes did not have recourse to Isocrates, the famous teacher of the day, because of inability to pay the high fee, 10 minae; another view was that Demosthenes was attracted by the peculiar virtues of Isaeus' style.

[4] *Vide* the speeches *Against Aphobus* and *Against Onetor*.

ment, the orator urges, its value might have been more than doubled, but owing to the neglect and fraud of the trustees the son received but a fractional part of the amount bequeathed by the father. Smarting under this injustice Demosthenes sought to vindicate his rights at law, and found himself involved by the subter-   Prosecution of his guar-dians. fuges of his guardians in a series of prosecutions[1]. But his talent for forensic argument found employment not on his own behalf alone. Attic practice required that the plaintiff and defendant in a suit should appear in person. Accordingly one who was himself without ability to plead his cause to the best effect had recourse to another whose inclination and training fitted him for such a task, and procured from him a speech in which to present his case to the jury. This profession of speech-writing (λογογραφεῖν), which Demosthenes pursued throughout his career, not only afforded him a source of income, but provided in his early days an oppor-   The Law-courts and the Assembly. tunity for the exercise and development of his powers of reasoning and expression. It should be observed that at Athens a political issue was often involved in the trial of an individual, particularly so as the proposer of a measure was held responsible for it throughout the space of one year, and was subject during that period to an indictment for an illegal proposal (γραφὴ παρανόμων)[2]. Thus a writer of speeches for the law-courts naturally became interested in the political questions of the day[3]. It was, moreover, the position of a prominent politician, influencing the votes of the citizens and controlling the policy of the city in the Assembly at Athens, which formed the object of Demosthenes' ambition.

[1] *Vide* the speeches *Against Aphobus* and *Against Onetor.*

[2] Cf. *Ol.* iii. 10 νομοθέτας *n.* and the circumstances of the speech *On the Crown, infr.* p. xxxix.

[3] Cf. p. xiv. n. 3. Similarly at Rome the conflict of opposing parties found expression on occasion in the trial of an individual, e.g. Rabirius, on whose behalf Cicero delivered his speech *pro Rabirio* (Mommsen, iv. 458 f.) ; and political matters were introduced in forensic pleadings, e.g. the defence of the *Optimates* in Cic. *pro Sestio* §§ 96–127.

His early efforts at addressing the sovereign body of the Athenians were however attended with failure.

Early failures and physical disadvantages. Inexperienced as he was, he was confounded by the clamour of the populace, while certain physical disabilities under which he laboured as a speaker now revealed themselves all too clearly and brought about his discomfiture. His voice was weak, his articulation indistinct[1]; his shortness of breath interfered with the even flow of his speech and rendered his delivery rough and broken. Disheartened by his ill success he is said to have complained on one occasion that, while ignorant and besotted sailors[2] could obtain a hearing from the Athenians, he himself failed to secure their attention in spite of an industry and pains that had come near to ruining his physical health. Yet encouragement was not wholly lacking. A certain Eunomus, who had in his boyhood listened to Pericles, compared the young speaker's oratory to that of the great statesman of the fifth century, and ascribed his failure to his lack of hardihood both of mind and body. The distinguished actor Satyrus exhibited how much a speech can gain or lose through the manner of its delivery, by causing Demosthenes to recite a passage of poetry and then himself repeating it in a tone and manner suitable to the character to whom it belonged and the circumstances in which it was uttered[3].

Determination to succeed. Demosthenes set himself resolutely to work with a view to remedying his defects. He built, so the story runs, a subterranean chamber,

---

[1] Hence the nickname Βάτταλος ("Stammerer") to which his enemies gave a more offensive signification. Cf. Aeschines, *Against Timarchus*, 126, 131; Dem. *On the Crown*, 180.

[2] The allusion was perhaps to Demades, a very successful public speaker, who had been a sailor and was addicted to drink.

[3] The importance which Demosthenes himself attached to this is shown by a story told in Plutarch's *Life*, c. xi. A man came to seek Demosthenes' advocacy, complaining that he had been assaulted. "Nay," said Demosthenes, "*you* have not suffered anything of what you tell me." Raising his voice the other shouted, "*I* not suffered anything, Demosthenes!" "Ah," replied the orator, "*now* I hear the voice

wherein he practised speaking for two and three months together, and in order to prevent interruption of his studies, he would shave the half of his head, so that shame should make him unable to appear in public, even if he were to desire to do so. Demetrius of Phalerum[1] heard Demosthenes himself in his later years recounting how he endeavoured to improve his articulation by reciting speeches with pebbles in his mouth ; how he sought to strengthen his voice and gain control of his breathing by speaking while running and ascending hills and by delivering passages of poetry and prose without pausing to respire ; and how with a view to securing a suitable manner he used to practise the delivery of his orations before a large mirror[2].

The elaborate care which Demosthenes bestowed upon his speeches was actually made a reproach against him. Like Pericles, perhaps in imitation of the deliberate reserve which that statesman cultivated, he hardly

Care in pre-paration.

of one who has been injured and has suffered." More often quoted is the anecdote related by many authors (e.g. Cicero, *de Or.* iii. 56) that in answer to the question what was most important in oratory Demosthenes replied "Delivery"; and then in response to further questions ascribed to "Delivery" the second and third places in importance also. It was perhaps his own early difficulties that led Demosthenes to set so much store by what Bacon declared to be "that part of an Oratour which is but superficiall" (Essays, *Of Boldnesse, ad init.*). Aristotle (*Rhet.* iii. 1. 3) alludes to its importance and the lack of a scientific treatment of it (ὃ δύναμιν μὲν ἔχει μεγίστην, οὔπω δ' ἐπικεχείρηται, τὰ περὶ τὴν ὑπόκρισιν).

[1] A distinguished orator, poet, philosopher and statesman, who flourished in the closing years of the fourth century B.C.

[2] Similarly it is said (Ps.-Plut. *Vit. X Orat.* 844 E) that in order to habituate himself to the roar of the Athenian Assembly Demosthenes used to practise beside the breaking waves at Phalerum. To his success *as a speaker* (κοσμοῦντος ἅπαντα καὶ χρηματίζοντος τῇ πρεπούσῃ ὑποκρίσει ἧς δεινότατος ἀσκητὴς ἐγένετο, Diony. Hal. περὶ Δημ. δεινότητος 66) there is abundant testimony; most striking is the story of Demosthenes' rival Aeschines (Cic. *de Or.* iii. 56) who, when his recital of Demosthenes' speech *On the Crown* was received by the Rhodians with the liveliest admiration, is said to have exclaimed, "If you had heard it from his own lips!" or, according to Pliny *Ep.* ii. 3, τί δέ, εἰ αὐτοῦ τοῦ θηρίου ἠκούσατε;

ever spoke *ex tempore*, but carefully selected the times and the subjects of his harangues. In this he offered a striking contrast to his contemporary, Demades, and it was remarked that while the latter often came on the spur of the moment to the assistance of Demosthenes, when he was assailed by an outcry in the Assembly, similar service was never rendered by Demosthenes to Demades. Yet at times Demosthenes delivered an impromptu oration with convincing effect[1].

An ex tempore success. One such occasion is recorded by Plutarch[2]. A certain sophist, by name Lamachus, had written, in praise of Philip and Alexander, a composition containing a violent attack upon the Thebans and Olynthians. This he proceeded to read to the Greeks assembled at the Olympian festival, when Demosthenes intervening expounded at length the services to Greece of the peoples attacked by Lamachus, and the evils wrought by those who endeavoured to curry favour for themselves with the Macedonian monarchs. So deeply did he move his hearers and so threatening did their cries become, that the sophist slunk terror-stricken away from the assemblage.

The public career of Demosthenes is said by Plutarch to have begun in the year of the outbreak of the Phocian War (355 B.C.). But it was not until some time later that he became politically prominent. During the four years 355—352 B.C. he not only composed for the law-courts speeches which had a political bearing[3], but himself addressed to the Assembly the orations *On the Symmories*

Early harangues.

---

[1] He was, moreover, on occasion responsible for a happy repartee. Pytheas, an opponent of Demosthenes and a notorious evil-liver, declared that Demosthenes' reflections "smelt of the lamp." "The lamp," replied Demosthenes, "sees you and me at different work." When Epicles complained that Demosthenes was "always considering," the other retorted that he would be ashamed to advise so great a people without consideration.

[2] *Vit. Dem.* ix.

[3] *Against Androtion* (355 B.C.), *Against the proposal of Leptines* (354 B.C.), *Against Timocrates* (353 B.C.), *Against Aristocrates* (352 B.C.). Only the speech *Against the proposal of Leptines* was delivered by Demosthenes himself.

(354 B.C.), *For the Megalopolitans* (353 B.C.), and *For the Liberty of the Rhodians*[1]. It was, however, as the champion of Athens and Greece against the aggression of Macedon under its able but unscrupulous ruler Philip that "he quickly won reputation, and was lifted by his speeches The opponent of Macedon. and outspokenness into notoriety, with the result that he excited the admiration of the Greeks and the attentions of the Great King, while Philip regarded him more seriously than he did any other statesman, and even those who hated him admitted that they had to deal with a man of distinction[2]." It becomes necessary therefore to direct our attention for a time to that new power which arose in the Greek world towards the middle of the fourth century B.C. For with the history of Macedon the career of Demosthenes is inextricably associated.

(ii) *The Uprising of Macedon.*

Stretched along the northern frontier of Thessaly, from Thrace on the east to Illyria in the west, Macedon had played hitherto but little part in the affairs of Greece. At the time of the Persian invasion the Macedonian king, Macedon in the fifth century B.C. Alexander I, had openly sided with Xerxes, while at the same time he sought in secret to secure his position with the Greeks by furnishing to them advantageous information[3]. During the Peloponnesian war Perdiccas II, who then occupied the Macedonian throne, had entered into relations with both Athenians and Lacedaemonians, but had lent effective aid to neither[4]. His successor, Archelaus, following the example of the tyrants of an earlier age, such as Hiero of Syracuse and Peisistratus of Athens, had

---

[1] Traditionally assigned to 351 B.C. but almost certainly earlier. For this and the other speeches mentioned *vide* Demosthenes, *Philippics*, ed. Davies (Pitt Press Series), pp. xx–xxi; Butcher, *Demosthenes*, pp. 32–49.

[2] Plut. *Vit. Dem.* xii.   [3] Herod. vii. 173; viii. 140.

[4] Thuc. Ind. s.v. Περδίκκας.

gathered to his court a number of men skilled in letters and the fine arts. Among these had been Euripides[1] and Agathon the tragedians, Timotheus, well known to us from the gibes of the comic poets as one of the leaders in a new school of music, and the painter Zeuxis. Archelaus had also erected buildings and constructed roads; but despite his efforts Macedonia still remained without the strict confines of the Greek world. The city-state (πόλις), that distinguishing mark of Greek

Character of the people. political organization, was replaced in the case of Macedonia by the tribal association (ἔθνος); the people were rude and wild, drinking deep and devoting themselves to hunting and fighting; and although their language, as its remains show, was a form of the Greek speech, and the ruling house had had its Greek birthright acknowledged at Olympia, the Macedonians were regarded by the Greeks in general as βάρβαροι[2]. Beset by turbulent neighbours—the Illyrians to the west, the Paeonians to the north, the Thracians to the east—disturbed by frequent faction and by the revolt of the tribes subject to her sway, Macedonia seemed little like to develop within the short space of half a century into the mightiest power, not in Greece alone, but in the world. Such

A feeble power. was her weakness that when the Boeotian Pelopidas, in retaliation for Macedonian interference in Thessaly, invaded the country in 368 B.C., he had little difficulty in bringing the Macedonian regent, Ptolemy, step-father of the king, to terms, and carried away with him to Thebes thirty youths of noble birth as hostages for the future good behaviour of Macedonia. One of their number was Philip, brother to the nominal ruler of the country, Perdiccas III.

Three years later Perdiccas succeeded in ridding himself

The maker of Macedon. of Ptolemy by assassination, and in the following year, 364 B.C., Philip returned to Macedon from

---

[1] His well-known play *The Bacchants* was composed in Macedonia, and probably inspired by Dionysiac worship there.

[2] Cf. *Ol.* iii. 16 οὐ βάρβαρος; *n.*

Thebes. He had lived there for four years during a period when, through the political skill and military genius of Epameinondas, Thebes had become the leading power of Greece. It would seem that Philip did not disregard the opportunity thus afforded him ; that he had learned well his lessons in statecraft and the art of war events were soon to prove.

In 359 B.C. Perdiccas III fell in battle against the Illyrians, and Philip, a young man of twenty-four, became guardian to the son of the late king, the child Amyntas, and regent of Macedonia. His position was a difficult one. On the west he was threatened by the Illyrians, **Early difficulties.** on the north by the Paeonians. On the east the Thracians were ready to advocate in arms the claims of a pretender to the throne, while another aspirant, Argaeus, had the active support of the Athenians, who despatched a fleet to his aid. In this early crisis the conduct of Philip was marked by that energy and shrewdness for which he was afterwards to become famous[1]. Gold, a weapon in which he always reposed great confidence[2], secured immunity, at least for a time, from Paeonians and Thracians. Argaeus was defeated ; but to escape, if possible, Athenian resentment, Philip allowed the Athenians who were captured to depart unharmed, and formally renounced all claim to Amphipolis, a mercantile and strategic position of great importance on the River Strymon and a lost possession of Athens which it was earnestly desired to recover[3]. Relieved from the more insistent perils Philip devoted the winter to reconstituting and training his troops ; then turning with reorganized forces, first against the Paeonians,

---

[1] *Ol.* i. 12 *et seq.*; ii. 23.

[2] Cf. Plut. *Apophthegm. Reg.* (*Philip.* 14); Cic. *ad Attic.* i. 16 neque auctoritate neque gratia pugnat (sc. Pompeius), sed quibus Philippus omnia castella expugnari posse dicebat, in quae modo asellus onustus auro posset ascendere; Hor. *Od.* iii. 16, 13–15 diffidit urbium | portas uir Macedo et subruit aemulos | reges muneribus.

[3] Amphipolis was founded as a colony by Athens in 436 B.C. In 424 B.C. it fell into the hands of Brasidas and was never regained by Athens. Perdiccas III had occupied it with a garrison.

and then against the Illyrians, he secured in both campaigns
a signal success.

The natural direction for the expansion of Macedonian

**Expansion of
Macedonian
power.**

power was southwards and eastwards. The
possession of Chalcidice and its harbours pro-
mised control of the Thermaic Gulf and Northern
Aegaean; the mountain range of Pangaeus to the east of
Macedonia offered bounteous store of gold wherewith to pay
troops and to ensure diplomatic successes; while in the Thracian
Chersonese, commanding the entrance to the Propontis and
the Euxine, was to be found a position of which the strategic
value was generally recognized and was, in fact, of no less
importance in ancient than in modern times. But there were
obstacles in the way. The passage eastward across the
Strymon was barred by Amphipolis, to which Philip had
abandoned his right. The shores of the Thermaic Gulf and
Chalcidice were fringed with cities, either autonomous, like
Olynthus and her sister towns, or subject to Athens, like
Poteidaea. Amphipolis was first attacked. She appealed for
aid to Athens, but in vain[1]. To prevent succour being sent
Philip had secretly arranged to hand over the city, when in his
possession, to the Athenians, on condition that they in return
allowed him to capture without interference the town of Pydna

**Capture of
Amphipolis
(357 B.C.),
Pydna and
Poteidaea
(356 B.C.).**

on the Thermaic Gulf[2]. Amphipolis fell; Pydna
followed suit; but Philip retained both. Know-
ing that war with Athens must follow he added
to his captures the Athenian dependency of
Poteidaea, which he bestowed as a gift upon the
people of Olynthus. Alarmed by Philip's aggression the Olynthians had sought an alliance with Athens, but owing to the
Athenians' secret arrangement with Philip their overtures had
been rejected[3]. By his present action Philip effectively pre-

---

[1] *Ol.* i. 8.

[2] *Ol.* ii. 6 τὸ θρυλούμενόν ποτ' ἀπόρρητον ἐκεῖνο.

[3] *Ibidem,* ὅτ' Ὀλυνθίους ἀπήλαυνόν τινες ἐνθένδε βουλομένους ὑμῖν
διαλεχθῆναι.

cluded them from joining hands with the Athenians against him.

Meanwhile the attention of the Athenians had been turned to Euboea, which had been since the battle of Leuctra in 371 B.C. under the control of Thebes. The ascendancy of Athens was now re-established in the island in a campaign in which Demosthenes volunteered his services as trierarch[1]. But shortly after Philip's successes in the north the city was distracted by the revolt of Chios, Cos, Rhodes and Byzantium, important members of the Athenian Confederacy, which, originating in a maritime league with Byzantium, Chalcedon and Rhodes in 390 B.C., had been considerably extended after 378 B.C. and had come eventually to include some 70 cities. The rebels were abetted by Mausolus of Caria, and after two years of warfare Athens was left with weakened resources and compelled to acknowledge their independence. The memory of the Carian tyrant has been perpetuated only by his magnificent sepulchre and the word "mausoleum"; yet in those days men seem to have looked to the east with at least as much alarm as to the north.

The "Social" War, 357—5 B.C.

The tone of Demosthenes' references to Philip in his earlier speeches betrays no grave apprehension of that monarch's growing power. In the speech *Against the proposal of Leptines* (354 B.C.) mention is made of the capture of Pydna and Poteidaea[2]; in that *On the Symmories* (354 B.C.) the passages which allude to the enemies with whom Athens is confronted *may* refer to Philip, although it is far from certain that they do so[3]. In the speech *For the liberty of the Rhodians* there is a passing warning against treating Philip as beneath contempt; but there is no grave

The disregard of Philip's advance.

---

[1] *Ol.* i. 8; *de Cor.* 99 σφετεριζομένων Θηβαίων τὴν Εὔβοιαν οὐ περιείδετε...ἀλλ᾽ ἐβοηθήσατε καὶ τούτοις, τῶν ἐθελοντῶν τριηράρχων τότε πρῶτον γενομένων τῇ πόλει, ὧν εἷς ἦν ἐγώ.

[2] § 61.

[3] § 11 τί τοὺς ὁμολογουμένως ἐχθροὺς ἔχοντες ἑτέρους ζητοῦμεν; § 41, παρασκευάζεσθαι πρὸς τοὺς ὑπάρχοντας ἐχθροὺς κελεύω.

insistence upon the admonition[1]. In the speech *Against Aristocrates* (352 B.C.) the name of the Macedonian king is mentioned more frequently and with a greater seriousness[2]. This oration was delivered against a proposal made in favour of Charidemus whereby the person of that leader of mercenaries was rendered less liable to attack. Charidemus was brother-in-law to the Thracian Cersobleptes, and the proposal seems to have been designed to secure the support of that chief against Macedonia[3]. Such had been the course of events that it might well suggest to thinking men what a formidable power Philip had by now become.

Under the influence of Thessaly and Thebes the members of the Delphian Amphictyony had condemned the Phocians to pay a heavy fine as indemnity for a sacrilege which, it was alleged, they had committed. The Phocians retaliated by seizing Delphi. By means of the treasure accumulated there they readily gathered to their support a large number of mercenary soldiers, and took the field against their foes under the leadership of Philomelus. After vanquishing the Locrians they suffered a severe defeat from the Thebans at Neon (354 B.C.), where Philomelus perished. His successor Onomarchus, however, by his military skill and free-handed use of the wealth at his command, reduced his adversaries to such straits

The "Sacred" or "Phocian" War, 356—46 B.C.

---

[1] ὁρῶ δ᾽ ὑμῶν ἐνίους Φιλίππου μὲν ὡς ἄρ᾽ οὐδενὸς ἀξίου ὀλιγωροῦντας, βασιλέα δ᾽ ὡς ἰσχυρὸν ἐχθρὸν οἷς ἂν προέληται φοβουμένους.

[2] §§ 107, 111, 116, 121 (ὁ μάλιστα δοκῶν νῦν ἡμῖν ἐχθρὸς εἶναι Φίλιππος οὑτοσί). "It is difficult not to read something of contempt in the words ἴστε δήπου Φίλιππον τουτονὶ τὸν Μακεδόνα (§ 111)," Butcher, *Demosthenes*, p. 50. But the contempt is of Philip's nationality, not of his power. Cf. *Phil.* i. 10 γένοιτο γὰρ ἄν τι καινότερον ἢ Μακεδὼν ἀνὴρ Ἀθηναίους καταπολεμῶν καὶ τὰ τῶν Ἑλλήνων διοικῶν; The same point barbed the inscription below Demosthenes' statue. *Vide infra*, p. xliv. Cf. i. 9 Μακεδονίας *n.*

[3] There appear to have been two parties at Athens, the one seeking to checkmate Philip by making Cersobleptes supreme in the Chersonese, the other believing that Athens' interest lay rather in maintaining a 'balance of power' there. For some account of Charidemus cf. *Ol.* iii. 5 *n.*

that the Thessalians turned for assistance to their northern neighbour Philip. He had been engaged in taking Methone, the last of the possessions of Athens on the Thermaic Gulf, and had lost an eye in the attack[1]. Now he at once availed himself of the opportunity of establishing a foothold in Greece. He drove the Phocians out of Thessaly and seized Pagasae[2]; but when Onomarchus himself appeared at the head of an overwhelming army, Philip in Thessaly, 353–2 B.C. Philip was compelled in his turn to retire. In the following year (352 B.C.) he reappeared. He had left a Macedonian garrison in Pagasae, and Onomarchus, aided by an Athenian fleet under Chares, was planning to dislodge it. But Philip obtained a complete victory; Onomarchus, with a large number of his followers, perished; his adherents among the Thessalians were forced to fly from their country, in which the Macedonian power now became supreme. Ever ready to press an advantage home Philip moved southward, intending to strike a decisive blow at his Phocian foes in their own land. But his advance had aroused the fears of the Greeks. Reinforced by allies from Sparta, Checked at Thermopylae. Achaea and Athens, and supported by an Athenian fleet, the Phocians barred his way at Thermopylae. Philip recognized that the time was not yet ripe for him and withdrew. Six years were to pass before the success now denied him was to be achieved.

(iii) *From the First Philippic to the Peace.*

Meanwhile he turned his attention to Thrace, where he laid siege to Heraeum Teichus[3], the capital of Cersobleptes, and soon reduced that chieftain to submission. The alarm which Philip's advance Threatens the Cherso-nese. to Thermopylae had created at Athens was intensified by the menace of his presence in the neighbourhood of the Chersonese.

---

[1] *Ol.* i. 9. Cf. *de Cor.* 67 ἑώρων δ᾽ αὐτὸν τὸν Φίλιππον...ὑπὲρ ἀρχῆς καὶ δυναστείας τὸν ὀφθαλμὸν ἐκκεκομμένον.

[2] *Ol.* i. 9 *n.*   [3] *Ol.* iii. 4 *n.*

The situation afforded Demosthenes his opportunity. He had
had already a considerable experience of public life and its
activities; study and practice had confirmed and established
his natural talent for oratory. He now came forward as a
political leader, the advocate of a policy the keynote of which
was opposition to Philip and the restoration to Athens of her
old imperial position[1]. It is easy, with the issue of events

The Demos-
thenic policy
and others.
before us, to condemn such a policy as "short-
sighted"; to declare it foredoomed to failure by
the hopeless degeneracy of the Athenians of the
fourth century B.C.; and to observe that "Demosthenes' orations
could not change the character of his countrymen." It was, at
least, an effort worth making. It was a more inspiring course
than that pursued by Eubulus and his friends[2], who, resigned
to the extinction of Athens as a power in the Greek world,
devoted their energies to the improvement of the condition
of the city and the provision of amusement for its citizens. It
was as practicable a course as that advocated by Isocrates, now
in his eighty-fifth year, who believed that the Greek states might
find a cure for their rivalries, if they should unite to satisfy
their several desires for aggrandisement at the expense of the
barbarians[3]. As Cicero looked back with admiration and regret
to the days of the Scipios[4], so Demosthenes was animated by
the ideal of Athens as she existed in the days of Pericles[5]. He
saw, as clearly as we see now, that the attainment of that ideal
involved a fundamental change in the character of his con-

---

[1] *Ol.* iii. 36 μὴ παραχωρεῖν, ὦ ἄνδρες Ἀθηναῖοι, τῆς τάξεως ἣν ὑμῖν
οἱ πρόγονοι τῆς ἀρετῆς μετὰ πολλῶν καὶ καλῶν κινδύνων κτησάμενοι
κατέλιπον.

[2] *Ol.* iii. 29.

[3] Cf. Isoc. *Phil.* 9 ηὕρισκον οὐδαμῶς ἂν ἄλλως αὐτὴν (sc. τὴν πόλιν
ἡμῶν) ἡσυχίαν ἄγουσαν, πλὴν εἰ δόξειε ταῖς πόλεσι ταῖς μεγίσταις
διαλυσαμέναις τὰ πρὸς σφᾶς αὐτοὺς εἰς τὴν Ἀσίαν τὸν πόλεμον ἐξενεγκεῖν
καὶ τὰς πλεονεξίας, ἃς νῦν παρὰ τῶν Ἑλλήνων ἀξιοῦσιν αὐταῖς γίγνεσθαι,
ταύτας εἰ παρὰ τῶν βαρβάρων ποιήσασθαι βουληθεῖεν.

[4] Cf. Tyrrell, *Cicero in his Letters*, p. xxxiii.

[5] Cf. *Ol.* iii. 21–6.

temporaries¹. But he had courage enough not to despair of being able to effect such a change.

The speech which marks Demosthenes' advance into the position of a leading politician is known as the *First Philippic*². The orator begins with an apology for addressing the Assembly before the recognized leaders of public opinion have expressed their views. His hearers, he declares, may be encouraged, not only by the fact of Athens' inaction in the past, but also by the history³ of her struggle with Sparta⁴, to hope that when action *is* taken against Philip, success will speedily follow. And surely the time for action has arrived. Even if fortune, "always more solicitous for us than we are for ourselves⁵," were to add to her past favours a fatal termination of Philip's present illness, the Athenians, "with their schemes and preparations far away⁶," would be unable even to accept what opportunity had offered to them. A definite proposition follows. The city should aim at a force of 50 triremes and a sufficient number of transports for half the knights. As a preliminary measure (πρὸ δὲ τούτων) Demosthenes urges the provision of a force of 2000 men (1500 mercenaries and 500 citizens, these latter serving in rotation for a short period); 10 swift triremes; and 200 cavalry with a suitable fleet of transports. He adds his reasons for not

---

¹ Cf. (*inter al.*) *Ol.* ii. 13 πολλὴν δὴ τὴν μετάστασιν καὶ μεγάλην δεικτέον τὴν μεταβολήν.

² Cf. Cic. *ad Atticum*, ii. 1 quod in eis orationibus, quae Philippicae nominantur, enituerat ciuis ille tuus (sc. Demosthenes). The speech is usually assigned to 351 B.C., but should perhaps be placed rather in 349 B.C.

³ A characteristic touch. Demosthenes found inspiration in the past. His favourite reading is said to have been the history of Thucydides, which he is declared by Lucian (*aduersus Indoctum* 4) to have copied out no less than eight times. Cf. *Ol.* iii. 23 οὐ γὰρ ἀλλοτρίοις ὑμῖν χρωμένοις παραδείγμασιν ἀλλ' οἰκείοις, ὦ ἄνδρες Ἀθηναῖοι, εὐδαίμοσιν ἔξεστι γενέσθαι.

⁴ The reference is not to the Peloponnesian War (431–04 B.C.) but to conflicts in the fourth century B.C., the so-called "Boeotian" War in 378 B.C., or, possibly, the "Corinthian" War in 395 B.C.

⁵ ἥπερ ἀεὶ βέλτιον ἢ ἡμεῖς ἡμῶν αὐτῶν ἐπιμελούμεθα, § 12.

⁶ ἀπηρτημένοι καὶ ταῖς παρασκευαῖς καὶ ταῖς γνώμαις, § 12.

embarking upon a more ambitious scheme and for insisting upon the presence of citizens among the troops; as well as a financial statement[1] showing how the expenses involved in his scheme might be discharged. The establishment of a standing force would enable Athens to seize opportunities for striking at Philip; would afford protection to commerce; and would prevent the success of those sudden expeditions which had already brought so much profit to their enemy.

A call to action.

The speech concludes with an urgent appeal for organized action and personal service in the field[2] in place of the fault-finding and the tittle-tattle with which the Athenians concerned themselves. Throughout there is a grave enough apprehension of the peril; warning is not neglected; but the spirit of hope predominates and "the effect of the whole is to stimulate, not to benumb[3]."

The speech however failed. In Thrace Philip had fallen sick[4]

Philip attacks Chalcidice.

and the Athenians perhaps hoped that a recurrence of the disease would rid them of their troublesome foe. But the Macedonian king's recovery had proved permanent, and he had soon engaged in fresh schemes of conquest. Olynthus and her confederate cities still remained to interfere with his complete control of the region of Chalcidice. The Olynthians had made their peace with Athens by recognizing her claim to Amphipolis, and had afforded shelter to Philip's half-brother who aspired to the Macedonian throne. Now Philip's demand that this pretender should be given up to him was met by a refusal. War followed, and Philip advanced against the Chalcidic cities. In most of these he was well served by his adherents and the gates were opened at his approach. Where resistance was offered, as at Aristotle's native city of Stagira, Philip gained an entrance by force.

As the danger of destruction approached nearer and nearer,

---

[1] This statement was comprised in a separate document, read to the Assembly, but not embodied in the speech.

[2] Cf. *Ol.* i. 2 τῶν πραγμάτων ὑμῖν ἐκείνων αὐτοῖς ἀντιληπτέον ἐστίν n. Index B, s. vv. αὐτός, ξένοι.

[3] Butcher, *Demosthenes*, p. 57.   [4] *Ol.* i. 13.

the citizens of Olynthus appealed for help to Athens. There was a general disposition to assist, and Demosthenes employed all the force of his eloquence to secure the despatch of a supporting expedition. The three speeches which   The he delivered in the course of the debates on the   *Olynthiac* question have received the title of the *Olynthiac*   *Speeches.* *Orations*[1]. The spirit of the *First Philippic* reveals itself again in these harangues in unabated vigour; encouragement and admonition are adroitly intermingled; and the orator earnestly implores his countrymen not to suffer this heaven-sent opportunity to escape them[2]. It was indeed a favourable moment for striking at Macedon. Cersobleptes had rebelled. Olynthus was a powerful ally. Athens sent to her assistance bodies of mercenary troops under Chares and Charidemus[3]. But Philip's statesmanship was equal to the occasion. Through his agents he had fomented faction in Euboea with the result that in the cities of that island, Eretria, Chalcis and Oreus, civil strife broke out, and those who favoured Athens were   Faction in expelled[4]. Now at a critical moment Euboean   Euboea. affairs seem to have distracted the thoughts of the Athenians from events in the north. Demosthenes protested in vain. When finally it was decided to send further help to Olynthus and a force of two thousand citizens was despatched, the doom of those whom they came to aid was already sealed. Aided by treachery which delivered into his hands the Olynthian cavalry[5] Philip had captured the city, to which he meted out a severe punishment. Many of its citizens were enslaved; its buildings   Olynthus were destroyed; seven years later, we are assured,   destroyed, it was difficult to recognize even its site[6].   348 B.C.

[1] The detailed succession of events is uncertain, as is the precise order in which the three speeches were delivered. *Vide* Appendix A. An analysis of the contents of the speeches is given pp. xlvi–l.

[2] τῶν ὑπὸ τῆς τύχης παρασκευασθέντων συμμάχων καὶ καιρῶν (ii. 2).

[3] Cf. *supr.* p. xx.   [4] *Phil.* iii. 57 ff.

[5] *Phil.* iii. 56.   Cf. Juv. xii. 47 callidus emptor Olynthi.

[6] *Phil.* iii. 26 ἁπάσας (sc. τὰς πόλεις) οὕτως ὠμῶς ἀνῄρηκεν ὥστε μηδ' εἰ πώποτ' ᾠκήθησαν προσελθόντ' εἶναι ῥᾴδιον εἰπεῖν.

Demosthenes must have been sorely tried by his inability to arouse the Athenians to effective action. To add to his misfortune he had suffered a personal affront which clearly excited in him strong feelings of anger and resentment. In the theatre, on the occasion of the great festival of Dionysus in 348 B.C., at which Demosthenes was acting as choregus for his tribe, one of his enemies, a wealthy and objectionable man named Meidias, struck the orator a blow. Owing to the position held by Demosthenes, and the time and place at which the blow was dealt him, the act was capable of being construed as impiety (ἀσέβεια) rather than simple outrage (ὕβρις). It is plain from the language which Demosthenes uses that he was deeply moved by the insult; but Plutarch tells us that in the end he compromised the action for thirty minae[1] owing to the strong position in which wealth and powerful friends had placed his adversary.

> The Speech *Against Meidias*, 347 B.C.

The capture and destruction of Olynthus created, for a time at least, a deep impression on the minds of the Athenians, and in order to consolidate the forces of Greece against Philip overtures were made to the cities of the Peloponnese. A speaker who emerged into prominence in connection with these embassies was Aeschines, Demosthenes' future rival, whose attitude towards Philip at this period was one of pronounced hostility.

> Embassies to Peloponnese.

Meanwhile the Sacred War[2] was being waged against Phocis by the Thebans and Thessalians, who unable to bring the conflict to a satisfactory conclusion sought assistance again from Philip as they had done six years before. Now, as then, Philip readily acceded to their request, while the Phocians on their side appealed to Sparta and Athens for help against their enemies. In response to the call addressed to them both Sparta and Athens sent troops to Thermopylae which was in

---

[1] *Vit. Dem.* xii. The same statement is made by Aeschines (*Against Ctesiphon*, 52) and is not contradicted by Demosthenes.

[2] *Supr.* p. xx.

the hands of the Phocian leader, Phalaecus.   But the situation
was complicated by faction amongst the Phocians   Phocian
themselves.   Phalaecus was at variance with the   quarrels;
party which had sent the appeal to Sparta and   Athens' diffi-
Athens; he had perhaps even been intriguing   cult position.
with the enemies of the latter city in Euboea; and he now
refused to allow either Athenians or Spartans to enter the pass.
A policy of active resistance to Philip thus became fraught with
the gravest possible consequences to Athens.   If Phalaecus
and his mercenaries were to make terms with Philip, the city
might be confronted by an overwhelming force within the
borders of Attica itself.   Philip, on the other hand, was not
unready to come to terms.   It was to his present interest to
reduce, so far as he might, the resistance to his progress into
central Greece.

On the proposition of Philocrates, from whom the peace
which followed has taken its name, an embassy,   1st Embassy
including among its members both Demosthenes   to Philip,
and Aeschines, was despatched to Philip in   347 B.C. (late).
347 B.C.   The terms which were arranged amounted to a recognition by both parties of the *status quo* at the time of the final
ratification of the peace.   Philip however stipulated that he
should be allowed to deal as he wished with the Phocians and
with Halus in Thessaly.   To these proposals the Athenian
Assembly agreed.   There was some reluctance about accepting
an arrangement which did not definitely secure the safety of
the Phocians; but Philip through his agents had given vogue
to the opinion that he was not in truth ill-disposed toward
Phocis, but would rather reduce the power of Thebes, a city
towards which the Athenians in general entertained no very
friendly feelings.   A second embassy now left   2nd Embassy,
Athens for Pella for the purpose of securing   346 B.C.
Philip's sworn adherence to the treaty.   This   (spring).
they only succeeded in obtaining after a considerable delay.
For Philip had employed himself during the interval in making
additions to his Thracian conquests, which under the terms
arranged thus remained in his hands.

After returning to Pella and taking the oath required from him the Macedonian king advanced southward into Thessaly. A peace was arranged with Halus and he proceeded on his way against Phocis. Phalaecus surrendered the pass of Thermopylae into his hands on condition that he himself and his troops were allowed to depart unmolested. The Athenian Assembly passed a decree summoning the Phocians to place the sanctuary of Delphi in the hands of the Amphictyons, on whose behalf Philip was avowedly acting. Thus betrayed by their military leader and deserted by Athens the Phocians were

The ruin of Phocis. left to the mercy of their ancient enemies, the Thessalians and Thebans, who possessed a predominant influence in the Council of the Amphictyons. That body decided that all the Phocian cities, with the exception of Abae, should be broken up into village communities; the sacred treasure which the Phocians had used was to be repaid at the rate of 60 talents a year; and the place formerly held by Phocis in the Amphictyonic League was assigned to Macedonia. Philip was elected President of the League and in that capacity celebrated the Pythian Games of 346 B.C. Athens marked her

Anger at Athens. displeasure by refusing to send representatives to the festival. The fate of the Phocians, whom she had been led to believe Philip would treat with consideration, had filled her with resentment and alarm. There was talk of war; but Demosthenes dissuaded his countrymen from

The Speech On the Peace. so rash a project in his speech *On the Peace.* It has been said of Demosthenes that "he was prone to lose sight of military necessities in his zeal for attaining some cherished political end." On this occasion, at least, he did not allow the bitterness of his hostility to Philip to blind him to the exigence of the situation[1].

[1] Demosthenes recognizes the present weakness of Athens (πολλὰ γὰρ προείμεθα, ὧν ὑπαρχόντων τότ' ἂν ἢ νῦν ἀσφαλέστερος καὶ ῥᾴων ἦν ἡμῖν ὁ πόλεμος, § 13) and the combination against her (ὅπως μὴ προαξύμεθ', ὦ ἄνδρες Ἀθηναῖοι, τοὺς συνεληλυθότας τούτους καὶ φάσκοντας Ἀμφικτύονας νῦν εἶναι εἰς ἀνάγκην καὶ πρόφασιν κοινοῦ πολέμου πρὸς ἡμᾶς, § 14).

(iv) *From the Peace to Chaeroneia.*

Thus peace was formally maintained, although neither the temper of the Athenians nor the restless energy of Philip[1] was favourable to its long continuance. The Macedonian king employed himself in consolidating his position in Thessaly and in seeking to extend his influence into the Peloponnese. From Sparta, rigid and conservative as she was, he had little to hope. He turned naturally to those states which were jealous of Lacedaemonian power, and concluded arrangements with Messenia, Megalopolis, Argos and Elis. Demosthenes viewed this development with alarm. He saw that his city might be confronted with foes from the south as well as from the north, and induced the Athenians to despatch embassies to the cities of the Peloponnesus in order to counteract the efforts of the agents of Macedon. He himself undertook the *rôle* of ambassador, and so successful was he that Philip was moved to send representatives to Athens asserting his peaceful intentions and protesting against what he declared to be a misconstruction of his actions. It was on the occasion of this Macedonian embassy's arrival and protest that Demosthenes delivered the short harangue known as the *Second Philippic.* In characteristic fashion he invites his audience to consider the fate of other peoples, such as the Olynthians and Thessalians[2], to whom Philip had come with fair words and gracious benefactions; and he draws from their history the lesson that "the nature of the wise possesses within itself one universal safeguard, which ensures safety and well-being to all, and especially to democracies in their dealings with tyrants." This safeguard is "Mistrust." "Treasure it, cling to it," he adjures the

Philip active in the Peloponnese.

The Second Philippic, 343 B.C.

[1] τὴν φιλοπραγμοσύνην ᾗ χρῆται καὶ συζῇ Φίλιππος, ὑφ' ἧς οὐκ ἔστιν ὅπως ἀγαπήσας τοῖς πεπραγμένοις ἡσυχίαν σχήσει. *Ol.* i. 14.

[2] For the Olynthians cf. *supr.* pp. xviii, xxv. For the Thessalians he expelled their tyrants; gave them Magnesia and Nicaea; and restored to them their Amphictyonic Presidency. But he reconstituted the government and appropriated the revenues. Cf. *Ol.* i. 22.

Athenians; "if you keep it intact, no harm will ever befall you[1]."

Not only in the Peloponnesus but nearer to Attica Mace-
Megara and Euboea. donian intrigue was busy. An attempt to overthrow the government in Megara failed, with the
result that that city took its stand with Athens. In Euboea
however oligarchies favourable to Philip were set up in Eretria
and Oreus; but in Chalcis the democratic *régime* maintained
its position, which was further secured by an Athenian alliance.
Unsuccessful on the whole upon the east Philip turned his
attention to the west. In Epirus his wife's brother, Alexander,
was disputing the throne with her uncle, Arybbas. Philip now
went to his aid, established him in his sovereignty, and extended
his dominion to the northern frontiers of Ambracia. Perhaps he
Philip in Epirus. meant to penetrate southward to the Corinthian
Gulf, where the possession of Naupactus would
have afforded him a way of crossing into the Peloponnese. But
his presence in those regions alarmed the peoples of the west.
Corcyra, Ambracia, Acarnania and Achaea united themselves
with Athens. Philip refrained from advancing further and be-
took himself to Thrace, where the course of events had made his
presence advisable.

At Athens the party hostile to Macedon was now in the
Philocrates impeached. ascendant. The peace of 346 B.C. was more
unpopular than ever, and Philocrates, who was
regarded as chiefly responsible for it, was impeached for treason.
His accuser was Hypereides, a supporter of Demosthenes. So
little hope had Philocrates of acquittal that he fled from the city
without standing his trial and in his absence was condemned
to death. Demosthenes himself revived against Aeschines a
charge of misconduct in connection with the second embassy
to Philip[2]. This charge he had brought three years before;
but his opponent had then countered the attack by assailing
Timarchus, a friend of Demosthenes associated with him in the
prosecution, for disreputable debauchery. Now however the

---

[1] *Phil.* ii. 24.   [2] *Supr.* p. xxvii.

accusation of misconduct was renewed; Aeschines was forced
to face the issue, and in spite of a skilful defence
only managed to escape condemnation by the
narrow margin of thirty votes[1]. It was inevitable
that hostilities against Philip would, sooner or
later, be resumed. There was more than one point still in
dispute which might serve as a pretext for a declaration of
war.

The Speech
*On the
Embassy,*
343 B.C.

Halonnesus, hard by the Thessalian coast, had formerly
belonged to Athens but had fallen into the hands of pirates.
These had been expelled by Philip who had possessed himself
of the place, the "restoration" of which was now, at Demosthenes' instigation, demanded by the Athenians. While refusing
to recognize the Athenians' claim and "restore"
(ἀποδοῦναι) the island Philip offered to "bestow"
(δοῦναι) it upon them as a free gift[2]. The Athenians further
asked that Philip should renounce all claim to those positions
in Thrace which he had captured between the arrangement
of the peace and his formal ratification of it[3]. So far from
acceding to this request Philip reappeared in Thrace, dethroned
Cersobleptes, and placed the country under the control of
Macedon. Hostilities broke out in the region of the Chersonese. Diopeithes, who had been despatched thither by the
Athenians to uphold their interests, made an attack upon

Bones of
contention.

---

[1] This is the statement of Idomeneus of Lampsacus (*fl. circ.* 300 B.C.).
From the absence of any reference to the result in the speeches of
Aeschines and Demosthenes, *On the Crown* (*infr.* p. xxxix), Plutarch
unjustifiably infers (c. xv.) that an actual trial never took place.

[2] The speech *On Halonnesus*, printed among Demosthenes' works,
was composed by his contemporary Hegesippus. The temper of the
Athenians is plainly exhibited by their acceptance of such a verbal
quibble (περὶ συλλαβῶν διαφερόμενος, Aeschines *Against Ctesiphon*, 83).
Cf. the gibe of Antiphanes the comedian (*fl. circ.* 350 B.C.), Νεοττίς
(Kock *fr.* 169).

> A. ὁ δεσπότης δὲ πάντα τὰ παρὰ τοῦ πατρὸς
> ἀπέλαβεν, οὐ παρέλαβεν. B. ἠγάπησέ γ' ἂν
> τὸ ῥῆμα τοῦτο παραλαβὼν Δημοσθένης.

[3] *Supr.* p. xxvii.

Cardia, a city allied with Philip, and pillaged and harried the Thracian seaboard. Too late to punish him with arms Philip

The Speech
On the
Chersonese
and the *Third*
Philippic,
341 B.C. sent a protest to Athens, where Demosthenes in the speech *On the Chersonese* defended the action of Diopeithes. He attacks Philip on the score that "he has broken the peace and is the enemy and foe of the whole city, aye of the very ground on which it stands[1]"; a view which found further expression in the *Third Philippic*, a harangue marked out by the clarity and vigour of its thought and language as a masterpiece of political oratory. Philip, he cries, "denies that he is making war; but so far am I from agreeing that, in these actions of his, he is keeping the peace which he made with you, that I say that in making an attempt upon Megara, in seeking to set up tyrannies in Euboea, in advancing now upon Thrace, in plotting and planning in the Peloponnese, in every use to which he puts his powers, he is breaking the peace and making war upon you; unless you mean to insist that those who are setting up engines of war against you are maintaining peace until they have brought them actually up to your walls[2]."

The energetic appeals of Demosthenes had their effect. Embassies were sent out. The orator himself proceeded to the Hellespont and there gained the adherence of the two important cities of Perinthus and Byzantium. Against Perinthus Philip brought to bear in vain all the resources which skill in

Athens at
war with
Philip. the conduct of sieges could suggest. An attack upon Byzantium followed. Two fleets were sent to its aid by the Athenians, who now openly declared war upon Macedon, and Philip was forced to abandon his campaign. The Scythians were causing trouble in the north and against them he now turned his arms. The tyrannies set up in the Macedonian interest in Eretria and Oreus had previously been overthrown, and the cities of Euboea had united themselves in an independent federation. In commemoration of these events and in recognition of his services

[1] *de Chersoneso,* 39.　　　　　[2] *Phil.* iii. 17.

Demosthenes had received from his grateful fellow-countrymen a golden crown at the festival of Dionysus. Thus the current of affairs seemed at last to have set against Philip. With a view to that struggle which must sooner or later decide the issue between Athens and Macedon, Demosthenes now applied himself to the carrying out of a reform in connection with the financial supply for the navy[1]. Previously the triremes of the Athenian fleet had been furnished to the state by its 1200 richest citizens. These were divided into 20 boards or symmories ($\sigma \upsilon \mu$- *Demosthenes and naval and military finance.* $\mu o \rho \iota a \iota$) of 60 members each, the division doubtless being made in such a way as to secure that the total wealth of each symmory was as nearly as possible the same. Demosthenes seems to have thought that the rights and duties of individual members of the symmories were not defined with sufficient precision; and that to this lack of elaboration in the system were ultimately to be attributed those delays and deficiencies in the completion of the naval programme which continually arose[2]. He now imposed the provision of a trireme as a charge on an estate of 10 talents; estates of lower or higher value had to bear the burden in due proportion. This was clearly a more practicable arrangement although resisted, as was to be expected, by the wealthier Athenians. Another scheme, which Demosthenes now saw realized, was the application to military purposes of the Theoric monies, a reform which he had already suggested in the *Olynthiac Orations*[3].

Meanwhile Philip was engaged in Thrace. It was concerns of the Amphictyons which once more afforded him an opportunity of intervening in the affairs of Greece. When the Amphictyonic synod met *An Amphictyonic dispute.*

---

[1] The subject had occupied him long before. Cf. the speech, *de Symmoriis* (354 B.C.), *supr.* p. xiv.

[2] This may be inferred from the *detailed* character of the reform suggested in the speech *On the Symmories* 17–23, the gist of which is a demand for *organization* (cf. εἴ τι παραλείπομεν νῦν...αὐτὸ τὸ πρᾶγμ' ἑαυτῷ εὑρήσει).

[3] Index A, *Theoric Fund.*

at Delphi in the autumn of 340 B.C., a charge[1] of cultivating land consecrate to Apollo was brought by Aeschines against the inhabitants of the Locrian town of Amphissa. An armed conflict took place between this people and the Amphictyons, and subsequently an Amphictyonic war against Amphissa was declared. Some of the states, notably Athens and Thebes, refrained from taking any part in the proceedings; the Amphictyonic forces met with but little success; and a proposal was made in the Amphictyonic synod by Thessalian and other representatives, probably at Philip's instigation, that the ruler of Macedon should be invited to conduct the war. The invitation was given and promptly accepted. In the spring of 338 B.C.

Philip advances to Elateia. Philip arrived in Phocis and fortified the town of Elateia, a strategic position south of Thermopylae and commanding the road southward into Boeotia and Attica. The news of Philip's presence at Elateia filled the Athenians with dismay[2]. If Thebes should take the Macedonian side—and between Athens and Thebes there was an old and bitter dislike—Attica lay open to Philip's attack. In this crisis Demosthenes' eloquence served his country well. With nine others he went to Thebes to plead for an alliance of that city with Athens; an embassy from Philip was present also; but in the end the offers and arguments of Demosthenes and his colleagues prevailed[3]. When Philip after capturing Amphissa and Naupactus entered the north-west of Boeotia,

Athens and Thebes. he was confronted at Chaeroneia by the united forces of Thebes and Athens. Demosthenes himself served in the ranks of the hoplites bearing a shield on

---

[1] According to Demosthenes the charge was part of a plot to create an opportunity for Philip in another "Sacred" War. Aeschines maintained that the people of Amphissa intended to make an accusation against Athens, and that by anticipating their charge he saved his country from a conflict with the Amphictyons.

[2] Cf. the famous picture of the scene at Athens in *de Cor.* 169 ff.

[3] A lively description of this embassy is to be found in *de Cor.* 211 ff. Demosthenes himself puts the achievement of this alliance in the forefront of his successes. Cf. *infr.* p. xxxix.

which were emblazoned in letters of gold the words *"Good Luck"* (ἀγαθῇ τύχῃ). But the generalship of Philip and the valour of his troops gained a decisive victory, although the Thebans in particular fought bravely and fell where they stood. If they were found false to Greece when the Persian invaded the land, they now made atonement by their prowess in this later struggle for liberty[1]. Demosthenes' courage failed him and he fled from the battle. As a man of words rather than deeds he has suffered criticism in modern, as in ancient, times. A contemporary comedian, with satiric paradox, wrote of him:

> B. "Demosthenes will cease to rage." A. "Who's he?" B. "'*Who's he?*' you say!
> A giant who has swords and guns for dinner every day.
> But words he hates. A neat antithesis—he'd rather die
> Than such a thing should pass *his* lips. There's bloodshed in his eye[2]."

It is well, therefore, to recall the judgment upon him of others who had most cause, perhaps, to appraise him justly. Amid the bacchanalian revelry in which he passed the night after the conflict, Philip amused himself with ridiculing his opponent by repeating, in a sarcastic jingle, the formula which had prefaced Demosthenes' proposals against himself[3]. "But when he was sobered and apprehended the magnitude of the crisis in which he had been placed, he shuddered at the ability and power of the orator, who had forced him to put to the hazard, in the

Demosthenes and his critics.

---

[1] Cf. Milton, *To the Lady Margaret Ley*:
    "That dishonest victory
    At Chaeroneia, fatal to liberty."

[2] Timocles (*fl. circ.* 340 B.C.), Ἥρωες (Kock, *fr.* 12):
    B. καὶ πρῶτα μέν σοι παύσεται Δημοσθένης
        ὀργιζόμενος. A. ὁ ποῖος; B. ὁποῖος; ὁ Βριάρεως
        ὁ τοὺς καταπέλτας τάς τε λόγχας ἐσθίων,
        μισῶν λόγους ἄνθρωπος οὐδὲ πώποτε
        ἀντίθετον εἰπὼν οὐδέν, ἀλλ' Ἄρη βλέπων.

[3] Plut. *Vit. Dem.* xx ᾖδε τὴν ἀρχὴν τοῦ Δημοσθένους ψηφίσματος πρὸς πόδα διαιρῶν καὶ ὑποκρούων, Δημοσθένης Δημοσθένους Παιανιεὺς τάδ' εἶπεν.

short space of a single day, his life and his empire[1]." And after
the battle had been fought and lost, the Athenians, as Plutarch
records, assigned to Demosthenes the task of reciting the
encomium over the bones of those who had fallen at Chaeroneia,
thus "showing by the especial honour and esteem which they
displayed towards their adviser that they did not repent of the
acts which he had advised[2]."

(v) *The Triumph of Macedon.*

The battle of Chaeroneia marked the beginning of a new
era in Greece[3]. Thebes suffered the loss of
her hegemony in Boeotia and a Macedonian
garrison was established in the Cadmeia. It had been expected
that Philip would follow up his success in the field with an
assault upon Athens; a body of commissioners, among whom
was Demosthenes, had been appointed to look to the fortifications of the city; but the conqueror, having in view, perhaps,
the difficulty of attacking a state that was still powerful at sea,
granted to the Athenians what Demosthenes himself admitted
to be not illiberal terms. What remained of the Athenian
confederacy[4] was to be dissolved and all claim to the Thracian
Chersonese was to be abandoned. Although Sparta remained
unconquered and defiant in the Peloponnese, the states of
Greece generally, in assembly at Corinth, agreed to furnish
contingents to the force which Philip designed to lead against
Persia. Greece was no longer to be a country in which a balance
of power was maintained among a number of independent and
self-centred city-states.

In 336 B.C. Philip fell by the assassin's hand[5]. The moment
seemed a favourable one for putting an end to
Macedonian domination. Thessaly was disaffected; Thebes endeavoured to expel the
garrison of Macedonians in her citadel. At

*After
Chaeroneia.*

*Death of
Philip, 336 B.C.
Unrest in
Greece.*

---

[1] Plut. *Vit. Dem.* xx.   [2] *Ibidem* xxi. Cf. *On the Crown* 285.

[3] It was as though 'a flood had swept over the world' (κατακλυσμὸν
γεγενῆσθαι τῶν πραγμάτων), *On the Crown* 214.   [4] *Supr.* p. xix.

[5] The crime was instigated by Philip's wife, Olympias, whom he proposed to put away in favour of Cleopatra, the niece of his general Attalus.

Athens Demosthenes had received private intelligence of Philip's murder, and presented himself in the Council with a cheerful countenance, pretending to have had a dream which boded great good for the city. When subsequently a public announcement of the event reached the city, the Athenians offered a sacrificial thanksgiving for the good tidings and voted a crown to the assassin, Pausanias. Although his daughter was newly dead, Demosthenes appeared in festive apparel with a wreath upon his head. But the joy was short-lived. Amid the dangers that beset him the new monarch, Alexander, acted with a promptitude that disconcerted his adversaries. He re-established his authority in Thessaly, and proceeding to Thermopylae was there recognized by the Amphictyons as the *Submission* head of their league. Thebes submitted; Athens *to Alexander.* sent a conciliatory embassy; and at a general assembly of the Greek states at the Isthmus he was acknowledged as the legitimate successor of Philip.

In the following year Alexander turned his arms against the Thracian and the Illyrian. In his absence the cities of Greece began once more to plot war against him, and Demosthenes did his utmost to fan the flame. He helped the Thebans to obtain arms with which they attacked the Macedonians in the Cadmeia, and the Athenians made preparations to lend assistance. The voice of Demosthenes held undisputed sway in *Vain effort* the Assembly; and he sought to rouse the satraps *at rebellion.* of the Great King to make war upon Alexander, whom he jeeringly described as "a boy," "a jack-of-all-trades-and-master-of-none[1]." But when Alexander appeared the opposition to him collapsed. The Athenians sent an embassy to deprecate his wrath. Demosthenes was appointed one of the ambassadors; but he feared to face the angry king, and when he reached Mt Cithaeron on the northern border of Attica turned back to

---

[1] Plut. *Vit. Dem.* xxiii παῖδα καὶ Μαργίτην ἀποκαλῶν. Margites, the hero of a burlesque poem attributed to Homer,

πόλλ' ἠπίστατο ἔργα, κακῶς δ' ἠπίστατο πάντα.

the city. Deserted by Athens Thebes was an easy prey; her
buildings were levelled with the ground; only
the house of the poet Pindar was left standing [1].
From Athens Alexander demanded the surrender
of those chiefly responsible for the movement
against him. Among their number were the orators Demosthenes and Lycurgus, as well as Charidemus [2] and Ephialtes,
who had been prominent as leaders of mercenary troops. When
the demand was submitted to the Athenians Demosthenes
reminded them of the story of the sheep that surrendered the
watch dogs to the wolves. As a merchant sold, not merely the
sample of wheat displayed to his customer, but the whole stock
of which it formed but a part, so, he warned them, they would
surrender, not merely the individuals specified by Alexander, but
the whole community of Athens as well. Eventually Demades,
whose sympathy with Macedon was well known, was induced [3]
to ask Alexander to abate his demand, and the king agreed to
be content with the expulsion of Charidemus and Ephialtes.

Demos-thenes' sur-render demanded.

After Alexander's departure to the east a fresh movement
against Macedon was set afoot in Greece. Agis,
king of Sparta, enlisted support from Arcadia,
Achaea and Elis, and an attack was made upon
Megalopolis, now the centre of Macedonian influence in the
Peloponnese. But Antipater, the regent of Macedonia, soon
advanced to the relief of the city and crushed the confederates
in battle. Agis perished on the field. Athens had taken no
part in the struggle. It would seem that the fortunes of
Demosthenes and his party were at a low ebb. Encouraged
by this Demosthenes' old adversary, Aeschines, now delivered

Battle of Megalopolis, 331 B.C.

---

[1] Cf. Milton, *Written on his door when the Assault was intended to the City,*

> "The great Emathian conqueror bid spare
> The house of Pindarus, when temple and tower
> Went to the ground."

[2] *Supr.* p. xx.

[3] It is said that he received five talents from the persons threatened. Plut. *Vit. Dem.* xxiii.

an attack which he had threatened six years before. When in 336 B.C. the murder of Philip had filled with new hope the opponents of Macedon at Athens[1], a certain Ctesiphon had proposed in the Council that the services of Demosthenes to the state, particularly in regard to the restoration of the city's fortifications[2], should be recognized by the bestowal of a golden crown; that the presentation of the crown should take place in the Theatre at the time of the Great Dionysia, and the reason for its bestowal be proclaimed by the herald to the assembled multitude. Before the proposal was brought before the Assembly Aeschines laid against Ctesiphon an indictment for having put forward a motion which contravened the Law[3]. The effect of Aeschines' action was to render the bestowal of the crown impossible until the validity of his charge against Ctesiphon had been decided. The illegality alleged was threefold: (*a*) the bestowal of a crown which had been decreed by the Council or the Assembly could not legally be made in the place or on the occasion proposed; (*b*) no crown could legally be conferred upon one who had not passed the official audit in connection with any office which he had held, and Demosthenes, as a commissioner for the repair of the fortifications (τειχοποιός), was still liable to such an audit (ὑπεύθυνος); (*c*) the services of Demosthenes did not merit such a recognition. The first two objections were technical, and as such Demosthenes deals but cursorily with them in the speech which he delivered on behalf of the defendant Ctesiphon[4]. All his eloquence is concentrated upon the third item in Aeschines' indictment. His answer is, in truth, a vindication of the policy to which he had given up his life. "It was due to my policy," he declares, "which the prosecutor assails, that instead of joining Philip in an invasion of our land, as all

The trial of Ctesiphon.

Demosthenes' speech On the Crown, 330 B.C.

---

[1] *Supr.* p. xxxvi. [2] *Supr.* p. xxxvi.

[3] γραφὴ παρανόμων, *supr.* p. xi.

[4] In accord with Attic practice (*supr.* p. xi.) Ctesiphon himself, as defendant, formally pleaded his cause.

men thought they would[1], the Thebans stood shoulder to shoulder with us and barred his path ; that instead of battle being joined in Attica, it was joined ninety miles away from the city on the frontier of Boeotia ; that instead of privateers from Euboea pillaging and ravaging us, no attack was made upon Attica from the sea during the whole of the war ; that instead of Philip laying hands upon Byzantium and having control of the Hellespont, the people of Byzantium fought with us against him[2]." In the end Demosthenes gained a signal triumph. Failing to secure one-fifth of the votes of the jury[3] Aeschines was mulcted in a fine of 1000 drachmae and incapacitated from bringing any future action. He failed to pay the amount required and withdrew to Rhodes, where, as a teacher and lecturer, he lived for the remainder of his days.

Yet although active in the law-courts and successful in obtaining a favourable verdict in the case against Ctesiphon, politically Demosthenes remained throughout these years in a subordinate position. The leading men in Athenian affairs were Phocion, Demades and Lycurgus, the last-named of whom, although, unlike the others, he had been opposed to Macedon, retained the control of financial affairs[4]. The relations between Athens and Macedon remained, outwardly at least, amicable enough until 324 B.C., when an event occurred which threatened once more to bring about a collision. A noble Macedonian named Harpalus had been left by Alexander at Babylon in charge of the royal treasury and the administration of the satrapy. Luxury and extravagance had led him to misappropriate the property of his master, and when he learned that Alexander was returning from India, he feared to face him

Ascendancy of Demosthenes' political opponents.

---

[1] Demosthenes had shared this opinion. Cf. *Ol.* i. 25–6 ἂν δ' ἐκεῖνα Φίλιππος λάβῃ, τίς αὐτὸν κωλύσει δεῦρο βαδίζειν; Θηβαῖοι; μὴ λίαν πικρὸν εἰπεῖν ᾖ—καὶ συνεισβαλοῦσιν ἑτοίμως.

[2] *de Cor.* 229-30.

[3] τὸ μέρος τῶν ψήφων.

[4] Lycurgus continued as Chancellor of the Exchequer (ταμίας τῆς κοινῆς προσόδου) from 338 B.C. to 326 B.C.

and fled with 6000 mercenaries and 5000 talents to Greece.
When he presented himself at Athens, the city was naturally
disinclined to receive so formidable a visitor. Thereupon
Harpalus withdrew to Taenarum, and returning later without
his armament found refuge in Athens. His
surrender was demanded; and the Athenians,
on the proposition of Demosthenes, agreed to de-
liver him up, if Alexander would send officers to
receive him into custody. But they refused to hand the fugitive

Harpalus
arrives at
Athens,
324 B.C.

over to Antipater, the regent of Macedon, or to Philoxenus, who
had control in western Asia ; and declared that they would hold
such monies as Harpalus had in his possession with a view to
restoring them to Alexander, from whom they had been stolen.
The amount in question was said to be 700
talents. It was deposited in the Acropolis under

The stolen
treasure.

the charge of commissioners, of whom Demosthenes was one ;
but no definite record was made of the actual sum. Harpalus
soon escaped, almost certainly with the connivance of those in
whose hands he was. It was discovered that the money in the
Acropolis was less by one-half than had formerly been supposed. Rumour was active, and Demosthenes sought to
counter it by proposing that the Council of the Areopagus be
deputed to hold an enquiry into the affair. After a considerable
interval that body reported that certain leading Athenians had
been guilty of receiving bribes. One of these was Demosthenes himself; he had received, it was asserted, 20 talents.
The orator was impeached in the law-courts and
condemned to pay a fine of 50 talents. So

Demosthenes
in exile.

heavy an obligation he was unable to discharge and was con-
sequently imprisoned; later he escaped into exile, which he
spent for the most part in Aegina and at Troezen on the coast
of Argolis, "gazing tearfully at Attica" and deploring the
misfortunes which beset the path of the politician[1].

---

[1] Plut. *Vit. Dem.* xxvi. The question of Demosthenes' guilt or
innocence has been much canvassed. On the whole it seems probable
that he received the 20 talents, but for political rather than personal

(vi) *The Last Effort.*

In 323 B.C. Alexander died at Babylon in his thirty-third

Death of Alexander, 323 B.C. year. A rising in Greece against Macedon followed, and Athens took an active part. When in the previous year (324 B.C.) Alexander, through his representative Nicanor, had bidden the Greeks assembled at the Olympian festival to suffer all exiles to return to the homes whence they had been driven, the official representatives of Athens, at whose head was Demosthenes as ἀρχιθέωρος, had protested against the king's command. Now supported by the Aetolians and other peoples of northern Greece the Athenians broke into open war. They had gathered a considerable army of mercenaries; and when Antipater marched southwards through Thessaly, he was outmanœuvred near Thermopylae and compelled to shut himself

Antipater besieged in Lamia. up with his forces in Lamia. There he was besieged by his enemies, who were commanded by the Athenian Leosthenes, a professional soldier and a brave and skilful captain. Meanwhile Athens was seeking aid from the Peloponnese. Embassies were despatched to the various cities, and Demosthenes, although an exile, supported their pleadings to the utmost of his power. Antipater, on his side, did not lack advocates; in particular, two fugitives from Athens, Pytheas and Callimedon, opposed the efforts of the Athenian representatives to rally the Peloponnesians to their cause. On one occasion Pytheas declared that an Athenian embassy in a city was like ass's milk in a house, a sign of "sickness"—in the former case, of the body politic,

An acute retort. in the latter, of an inmate of the dwelling. But Demosthenes neatly turned the comparison upon ends. The appearance of his associate Hypereides as a prosecutor of Demosthenes may have been designed to clear from suspicion of dealings with Harpalus the party to which both accuser and accused belonged. The comedians of course took Demosthenes' venality for granted. Cf. Timocles, Δῆλος (? Δήλιος) *circ.* 325 B.C. (Kock *fr.* 4).

> A. Δημοσθένης τάλαντα πεντήκοντ' ἔχει.
>
> B. μακάριος, εἴπερ μεταδίδωσι μηδενί.

its author by observing that there was indeed a resemblance between the Athenian embassy and the ass's milk, inasmuch as it was the object of both to replace "sickness" by "health[1]." The orator's services were recognized by his recall from banishment. A trireme was sent to bring him from Aegina; the civic and religious officers, as well as the whole population of the city, welcomed him home. When he landed once more upon his native soil, he lifted up his hands in thanks to   Demosthenes' Heaven, declaring that he had been vouchsafed   return. a return more glorious than that of Alcibiades, since it was due to persuasion and not to force.

The siege of Lamia was pressed vigorously by Leosthenes. But while inspecting the blockading trenches he was slain by a stone, and early in the year 322 B.C. Leonnatus, the governor of Hellespontine Phrygia, arrived with an army in Thessaly, and compelled the Greeks to withdraw their forces from Lamia in order to give him battle. The Macedonians were defeated and Leonnatus fell. But Antipater succeeded   Antipater in joining hands with the survivors, and together   relieved and victorious at they retreated into Macedonia to wait until   Crannon, reinforcements should reach them. Craterus   322 B.C. with an army of veterans was already on his way from the east; his troops united with those of Antipater and advanced into Thessaly; at Crannon in the late summer they achieved a complete triumph. The Greek resistance collapsed. When the victorious Macedonians arrived at Thebes, Athens made her submission; Demosthenes, Hypereides and others of their party fled from the city; and a Macedonian garrison was established in Munychia. On the proposition of Demades sentence of death was passed upon the fugitives. Demosthenes had taken sanctuary in the temple of Poseidon on Calauria, a small island off the coast of Argolis. There he was confronted by an emissary of Antipater, a certain Archias, who had formerly been an actor, but from his subsequent activities earned the sobriquet of "the exile-hunter" (ὁ φυγαδοθήρας). Archias at first sought to induce Demosthenes to leave his refuge by blandishments

---

[1] Plut. *Vit. Dem.* xxvii.

and fair words. "Your acting never convinced me, Archias," replied the orator, "nor will your promises do so now." The fair-spoken words were succeeded by threats. "This," observed Demosthenes, "is the *real* voice of Macedon; the other was a feigned one." Retiring within the temple he made as if to write, biting his pen as though in thought. Presently covering up his head he lay down. Archias bade him arise and renewed his professions and promises. But Demosthenes had no thought of falling into his hands alive. He had taken the poison which he had long kept in readiness[1], and now felt that he was near his end. Looking steadily at Archias he bade him, with a last gibe at his old profession, now play the part of Creon in the tragedy and refuse burial to his body[2]. With stumbling footsteps, supported by his captors, he went forth from the temple, lest by dying within it he should pollute Poseidon's holy place which Macedonian violence had profaned. As he passed the altar, which stood outside in front of the temple, he fell to the earth and with a groan breathed his last.

Death of Demosthenes.

Not many years later, by decree of the Athenian people, it was resolved that the right of maintenance at the public expense should belong for ever, from generation to generation, to the eldest member of the family of Demosthenes. In the market place there was set up a bronze image of the orator, standing with fingers interlaced[3]; upon the base of it was written,

The statue of Polyeuctus, 280 B.C.

"Had but thy power, Demosthenes, been equal to thy will,
  Hellas by Macedonian wight had been unconquered still[4]."

---

[1] The poison was concealed, according to different stories, in the pen, in a ring, and in a piece of cloth.

[2] Creon refused burial to the body of Polyneices. Cf. Soph. *Antigone* 198–206.

[3] The statue was the work of Polyeuctus. The marble statue of Demosthenes in the Vatican at Rome and a statue in Lord Sackville's collection at Knole are believed to be based upon it.

[4]
  εἴπερ ἴσην γνώμῃ ῥώμην, Δημόσθενες, εἶχες,
    οὔποτ' ἂν Ἑλλήνων ἦρξεν ἀνὴρ Μακεδών.
For the contempt in ἀνὴρ Μακεδών cf. p. xx, *n.* 2.

ANALYSIS

THE main object of the following analysis of the speeches is to throw some light upon the plan upon which they have been composed.

No attempt has been made to discriminate formally between narrative (διήγησις) and proof (πίστις), since the two are almost everywhere merged in each other, the orator finding the ground for his views in the story of the past or the survey of the present[1].

In each speech a practical proposal constitutes the central nucleus (cf. i. 16–20 ; ii. 11–13 ; iii. 10–20). A prefatory notice of this proposal may appear at the opening of the speech (e.g. the expedition to Olynthus, suggested in i. § 2, is fully expounded in §§ 16–18), or towards the close some aspect of it may undergo further development (e.g. in *Ol.* iii. the application of the Theoric fund to the public service suggested in the central passage of the speech, §§ 10–20, is elaborated in §§ 33–35).

The portions of the speech on either side of this nucleus are designed to exhibit the position of affairs which has given rise to the proposal. The speaker dwells on the situation in its brighter or its darker aspect according as he desires to appeal to his audience through their hopes or through their fears. In *Ol.* i. encouragement and warning are intermingled ; in *Ol.* ii. encouragement predominates; in *Ol.* iii. the tone is mainly one of grave admonition. In the latter part of his speech Demosthenes not infrequently returns to a point already insisted upon in the earlier part, reinforcing his previous argument by approaching the topic afresh from a different

[1] Cf. Butcher, *Demosthenes*, p. 156, "Narrative, refutation, and proof are blended or displaced according to the requirements of the case."

point of view[1]. For example, in *Ol.* ii. the weakness of Philip is shown, first (§§ 5–10), by a review of his relations with other powers, and, secondly (§§ 14–21), by a consideration of the condition of Macedonia and the character of the king's entourage.

Each speech commences with a formal introductory passage and ends with a conclusion designed to be of happy omen.

Ol. I.

§ 1. *Introduction.* You would give much to learn the policy which is to your interest. Listen to your advisers' counsels, both meditated and spontaneous, and it will be easy to select the course which is to your advantage.

§§ 2–5. *Philip's strength and weakness.* Action is imperative. We must send a force to help Olynthus and ambassadors to watch events. Philip has advantages, but he has disadvantages too. He has an ill record in the past, and, as a tyrant, is regarded with distrust.

§§ 6–9. *Athens' opportunity.* Action cannot be deferred. In Olynthus we have a stable ally. Had we used our past opportunities, we should have escaped our present difficulties *We* have made Philip great.

§§ 9–13. *The danger of neglect.* Heaven has been kind, though, like the spendthrift, we have not recognized our blessings. If Philip secures Olynthus, he will be invincible. Recall the energy and ambition which have marked his career.

§§ 14, 15. *The price of present ease.* Philip is active, we are remiss. Like those who borrow at high interest we shall have to pay a heavy reckoning.

§§ 16–18. *A plan of campaign.* Although your anger at failure does not always fall upon those responsible, I will put before you my plan. Despatch *two* armies—one to succour

---

[1] Cf. Butcher, *op. cit.* p. 157, "Demosthenes preferred repetition to copiousness; but in this sense, that he frequently came back upon the dominant idea, and enforced it, not with verbal repetition, but with fresh illustration."

Olynthus, one to attack Macedonia. Either alone will be in-effective.

§§ 19, 20. *A financial suggestion.* Money you have in plenty—if you will use it for war instead of festivals. Other-wise a special tax must be levied.

§§ 21–24. *Philip's difficulties Athens' chance.* Philip's expectations have not been fulfilled. His financial resources are in some degree threatened ; his subjects are ready to revolt. Success has made him reckless. Seize the occasion ; fight and summon others to the fray.

§§ 25–27. *Invasion the penalty of inaction.* War must come, if not now abroad, hereafter at home. Olynthus is the only bar to Philip's advance. An invasion of Attica would both ruin and disgrace us.

§ 28. *Conclusion.* Let all combine to keep the war abroad —men of wealth, men of military age, men of affairs. The acts of these last you will estimate according to the fortune in which you find yourselves. Heaven grant that fortune be fair !

Ol. II.

§§ 1, 2. *Introduction.* In offering us such allies as the Olynthians Heaven itself has helped us. It is now for us to help ourselves.

§§ 3, 4. *Philip's glory Athens' shame.* I will not speak of Philip's power. It is a glory to him but a disgrace to us, for it is to some among us that he owes it. I will speak rather of what is to his discredit.

§§ 5–8. *Philip's duplicity and its consequence.* A review of his actions will exhibit his past treachery and prove that it can no longer serve him in the future. He rose through deceiving all with whom he dealt. Their eyes have now been opened and he will fall.

§§ 9, 10. *The insecurity of Philip's power.* Force cannot keep what fraud has won. Power founded on wickedness and greed collapses of itself.

§§ 11–13. *Demosthenes' plan.* Send help to Olynthus and an embassy to Thessaly to foment opposition to Philip. Words —especially *our* words—without deeds are vain. Act, raise money, fight, and Philip's weakness will reveal itself.

§§ 14–21. *Macedonia's unsound condition.* United with another power Macedonia may have been of some account ; alone she is weak. Her people are distressed by ceaseless campaigning and loss of trade. Philip has surrounded himself with inefficiency and profligacy. As in the physical body, so in the body politic, latent evil will, under stress, make its presence apparent.

§§ 22–26. *Athens' inaction.* Fortune is not kinder to Philip than to us, but *he* acts while *we* are idle. It is not strange that he wins, but that we, with our past record, now fail to act. Our present case is due to mutual recrimination and hoping that others will act. Persistence in what has ruined us cannot lead to improvement.

§§ 27–30. *Evils to be reformed.* We must change our policy and play our part. At present your generals have to employ their troops where they can obtain pay for them. Your politics are dominated by factions. Be your own masters. If all the burdens are thrown upon one section alone, that section will fail you.

§ 31. *Conclusion.* In a word—All must bear their fair share of taxation and military service. All must have equal right to be heard. Advice must be accepted, not because of its author, but on its merits. So will your whole position change for the better.

Ol. III.

§§ 1, 2. *Introduction.* We have to consider, not retaliation upon Philip, but the safety of ourselves and our allies.

§ 3. *The need of frankness.* It is difficult to address you. You lack will, not knowledge. Honest speech may improve your position ; speech designed only to please has ruined it.

§§ 4, 5. *Athens' remissness in the past.* Two or three years ago an ambitious scheme was followed by inadequate action. Philip's illness gave you your chance. Instead of seizing it you abandoned your effort.

§§ 6-9. *Athens' present opportunity.* Now the Olynthians are at war with Philip. Lend prompt and vigorous aid. To fail to do so will involve, not disgrace alone, but peril. There is no other power to stand between us and Philip.

§§ 10-13. *Legal reforms the first step.* At present certain laws are a bar to salutary proposals. Compel those who introduced those laws to secure their repeal.

§§ 14, 15. *Action the supreme necessity.* Decrees alone are useless. Otherwise your position would be a far different one. Action alone is wanting to ensure success.

§§ 16-18. *The call is to every man.* We have every reason to oppose Philip. It is we who have made him powerful, though, like fugitives in a rout, we shall blame any one but ourselves. Cease recrimination and unite in discovering the best policy. If that policy involves burdens, that is not the fault of its advocate.

§§ 19, 20. *The deceitfulness of wishes.* We cannot spend the same money on festivals and on war. Let us disregard wishes and face facts. It would be shameful to suffer lack of means to prevent us from opposing Philip.

§§ 21-26. *The story of the Past.* I seek, not personal popularity as do modern statesmen, but the city's safety as did the statesmen of old. Consider their achievements—supremacy in Greece, wealth, power abroad, triumphs on land and sea. Their private fortunes remained humble ; their object was the city's weal, not their own ; their means good faith, religion and equity.

§§ 27-29. *The contrast of the Present.* Under our modern statesmen, with a clear field, we have lost territory and allies; have spent treasure in vain; and have raised up against ourselves a powerful enemy. While the state's fortunes have declined, those of her statesmen have prospered.

§§ 30-32. *The Reason.* The change is due to your lack of control over your leaders. You are their servants and cringe to them. How then can you have the lofty spirit of old? A man's *morale* is determined by his habits. You do not like to hear the truth; I am surprised you have suffered it from me.

§§ 33-36. *The Remedy.* Reform your ways. Serve, act, put your monies to a proper use. At present these do you no real good. Service in some capacity should be the condition of receiving payment from the state. Thus both the state and the individual are benefited. Do not talk about your *mercenaries'* successes, but serve *yourselves*. Stand firm in the post of honour which your forefathers won and bequeathed to you.

§ 36. *Conclusion.* "I have stated roughly what I think of advantage. God grant you choose what is best for the state and for us all!"

THE SOURCES OF THE TEXT

THE MSS. of Demosthenes exceed 150 in number. The tradition which they represent is derived from the recension of the text made by the scholars of Alexandria in the third century B.C., but the oldest of the existing MSS was not written earlier than the tenth century A.D. There have been found in Egypt small portions of the Demosthenic writings, which were inscribed upon papyrus prior to the Christian era. Two such fragments contain parts of *Ol.* ii. § 10 and § 15, but exhibit no reading unknown to the MSS.[1]

[1] Reproduced by Sir F. G. Kenyon in the *Classical Review* for Dec. 1892 (Vol. VI), "The only noticeable point here is the confirmation of the vulgate reading ἄλλος Μακεδόνων βασιλεύς as against the reading ἄλλος Μακεδόνων adopted by Blass from the scholia."

The most important MS., usually denominated by the letter S[1], is in the Bibliothèque Nationale at Paris. It is written on parchment in minuscule letters, and is ascribed to the early part of the tenth century A.D. It has been corrected, not only by the original scribe but by several later hands as well, and contains in the margin a large number of alternative readings and notes. As compared with other MSS. it presents, generally speaking, a terser and more vigorous text, being comparatively free from interpolation and the admixture of glosses. Such mistakes as occur are almost without exception clerical errors which can be readily corrected[2].

Apart from this Paris MS. chief authority is generally ascribed to a MS. denominated A (i.e. Augustanus), which was written on parchment probably in the eleventh century A.D. This MS., which was formerly at Augsburg[3] and is now at Munich, has suffered from mutilation, one result of which is that it now lacks a considerable portion of the text of the Olynthiac speeches. There exist, however, some sheets, evidently of a later date, which contain the whole of the missing portions with the exception of the earlier part of *Ol.* i.

Another MS. which is of considerable value in the establishment of the text is M (i.e. Marcianus), to be found in the Library of St Mark at Venice. It is an eleventh century MS, written on parchment, and containing a large number of notes in the margin as well as frequent corrections by various hands in the text.

The speeches of Demosthenes were well known to, and freely quoted by, later writers. Such quotations however, while they may occasionally serve to confirm a reading, cannot fairly be employed to set aside the evidence of the MSS. If made from memory the quotation may be inaccurate ; if made from

---

[1] The MS. formerly belonged to a "Sosandrian" monastery.

[2] A facsimile has been published at Paris by M. Omont.

[3] Hence the name of the MS. since Augsburg = Augusta Vindelicorum.

the written words, we have no means of estimating the value of that text from which it was drawn. It has been pointed out that Dionysius of Halicarnassus [1], who quotes the opening of Demosthenes' *Third Philippic* four times, presents us with *three* varieties of text. Still less trustworthy as sources of information concerning the text are those echoes of Demosthenes' writings to be found in rhetoricians, like Libanius (fourth century A.D.), and parodists, like Lucian [2] (second century A.D.). In such compositions it is clearly impossible to disentangle with confidence the original words of Demosthenes from the accretions and alterations due to the writer of a later age.

[1] A learned and excellent literary critic, who died at Rome in the year 7 B.C.

[2] Index A, s.v. Lucian.

ΟΛΥΝΘΙΑΚΟΣ Α

ΛΙΒΑΝΙΟΥ ΥΠΟΘΕΣΙΣ

Ὄλυνθος ἦν πόλις ἐπὶ Θρᾴκης, Ἑλληνικὸν δὲ ταύτῃ τῶν ἐνοικούντων τὸ γένος, ἀπὸ Χαλκίδος τῆς ἐν Εὐβοίᾳ· ἡ δὲ Χαλκὶς Ἀθηναίων ἄποικος. πολλοὶ δὲ πόλεμοι καὶ ἔνδοξοι τῆς Ὀλύνθου· Ἀθηναίοις τε γὰρ ἐπολέμησεν ἄρχουσι τῶν Ἑλλήνων τὸ παλαιὸν καὶ αὖθις Λακεδαιμονίοις· χρόνῳ τ᾽ εἰς δύναμιν προῆλθε μεγάλην καὶ τῶν συγγενῶν πόλεων ἐπῆρχεν· ἦν γὰρ ἐπὶ Θρᾴκης πολύ τι γένος Χαλκιδικόν. Φιλίππῳ δὲ 2 τῷ Μακεδόνων βασιλεῖ συμμαχίαν οἱ Ὀλύνθιοι ποιησάμενοι καὶ πολεμοῦντες μετ᾽ αὐτοῦ πρὸς Ἀθηναίους τὸ κατ᾽ ἀρχάς, καὶ τοῦτο μὲν Ἀνθεμοῦντα παρὰ τοῦ Μακεδόνος εἰληφότες, πόλιν ἀμφισβητήσιμον Μακεδόσι καὶ Ὀλυνθίοις, τοῦτο δὲ Ποτείδαιαν, ἣν Ἀθηναίων ἐχόντων ἐκπολιορκήσας ὁ Φίλιππος Ὀλυνθίοις παρέδωκεν, ὕστερον ὑποπτεύειν ἤρξαντο τὸν βασιλέα, ὁρῶντες αὐτοῦ ταχεῖαν καὶ πολλὴν τὴν αὔξησιν, οὐ πιστὴν δὲ τὴν γνώμην. ἀποδημοῦντα δὲ τηρήσαντες αὐτόν, πέμψαντες πρέσβεις πρὸς Ἀθηναίους κατελύσαντο τὸν πρὸς αὐτοὺς πόλεμον, ποιοῦντες τοῦτο παρὰ τὰς συνθήκας τὰς πρὸς Φίλιππον· συνετέθειντο γὰρ καὶ κοινῇ πολεμεῖν πρὸς Ἀθηναίους, κἂν ἄλλο τι δόξῃ, κοινῇ σπείσασθαι. ὁ δὲ Φίλιππος πάλαι 3 μὲν προφάσεως ἐπ᾽ αὐτοὺς δεόμενος, τότε δὲ ταύτην λαβών, ὡς τὰς συνθήκας παραβεβηκόσι καὶ πρὸς τοὺς ἐχθροὺς τοὺς ἑαυτοῦ φιλίαν ἐσπεισμένοις πόλεμον ἐπήνεγκεν. οἱ δὲ πεπόμφασι πρέσβεις εἰς Ἀθήνας περὶ βοηθείας, οἷς ὁ Δημοσθένης συναγορεύει, βοηθεῖν κελεύων τοῖς Ὀλυνθίοις. καί φησι τὴν Ὀλυνθίων σωτηρίαν ἀσφάλειαν τῶν Ἀθηναίων εἶναι· σῳζομένων γὰρ τῶν Ὀλυνθίων οὐδέποθ' ἥξειν εἰς τὴν Ἀττικὴν Φίλιππον, ἀλλὰ τοῖς Ἀθηναίοις ἐξουσίαν ἔσεσθαι πλεῖν ἐπὶ τὴν Μακεδονίαν κἀκεῖ ποιεῖσθαι τὸν πόλεμον· εἰ δ' ὑπὸ Φιλίππῳ γένοιθ' ἡ πόλις αὕτη, ἀνεῖσθαι τὴν ἐπὶ τὰς Ἀθήνας ὁδὸν τῷ βασιλεῖ. φησὶ δὲ δύσμαχον εἶναι τὸν Φίλιππον οὐχ ὡς ὑπείληπται, θαρσύνων ἐπ' αὐτὸν τοὺς Ἀθηναίους.

4 Διείλεκται δὲ καὶ περὶ τῶν δημοσίων χρημάτων, συμβουλεύων αὐτὰ ποιῆσαι στρατιωτικὰ ἀντὶ θεωρικῶν. καὶ τὸ ἔθος οὐ πρόδηλον ὄν, ᾧ ἐχρῶνθ' οἱ Ἀθηναῖαι, ἀνάγκη σαφηνίσαι. οὐκ ὄντος τὸ παλαιὸν θεάτρου λιθίνου παρ' αὐτοῖς, ἀλλὰ ξυλίνων συμπηγνυμένων ἰκρίων καὶ πάντων καταλαμβάνειν τόπον σπευδόντων, πληγαί τ' ἐγίνοντο καί που καὶ τραύματα. τοῦτο κωλῦσαι βουληθέντες οἱ προεστῶτες τῶν Ἀθηναίων ὠνητοὺς ἐποιήσαντο τοὺς τόπους, καὶ ἕκαστον ἔδει [διδόναι] δύ' ὀβολοὺς καταβαλόντα θέαν ἔχειν· ἵνα δὲ μὴ δοκῶσιν οἱ πένητες τῷ ἀναλώματι λυπεῖσθαι, ἐκ τοῦ δημοσίου λαμβάνειν ἕκαστον ἐτάχθη τοὺς δύ' ὀβολούς. ἐντεῦθεν μὲν οὖν τὸ ἔθος ἤρξατο, προῆλθε δ' εἰς τοῦτο, ὥστ' οὐκ εἰς τοὺς τόπους μόνον ἐλάμβανον, ἀλλ' ἁπλῶς πάντα τὰ δημόσια χρήματα διενέμοντο. ὅθεν καὶ περὶ τὰς στρατείας ὀκνηροὶ κατέστησαν. 5 πάλαι μὲν γὰρ στρατευόμενοι μισθὸν παρὰ τῆς πόλεως ἐλάμβανον, τότε δ' ἐν ταῖς θεωρίαις καὶ ταῖς ἑορταῖς οἴκοι μένοντες διενέμοντο τὰ χρήματα· οὐκέτ' οὖν ἤθελον ἐξιέναι καὶ κινδυνεύειν, ἀλλὰ καὶ νόμον ἔθεντο περὶ τῶν θεωρικῶν τούτων χρημάτων, θάνατον ἀπειλοῦντα τῷ γράψαντι μετατεθῆναί τε ταῦτ' εἰς τὴν ἀρχαίαν τάξιν καὶ γενέσθαι στρατιωτικά. διὸ Δημοσθένης εὐλαβῶς ἅπτεται τῆς περὶ τούτου συμβουλῆς, καὶ ὑπερωτήσας ἑαυτὸν ὅτι "σὺ γράφεις ταῦτ' εἶναι στρατιωτικά;" ἐπιφέρει "μὰ Δί' οὐκ ἔγωγε." ταῦτα μὲν περὶ τῶν θεωρικῶν.

Διείλεκται δ' ὁ ῥήτωρ καὶ περὶ πολιτικῆς δυνάμεως, 6 ἀξιῶν αὐτοὺς στρατεύεσθαι, καὶ μὴ διὰ ξένων, ὥσπερ εἰώθεσαν, ποιεῖσθαι τὴν βοήθειαν· τοῦτο γὰρ αἴτιον εἶναί φησι τοῦ τὰ πράγματ' ἀπόλλυσθαι.

Ἀντὶ πολλῶν ἄν, ὦ ἄνδρες Ἀθηναῖοι, χρημάτων 1 ὑμᾶς ἑλέσθαι νομίζω, εἰ φανερὸν γένοιτο τὸ μέλλον συνοίσειν τῇ πόλει περὶ ὧν νυνὶ σκοπεῖτε. ὅτε τοίνυν τοῦθ' οὕτως ἔχει, προσήκει προθύμως ἐθέλειν ἀκούειν τῶν βουλομένων συμβουλεύειν· οὐ γὰρ μόνον εἴ τι χρήσιμον ἐσκεμμένος ἥκει τις, τοῦτ' ἂν ἀκούσαντες λάβοιτε, ἀλλὰ καὶ τῆς ὑμετέρας τύχης ὑπολαμβάνω πολλὰ τῶν δεόντων ἐκ τοῦ παραχρῆμ' ἐνίοις ἂν ἐπελθεῖν εἰπεῖν, ὥστ' ἐξ ἁπάντων ῥᾳδίαν τὴν τοῦ συμφέροντος ὑμῖν αἵρεσιν γενέσθαι.

Ὁ μὲν οὖν παρὼν καιρός, ὦ ἄνδρες Ἀθηναῖοι, 2 μόνον οὐχὶ λέγει φωνὴν ἀφιεὶς ὅτι τῶν πραγμάτων ὑμῖν ἐκείνων αὐτοῖς ἀντιληπτέον ἐστίν, εἴπερ ὑπὲρ σωτηρίας αὐτῶν φροντίζετε· ἡμεῖς δ' οὐκ οἶδ' ὅντινά μοι δοκοῦμεν ἔχειν τρόπον πρὸς αὐτά. ἔστι δὴ τά γ' ἐμοὶ δοκοῦντα, ψηφίσασθαι μὲν ἤδη τὴν βοήθειαν καὶ παρασκευάσασθαι τὴν ταχίστην, ὅπως ἐνθένδε βοηθήσητε καὶ μὴ πάθητε ταὐτὸν ὅπερ καὶ πρότερον, πρεσβείαν δὲ πέμπειν, ἥτις ταῦτ' ἐρεῖ καὶ παρέσται τοῖς πράγμασιν. ὡς ἔστι μάλιστα τοῦτο δέος, μὴ 3 πανοῦργος ὢν καὶ δεινὸς ἄνθρωπος πράγμασι χρῆσθαι, τὰ μὲν εἴκων, ἡνίκ' ἂν τύχῃ, τὰ δ' ἀπειλῶν (ἀξιόπιστος δ' ἂν εἰκότως φαίνοιτο), τὰ δ' ἡμᾶς διαβάλλων καὶ τὴν ἀπουσίαν τὴν ἡμετέραν, τρέψηται καὶ παρασπάσηταί τι τῶν ὅλων πραγμάτων. οὐ μὴν 4 ἀλλ' ἐπιεικῶς, ὦ ἄνδρες Ἀθηναῖοι, τοῦθ' ὃ δυσμαχώ-

τατόν ἐστι τῶν Φιλίππου πραγμάτων, καὶ βέλτιστον
ὑμῖν· τὸ γὰρ εἶναι πάντων ἐκεῖνον ἕν᾽ ὄντα κύριον
καὶ ῥητῶν καὶ ἀπορρήτων, καὶ ἅμα στρατηγὸν καὶ
δεσπότην καὶ ταμίαν, καὶ πανταχοῦ αὐτὸν παρεῖναι
τῷ στρατεύματι, πρὸς μὲν τὸ τὰ τοῦ πολέμου ταχὺ
καὶ κατὰ καιρὸν πράττεσθαι πολλῷ προέχει, πρὸς δὲ
τὰς καταλλαγάς, ἃς ἂν ἐκεῖνος ποιήσαιθ᾽ ἄσμενος
5 πρὸς Ὀλυνθίους, ἐναντίως ἔχει. δῆλον γάρ ἐστι τοῖς
Ὀλυνθίοις ὅτι νῦν οὐ περὶ δόξης οὐδ᾽ ὑπὲρ μέρους
χώρας κινδυνεύουσιν, ἀλλ᾽ ἀναστάσεως καὶ ἀνδραποδισμοῦ τῆς πατρίδος, καὶ ἴσασιν ἅ τ᾽ Ἀμφιπολιτῶν ἐποίησε τοὺς παραδόντας αὐτῷ τὴν πόλιν καὶ
Πυδναίων τοὺς ὑποδεξαμένους· καὶ ὅλως ἄπιστον,
οἶμαι, ταῖς πολιτείαις ἡ τυραννίς, ἄλλως τε κἂν
ὅμορον χώραν ἔχωσι.
6 Ταῦτ᾽ οὖν ἐγνωκότας ὑμᾶς, ὦ ἄνδρες Ἀθηναῖοι,
καὶ τἄλλ᾽ ἃ προσήκει πάντ᾽ ἐνθυμουμένους φημὶ δεῖν
ἐθελῆσαι καὶ παροξυνθῆναι καὶ τῷ πολέμῳ προσ-
έχειν εἴπερ ποτὲ καὶ νῦν, χρήματ᾽ εἰσφέροντας
προθύμως καὶ αὐτοὺς ἐξιόντας καὶ μηδὲν ἐλλείποντας. οὐδὲ γὰρ λόγος οὐδὲ σκῆψις ἔθ᾽ ὑμῖν τοῦ μὴ
7 τὰ δέοντα ποιεῖν ἐθέλειν ὑπολείπεται. νυνὶ γὰρ ὃ
πάντες ἐθρυλεῖτε, ὡς Ὀλυνθίους ἐκπολεμῶσαι δεῖ
Φιλίππῳ, γέγονεν αὐτόματον, καὶ ταῦθ᾽ ὡς ἂν ὑμῖν
μάλιστα συμφέροι. εἰ μὲν γὰρ ὑφ᾽ ὑμῶν πεισθέντες
ἀνείλοντο τὸν πόλεμον, σφαλεροὶ σύμμαχοι καὶ μέχρι
του ταῦτ᾽ ἂν ἐγνωκότες ἦσαν ἴσως· ἐπειδὴ δ᾽ ἐκ τῶν
πρὸς αὐτοὺς ἐγκλημάτων μισοῦσιν, βεβαίαν εἰκὸς
τὴν ἔχθραν αὐτοὺς ὑπὲρ ὧν φοβοῦνται καὶ πεπόνθα-
8 σιν ἔχειν. οὐ δεῖ δὴ τοιοῦτον, ὦ ἄνδρες Ἀθηναῖοι,
παραπεπτωκότα καιρὸν ἀφεῖναι, οὐδὲ παθεῖν ταὐτὸν

ὅπερ ἤδη πολλάκις πρότερον πεπόνθατε. εἰ γὰρ ὅθ᾽
ἥκομεν Εὐβοεῦσιν βεβοηθηκότες καὶ παρῆσαν Ἀμφιπολιτῶν Ἱέραξ καὶ Στρατοκλῆς ἐπὶ τουτὶ τὸ βῆμα
κελεύοντες ἡμᾶς πλεῖν καὶ παραλαμβάνειν τὴν πόλιν,
τὴν αὐτὴν παρειχόμεθ᾽ ἡμεῖς ὑπὲρ ἡμῶν αὐτῶν προ-
θυμίαν ἥνπερ ὑπὲρ τῆς Εὐβοέων σωτηρίας, εἴχετ᾽ ἂν
Ἀμφίπολιν τότε καὶ πάντων τῶν μετὰ ταῦτ᾽ ἂν ἦτ᾽
ἀπηλλαγμένοι πραγμάτων. καὶ πάλιν ἡνίκα Πύδνα, 9
Ποτείδαια, Μεθώνη, Παγασαί, τἆλλ᾽, ἵνα μὴ καθ᾽
ἕκαστα λέγων διατρίβω, πολιορκούμεν᾽ ἀπηγγέλλετο,
εἰ τότε τούτων ἑνὶ τῷ πρώτῳ προθύμως καὶ ὡς προσ-
ῆκεν ἐβοηθήσαμεν αὐτοί, ῥᾴονι καὶ πολὺ ταπεινο-
τέρῳ νῦν ἂν ἐχρώμεθα τῷ Φιλίππῳ. νῦν δὲ τὸ μὲν
παρὸν ἀεὶ προϊέμενοι, τὰ δὲ μέλλοντ᾽ αὐτόματ᾽ οἰόμενοι σχήσειν καλῶς, ηὐξήσαμεν, ὦ ἄνδρες Ἀθηναῖοι,
Φίλιππον ἡμεῖς καὶ κατεστήσαμεν τηλικοῦτον, ἡλίκος
οὐδείς πω βασιλεὺς γέγονε Μακεδονίας.

Νυνὶ δὴ καιρὸς ἥκει τις, οὗτος ὁ τῶν Ὀλυνθίων,
αὐτόματος τῇ πόλει, ὃς οὐδενός ἐστιν ἐλάττων τῶν
προτέρων ἐκείνων. καὶ ἔμοιγε δοκεῖ τις ἄν, ὦ ἄνδρες 10
Ἀθηναῖοι, δίκαιος λογιστὴς τῶν παρὰ τῶν θεῶν ἡμῖν
ὑπηργμένων καταστάς, καίπερ οὐκ ἐχόντων ὡς δεῖ
πολλῶν, ὅμως μεγάλην ἂν ἔχειν αὐτοῖς χάριν, εἰκό-
τως· τὸ μὲν γὰρ πόλλ᾽ ἀπολωλεκέναι κατὰ τὸν
πόλεμον τῆς ἡμετέρας ἀμελείας ἄν τις θείη δικαίως,
τὸ δὲ μήτε πάλαι τοῦτο πεπονθέναι πεφηνέναι τέ τιν᾽
ἡμῖν συμμαχίαν τούτων ἀντίρροπον, ἂν βουλώμεθα
χρῆσθαι, τῆς παρ᾽ ἐκείνων εὐνοίας εὐεργέτημ᾽ ἂν
ἔγωγε θείην. ἀλλ᾽, οἶμαι, παρόμοιόν ἐστιν ὅπερ καὶ 11
περὶ τῆς τῶν χρημάτων κτήσεως· ἂν μὲν γάρ, ὅσ᾽
ἄν τις λάβῃ, καὶ σώσῃ, μεγάλην ἔχει τῇ τύχῃ τὴν

χάριν, ἂν δ' ἀναλώσας λάθῃ, συνανήλωσε καὶ τὸ
μεμνῆσθαι [τὴν χάριν]. καὶ περὶ τῶν πραγμάτων
οὕτως· οἱ μὴ χρησάμενοι τοῖς καιροῖς ὀρθῶς, οὐδ' εἰ
συνέβη τι παρὰ τῶν θεῶν χρηστόν, μνημονεύουσι·
πρὸς γὰρ τὸ τελευταῖον ἐκβὰν ἕκαστον τῶν πρὶν
ὑπαρξάντων κρίνεται. διὸ καὶ σφόδρα δεῖ τῶν λοιπῶν ὑμᾶς, ὦ ἄνδρες Ἀθηναῖοι, φροντίσαι, ἵνα ταῦτ'
ἐπανορθωσάμενοι τὴν ἐπὶ τοῖς πεπραγμένοις ἀδοξίαν
12 ἀποτριψώμεθα. εἰ δὲ προησόμεθ', ὦ ἄνδρες Ἀθηναῖοι, καὶ τούτους τοὺς ἀνθρώπους, εἶτ' Ὄλυνθον
ἐκεῖνος καταστρέψεται, φρασάτω τις ἐμοὶ τί τὸ
κωλῦον ἔτ' αὐτὸν ἔσται βαδίζειν ὅποι βούλεται. ἆρα
λογίζεταί τις ὑμῶν, ὦ ἄνδρες Ἀθηναῖοι, καὶ θεωρεῖ
τὸν τρόπον δι' ὃν μέγας γέγονεν ἀσθενὴς ὢν τὸ κατ'
ἀρχὰς Φίλιππος; τὸ πρῶτον Ἀμφίπολιν λαβών,
μετὰ ταῦτα Πύδναν, πάλιν Ποτείδαιαν, Μεθώνην
13 αὖθις, εἶτα Θετταλίας ἐπέβη· μετὰ ταῦτα Φεράς,
Παγασάς, Μαγνησίαν, πάνθ' ὃν ἐβούλετ' εὐτρεπίσας
τρόπον ᾤχετ' εἰς Θρᾴκην· εἶτ' ἐκεῖ τοὺς μὲν ἐκβαλών,
τοὺς δὲ καταστήσας τῶν βασιλέων, ἠσθένησεν· πάλιν
ῥάσας οὐκ ἐπὶ τὸ ῥαθυμεῖν ἀπέκλινεν, ἀλλ' εὐθὺς
Ὀλυνθίοις ἐπεχείρησεν. τὰς δ' ἐπ' Ἰλλυριοὺς καὶ
Παίονας αὐτοῦ καὶ πρὸς Ἀρύββαν καὶ ὅποι τις ἂν
εἴποι παραλείπω στρατείας.

14   Τί οὖν, ἄν τις εἴποι, ταῦτα λέγεις ἡμῖν νῦν; ἵνα
γνῶτ', ὦ ἄνδρες Ἀθηναῖοι, καὶ αἴσθησθ' ἀμφότερα,
καὶ τὸ προΐεσθαι καθ' ἕκαστον ἀεί τι τῶν πραγμάτων ὡς ἀλυσιτελές, καὶ τὴν φιλοπραγμοσύνην ᾗ
χρῆται καὶ συζῇ Φίλιππος, ὑφ' ἧς οὐκ ἔστιν ὅπως
ἀγαπήσας τοῖς πεπραγμένοις ἡσυχίαν σχήσει. εἰ δ'
ὁ μὲν ὡς ἀεί τι μεῖζον τῶν ὑπαρχόντων δεῖ πράττειν

ἐγνωκὼς ἔσται, ἡμεῖς δ᾿ ὡς οὐδενὸς ἀντιληπτέον
ἐρρωμένως τῶν πραγμάτων, σκοπεῖσθ᾿ εἰς τί ποτ᾿
ἐλπὶς ταῦτα τελευτῆσαι. πρὸς θεῶν, τίς οὕτως 15
εὐήθης ἐστὶν ὑμῶν ὅστις ἀγνοεῖ τὸν ἐκεῖθεν πόλεμον
δεῦρ᾿ ἥξοντα, ἂν ἀμελήσωμεν; ἀλλὰ μήν, εἰ τοῦτο
γενήσεται, δέδοικ᾿, ὦ ἄνδρες Ἀθηναῖοι, μὴ τὸν αὐτὸν
τρόπον ὥσπερ οἱ δανειζόμενοι ῥᾳδίως ἐπὶ τοῖς μεγά-
λοις [τόκοις] μικρὸν εὐπορήσαντες χρόνον ὕστερον
καὶ τῶν ἀρχαίων ἀπέστησαν, οὕτως καὶ ἡμεῖς [ἂν]
ἐπὶ πολλῷ φανῶμεν ἐρρᾳθυμηκότες, καὶ ἅπαντα πρὸς
ἡδονὴν ζητοῦντες πολλὰ καὶ χαλεπὰ ὧν οὐκ ἐβουλό-
μεθ᾿ ὕστερον εἰς ἀνάγκην ἔλθωμεν ποιεῖν, καὶ κινδυνεύσωμεν περὶ τῶν ἐν αὐτῇ τῇ χώρᾳ.

Τὸ μὲν οὖν ἐπιτιμᾶν ἴσως φήσαι τις ἂν ῥᾴδιον 16
καὶ παντὸς εἶναι, τὸ δ᾿ ὑπὲρ τῶν παρόντων ὅ τι δεῖ
πράττειν ἀποφαίνεσθαι, τοῦτ᾿ εἶναι συμβούλου. ἐγὼ
δ᾿ οὐκ ἀγνοῶ μέν, ὦ ἄνδρες Ἀθηναῖοι, τοῦθ᾿, ὅτι
πολλάκις ὑμεῖς οὐ τοὺς αἰτίους ἀλλὰ τοὺς ὑστάτους
περὶ τῶν πραγμάτων εἰπόντας ἐν ὀργῇ ποιεῖσθε, ἄν
τι μὴ κατὰ γνώμην ἐκβῇ· οὐ μὴν οἶμαι δεῖν τὴν ἰδίαν
ἀσφάλειαν σκοποῦνθ᾿ ὑποστείλασθαι περὶ ὧν ὑμῖν
συμφέρειν ἡγοῦμαι. φημὶ δὴ διχῇ βοηθητέον εἶναι 17
τοῖς πράγμασιν ὑμῖν, τῷ τε τὰς πόλεις τοῖς Ὀλυνθίοις σῴζειν καὶ τοὺς τοῦτο ποιήσοντας στρατιώτας
ἐκπέμπειν, καὶ τῷ τὴν ἐκείνου χώραν κακῶς ποιεῖν
καὶ τριήρεσι καὶ στρατιώταις ἑτέροις· εἰ δὲ θατέρου
τούτων ὀλιγωρήσετε, ὀκνῶ μὴ μάταιος ἡμῖν ἡ στρα-
τεία γένηται. εἴτε γὰρ ὑμῶν τὴν ἐκείνου κακῶς 18
ποιούντων, ὑπομείνας τοῦτ᾿ Ὄλυνθον παραστήσεται,
ῥᾳδίως ἐπὶ τὴν οἰκείαν ἐλθὼν ἀμυνεῖται· εἴτε βοηθησάντων μόνον ὑμῶν εἰς Ὄλυνθον, ἀκινδύνως ὁρῶν

ἔχοντα τὰ οἴκοι προσκαθεδεῖται καὶ προσεδρεύσει
τοῖς πράγμασι, περιέσται τῷ χρόνῳ τῶν πολιορκου-
μένων. δεῖ δὴ πολλὴν καὶ διχῇ τὴν βοήθειαν εἶναι.

19   Καὶ περὶ μὲν τῆς βοηθείας ταῦτα γιγνώσκω·
περὶ δὲ χρημάτων πόρου. ἔστιν, ὦ ἄνδρες Ἀθηναῖοι,
χρήμαθ᾽ ὑμῖν, ἔστιν ὅσ᾽ οὐδενὶ τῶν ἄλλων ἀνθρώπων
στρατιωτικά· ταῦτα δ᾽ ὑμεῖς οὕτως ὡς βούλεσθε
λαμβάνετε. εἰ μὲν οὖν ταῦτα τοῖς στρατευομένοις
ἀποδώσετε, οὐδενὸς ὑμῖν προσδεῖ πόρου, εἰ δὲ μή,
προσδεῖ, μᾶλλον δ᾽ ἅπαντος ἐνδεῖ τοῦ πόρου. τί
οὖν; ἄν τις εἴποι, σὺ γράφεις ταῦτ᾽ εἶναι στρατιω-
20 τικά; μὰ Δί᾽ οὐκ ἔγωγε. ἐγὼ μὲν γὰρ ἡγοῦμαι
στρατιώτας δεῖν κατασκευασθῆναι καὶ ταῦτ᾽ εἶναι
στρατιωτικὰ καὶ μίαν σύνταξιν εἶναι τὴν αὐτὴν τοῦ
τε λαμβάνειν καὶ τοῦ ποιεῖν τὰ δέοντα, ὑμεῖς δ᾽ οὕτω
πως ἄνευ πραγμάτων λαμβάνειν εἰς τὰς ἑορτάς.
ἔστι δὴ λοιπόν, οἶμαι, πάντας εἰσφέρειν, ἂν πολλῶν
δέῃ, πολλά, ἂν ὀλίγων, ὀλίγα. δεῖ δὲ χρημάτων, καὶ
ἄνευ τούτων οὐδὲν ἔστι γενέσθαι τῶν δεόντων.
λέγουσι δὲ καὶ ἄλλους τινὰς ἄλλοι πόρους, ὧν
ἕλεσθ᾽ ὅστις ὑμῖν συμφέρειν δοκεῖ· καὶ ἕως ἐστὶ
καιρός, ἀντιλάβεσθε τῶν πραγμάτων.

21   Ἄξιον δ᾽ ἐνθυμηθῆναι καὶ λογίσασθαι τὰ πράγ-
ματ᾽ ἐν ᾧ καθέστηκε νυνὶ τὰ Φιλίππου. οὔτε γάρ,
ὡς δοκεῖ καὶ φήσειέ τις ἂν μὴ σκοπῶν ἀκριβῶς,
εὐτρεπῶς οὐδ᾽ ὡς ἂν κάλλιστ᾽ αὐτῷ τὰ παρόντ᾽ ἔχει,
οὔτ᾽ ἂν ἐξήνεγκε τὸν πόλεμόν ποτε τοῦτον ἐκεῖνος, εἰ
πολεμεῖν ᾠήθη δεήσειν αὐτόν, ἀλλ᾽ ὡς ἐπιὼν ἅπαντα
τότ᾽ ἤλπιζε τὰ πραγματ᾽ ἀναιρήσεσθαι, κᾆτα διέ-
ψευσται. τοῦτο δὴ πρῶτον αὐτὸν ταράττει παρὰ
γνώμην γεγονὸς καὶ πολλὴν ἀθυμίαν αὐτῷ παρέχει,

εἶτα τὰ τῶν Θετταλῶν· ταῦτα γὰρ ἄπιστα μὲν ἦν 22
δήπου φύσει καὶ ἀεὶ πᾶσιν ἀνθρώποις, κομιδῇ δ',
ὥσπερ ἦν, καὶ ἔστι νῦν τούτῳ. καὶ γὰρ Παγασὰς
ἀπαιτεῖν αὐτόν εἰσιν ἐψηφισμένοι, καὶ Μαγνησίαν
κεκωλύκασι τειχίζειν. ἤκουον δ' ἔγωγέ τινων ὡς
οὐδὲ τοὺς λιμένας καὶ τὰς ἀγορὰς ἔτι δώσοιεν αὐτῷ
καρποῦσθαι· τὰ γὰρ κοινὰ τὰ Θετταλῶν ἀπὸ τούτων
δέοι διοικεῖν, οὐ Φίλιππον λαμβάνειν. εἰ δὲ τούτων
ἀποστερήσεται τῶν χρημάτων, εἰς στενὸν κομιδῇ τὰ
τῆς τροφῆς τοῖς ξένοις αὐτῷ καταστήσεται. ἀλλὰ 23
μὴν τόν γε Παίονα καὶ τὸν Ἰλλυριὸν καὶ ἁπλῶς
τούτους ἅπαντας ἡγεῖσθαι χρὴ αὐτονόμους ἥδιον ἂν
καὶ ἐλευθέρους ἢ δούλους εἶναι· καὶ γὰρ ἀήθεις τοῦ
κατακούειν τινός εἰσι, καὶ ἄνθρωπος ὑβριστής, ὥς
φασιν. καὶ μὰ Δί' οὐδὲν ἄπιστον ἴσως· τὸ γὰρ εὖ
πράττειν παρὰ τὴν ἀξίαν ἀφορμὴ τοῦ κακῶς φρονεῖν
τοῖς ἀνοήτοις γίγνεται, διόπερ πολλάκις δοκεῖ τὸ
φυλάξαι τἀγαθὰ τοῦ κτήσασθαι χαλεπώτερον εἶναι.
δεῖ τοίνυν ὑμᾶς, ὦ ἄνδρες Ἀθηναῖοι, τὴν ἀκαιρίαν 24
τὴν ἐκείνου καιρὸν ὑμέτερον νομίσαντας ἑτοίμως
συνάρασθαι τὰ πράγματα, καὶ πρεσβευομένους ἐφ'
ἃ δεῖ καὶ στρατευομένους αὐτοὺς καὶ παροξύνοντας
τοὺς ἄλλους ἅπαντας, λογιζομένους, εἰ Φίλιππος
λάβοι καθ' ἡμῶν τοιοῦτον καιρὸν καὶ πόλεμος γένοιτο πρὸς τῇ χώρᾳ, πῶς ἂν αὐτὸν οἴεσθ' ἑτοίμως ἐφ'
ὑμᾶς ἐλθεῖν; εἶτ' οὐκ αἰσχύνεσθε, εἰ μηδ' ἃ πάθοιτ'
ἄν, εἰ δύναιτ' ἐκεῖνος, ταῦτα ποιῆσαι καιρὸν ἔχοντες
οὐ τολμήσετε;
   Ἔτι τοίνυν, ὦ ἄνδρες Ἀθηναῖοι, μηδὲ τοῦθ' ὑμᾶς 25
λανθανέτω, ὅτι νῦν αἵρεσίς ἐστιν ὑμῖν πότερ' ὑμᾶς
ἐκεῖ χρὴ πολεμεῖν ἢ παρ' ὑμῖν ἐκεῖνον. ἐὰν μὲν γὰρ
ἀντέχῃ τὰ τῶν Ὀλυνθίων, ὑμεῖς ἐκεῖ πολεμήσετε καὶ

τὴν ἐκείνου κακῶς ποιήσετε, τὴν ὑπάρχουσαν καὶ τὴν
οἰκείαν ταύτην ἀδεῶς καρπούμενοι· ἂν δ᾽ ἐκεῖνα
Φίλιππος λάβῃ, τίς αὐτὸν κωλύσει δεῦρο βαδίζειν ;
26 Θηβαῖοι ; μὴ λίαν πικρὸν εἰπεῖν ᾖ—καὶ συνεισβαλοῦσιν ἑτοίμως. ἀλλὰ Φωκεῖς ; οἱ τὴν οἰκείαν οὐχ
οἷοί τ᾽ ὄντες φυλάττειν, ἐὰν μὴ βοηθήσηθ᾽ ὑμεῖς ἢ
ἄλλος τις. ἀλλ᾽, ὦταν, οὐχὶ βουλήσεται. τῶν
ἀτοπωτάτων μεντἂν εἴη, εἰ ἃ νῦν ἄνοιαν ὀφλισκάνων
27 ὅμως ἐκλαλεῖ, ταῦτα δυνηθεὶς μὴ πράξει. ἀλλὰ μὴν
ἡλίκα γ᾽ ἐστὶν τὰ διάφορ᾽ ἐνθάδ᾽ ἢ ἐκεῖ πολεμεῖν οὐδὲ
λόγου προσδεῖν ἡγοῦμαι. εἰ γὰρ ὑμᾶς δεήσειεν
αὐτοὺς τριάκονθ᾽ ἡμέρας μόνας ἔξω γενέσθαι καὶ ὅσ᾽
ἀνάγκη στρατοπέδῳ χρωμένους τῶν ἐκ τῆς χώρας
λαμβάνειν, μηδενὸς ὄντος ἐν αὐτῇ πολεμίου λέγω,
πλέον ἂν οἶμαι ζημιωθῆναι τοὺς γεωργοῦντας ὑμῶν
ἢ ὅσ᾽ εἰς ἅπαντα τὸν πρὸ τοῦ πόλεμον δεδαπάνησθε.
εἰ δὲ δὴ πόλεμός τις ἥξει, πόσα χρὴ νομίσαι ζημιώσεσθαι ; καὶ πρόσεσθ᾽ ἡ ὕβρις καὶ ἔθ᾽ ἡ τῶν
πραγμάτων αἰσχύνη, οὐδεμιᾶς ἐλάττων ζημία τοῖς
γε σώφροσιν.
28   Πάντα δὴ ταῦτα δεῖ συνιδόντας ἅπαντας βοηθεῖν
καὶ ἀπωθεῖν ἐκεῖσε τὸν πόλεμον, τοὺς μὲν εὐπόρους,
ἵν᾽ ὑπὲρ τῶν πολλῶν ὧν καλῶς ποιοῦντες ἔχουσι
μίκρ᾽ ἀναλίσκοντες τὰ λοιπὰ καρπῶνται ἀδεῶς, τοὺς
δ᾽ ἐν ἡλικίᾳ, ἵνα τὴν τοῦ πολεμεῖν ἐμπειρίαν ἐν τῇ
Φιλίππου χώρᾳ κτησάμενοι φοβεροὶ φύλακες τῆς
οἰκείας ἀκεραίου γένωνται, τοὺς δὲ λέγοντας, ἵν᾽ αἱ
τῶν πεπολιτευμένων αὐτοῖς εὔθυναι ῥᾴδιαι γένωνται,
ὡς ὁποῖ᾽ ἄττ᾽ ἂν ὑμᾶς περιστῇ τὰ πράγματα, τοιοῦτοι κριταὶ καὶ τῶν πεπραγμένων αὐτοῖς ἔσεσθε.
χρηστὰ δ᾽ εἴη παντὸς εἵνεκα.

ΟΛΥΝΘΙΑΚΟΣ Β

ΥΠΟΘΕΣΙΣ

Προσήκαντο μὲν τὴν πρεσβείαν τῶν Ὀλυνθίων οἱ Ἀθηναῖοι καὶ βοηθεῖν αὐτοῖς κεκρίκασι· μέλλουσι δὲ περὶ τὴν ἔξοδον καὶ δεδιόσιν ὡς δυσπολεμήτου τοῦ Φιλίππου παρελθὼν ὁ Δημοσθένης πειρᾶται θαρσύνειν τὸν δῆμον, ἐπιδεικνὺς ὡς ἀσθενῆ τὰ τοῦ Μακεδόνος πράγματα. καὶ γὰρ τοῖς συμμάχοις ὕποπτον αὐτὸν εἶναί φησι καὶ κατὰ τὴν ἰδίαν δύναμιν οὐκ ἰσχυρόν· τοὺς γὰρ Μακεδόνας ἀσθενεῖς εἶναι καθ᾽ ἑαυτούς.

Ἐπὶ πολλῶν μὲν ἄν τις ἰδεῖν, ὦ ἄνδρες Ἀθηναῖοι, δοκεῖ μοι τὴν παρὰ τῶν θεῶν εὔνοιαν φανερὰν γιγνομένην τῇ πόλει, οὐχ ἥκιστα δ᾽ ἐν τοῖς παροῦσι πράγμασι· τὸ γὰρ τοὺς πολεμήσοντας Φιλίππῳ γεγενῆσθαι καὶ χώραν ὅμορον καὶ δύναμίν τινα κεκτημένους, καὶ τὸ μέγιστον ἁπάντων, τὴν ὑπὲρ τοῦ πολέμου γνώμην τοιαύτην ἔχοντας, ὥστε τὰς πρὸς ἐκεῖνον διαλλαγὰς πρῶτον μὲν ἀπίστους, εἶτα τῆς ἑαυτῶν πατρίδος νομίζειν ἀνάστασιν, δαιμονίᾳ τινὶ καὶ θείᾳ παντάπασιν ἔοικεν εὐεργεσίᾳ. δεῖ 2 τοίνυν, ὦ ἄνδρες Ἀθηναῖοι, τοῦτ᾽ ἤδη σκοπεῖν αὐτούς, ὅπως μὴ χείρους περὶ ἡμᾶς αὐτοὺς εἶναι δόξομεν τῶν ὑπαρχόντων, ὡς ἔστι τῶν αἰσχρῶν, μᾶλλον δὲ τῶν

αἰσχίστων, μὴ μόνον πόλεων καὶ τόπων ὧν ἠμέν
ποτε κύριοι φαίνεσθαι προϊεμένους, ἀλλὰ καὶ τῶν
ὑπὸ τῆς τύχης παρασκευασθέντων συμμάχων καὶ
καιρῶν.

3 Τὸ μὲν οὖν, ὦ ἄνδρες Ἀθηναῖοι, τὴν Φιλίππου
ῥώμην διεξιέναι καὶ διὰ τούτων τῶν λόγων προτρέ-
πειν τὰ δέοντα ποιεῖν ὑμᾶς, οὐχὶ καλῶς ἔχειν ἡγοῦμαι. διὰ τί; ὅτι μοι δοκεῖ πάνθ᾽ ὅσ᾽ ἂν εἴποι τις
ὑπὲρ τούτων, ἐκείνῳ μὲν ἔχειν φιλοτιμίαν, ἡμῖν δ᾽
οὐχὶ καλῶς πεπρᾶχθαι ὁ μὲν γὰρ ὅσῳ πλείον᾽
ὑπὲρ τὴν ἀξίαν πεποίηκε τὴν αὑτοῦ, τοσούτῳ θαυ-
μαστότερος παρὰ πᾶσι νομίζεται· ὑμεῖς δ᾽ ὅσῳ
χεῖρον ἢ προσῆκε κέχρησθε τοῖς πράγμασιν, τοσούτῳ
4 πλείον᾽ αἰσχύνην ὠφλήκατε. ταῦτα μὲν οὖν παραλείψω. καὶ γὰρ εἰ μετ᾽ ἀληθείας τις, ὦ ἄνδρες
Ἀθηναῖοι, σκοποῖτο, ἐνθένδ᾽ ἂν αὐτὸν ἴδοι μέγαν γε-
γενημένον, οὐχὶ παρ᾽ αὑτοῦ. ὧν οὖν ἐκεῖνος μὲν
ὀφείλει τοῖς ὑπὲρ αὑτοῦ πεπολιτευμένοις χάριν, ὑμῖν
δὲ δίκην προσήκει λαβεῖν, οὐχὶ νῦν ὁρῶ τὸν καιρὸν
τοῦ λέγειν· ἃ δὲ καὶ χωρὶς τούτων ἔνι, καὶ βέλτιόν
ἐστιν ἀκηκοέναι πάντας ὑμᾶς, καὶ μεγάλ᾽, ὦ ἄνδρες
Ἀθηναῖοι, κατ᾽ ἐκείνου φαίνοιτ᾽ ἂν ὀνείδη βουλομένοις ὀρθῶς δοκιμάζειν, ταῦτ᾽ εἰπεῖν πειράσομαι.

5 Τὸ μὲν οὖν ἐπίορκον κἄπιστον καλεῖν ἄνευ τοῦ
τὰ πεπραγμένα δεικνύναι, λοιδορίαν εἶναί τις ἂν
φήσειεν κενὴν δικαίως· τὸ δὲ πάνθ᾽ ὅσα πώποτ᾽
ἔπραξε διεξιόντ᾽ ἐφ᾽ ἅπασι τούτοις ἐλέγχειν, καὶ
βραχέος λόγου συμβαίνει δεῖσθαι, καὶ δυοῖν ἕνεχ᾽
ἡγοῦμαι συμφέρειν εἰρῆσθαι, τοῦ τ᾽ ἐκεῖνον, ὅπερ καὶ
ἀληθὲς ὑπάρχει, φαῦλον φαίνεσθαι, καὶ τοὺς ὑπερεκπεπληγμένους ὡς ἄμαχόν τινα τὸν Φίλιππον ἰδεῖν

ὅτι πάντα διεξελήλυθεν οἷς πρότερον παρακρουόμενος
μέγας ηὐξήθη, καὶ πρὸς αὐτὴν ἥκει τὴν τελευτὴν τὰ
πράγματ᾽ αὐτοῦ. ἐγὼ γάρ, ὦ ἄνδρες Ἀθηναῖοι, 6
σφόδρ᾽ ἂν ἡγούμην καὶ αὐτὸς φοβερὸν τὸν Φίλιππον
καὶ θαυμαστόν, εἰ τὰ δίκαια πράττονθ᾽ ἑώρων ηὐξη-
μένον· νῦν δὲ θεωρῶν καὶ σκοπῶν εὑρίσκω τὴν μὲν
ἡμετέραν εὐήθειαν τὸ κατ᾽ ἀρχάς, ὅτ᾽ Ὀλυνθίους
ἀπήλαυνόν τινες ἐνθένδε βουλομένους ὑμῖν διαλεχθῆναι, τῷ τὴν Ἀμφίπολιν φάσκειν παραδώσειν καὶ
τὸ θρυλούμενόν ποτ᾽ ἀπόρρητον ἐκεῖνο κατασκευάσαι,
τούτῳ προσαγαγόμενον, τὴν δ᾽ Ὀλυνθίων φιλίαν μετὰ 7
ταῦτα τῷ Ποτείδαιαν οὖσαν ὑμετέραν ἐξελεῖν καὶ
τοὺς μὲν πρότερον συμμάχους [ὑμᾶς] ἀδικῆσαι,
παραδοῦναι δ᾽ ἐκείνοις, Θετταλοὺς δὲ νῦν τὰ τελευταῖα τῷ Μαγνησίαν παραδώσειν ὑποσχέσθαι καὶ
τὸν Φωκικὸν πόλεμον πολεμήσειν ὑπὲρ αὐτῶν ἀναδέξ-
ασθαι. ὅλως δ᾽ οὐδεὶς ἔστιν ὅντιν᾽ οὐ πεφενάκικ᾽
ἐκεῖνος τῶν αὐτῷ χρησαμένων· τὴν γὰρ ἑκάστων
ἄνοιαν ἀεὶ τῶν ἀγνοούντων αὐτὸν ἐξαπατῶν καὶ
προσλαμβάνων οὕτως ηὐξήθη. ὥσπερ οὖν διὰ τούτ- 8
ων ἤρθη μέγας, ἡνίχ᾽ ἕκαστοι συμφέρον αὐτὸν ἑαυτοῖς
ᾤοντό τι πράξειν, οὕτως ὀφείλει διὰ τῶν αὐτῶν
τούτων καὶ καθαιρεθῆναι πάλιν, ἐπειδὴ πάνθ᾽ ἕνεχ᾽
ἑαυτοῦ ποιῶν ἐξελήλεγκται. καιροῦ μὲν δή, ὦ ἄνδρες
Ἀθηναῖοι, πρὸς τοῦτο πάρεστι Φιλίππῳ τὰ πράγ-
ματα· ἢ παρελθών τις ἐμοί, μᾶλλον δ᾽ ὑμῖν δειξάτω,
ὡς οὐκ ἀληθῆ ταῦτ᾽ ἐγὼ λέγω, ἢ ὡς οἱ τὰ πρῶτ᾽
ἐξηπατημένοι τὰ λοιπὰ πιστεύσουσιν. ἢ ὡς οἱ παρὰ
τὴν αὐτῶν ἀξίαν δεδουλωμένοι [Θετταλοὶ] νῦν οὐκ
ἂν ἐλεύθεροι γένοινθ᾽ ἅσμενοι.

Καὶ μὴν εἴ τις ὑμῶν ταῦτα μὲν οὕτως ἔχειν 9

ἡγεῖται, οἴεται δὲ βίᾳ καθέξειν αὐτὸν τὰ πράγματα
τῷ τὰ χωρία καὶ λιμένας καὶ τὰ τοιαῦτα προειλη-
φέναι, οὐκ ὀρθῶς οἴεται ὅταν μὲν γὰρ ὑπ' εὐνοίας
τὰ πράγματα συστῇ καὶ πᾶσι ταὐτὰ συμφέρῃ τοῖς
μετέχουσι τοῦ πολέμου, καὶ συμπονεῖν καὶ φέρειν
τὰς συμφορὰς καὶ μένειν ἐθέλουσιν ἄνθρωποι· ὅταν
δ' ἐκ πλεονεξίας καὶ πονηρίας τις ὥσπερ οὗτος
ἰσχύσῃ, ἡ πρώτη πρόφασις καὶ μικρὸν πταῖσμ'
10 ἅπαντ' ἀνεχαίτισε καὶ διέλυσεν. οὐ γὰρ ἔστιν, οὐκ
ἔστιν, ὦ ἄνδρες Ἀθηναῖοι, ἀδικοῦντα κἀπιορκοῦντα
καὶ ψευδόμενον δύναμιν βεβαίαν κτήσασθαι, ἀλλὰ
τὰ τοιαῦτ' εἰς μὲν ἅπαξ καὶ βραχὺν χρόνον ἀντέχει,
καὶ σφόδρα γ' ἤνθησεν ἐπὶ ταῖς ἐλπίσιν, ἂν τύχῃ, τῷ
χρόνῳ δὲ φωρᾶται καὶ περὶ αὐτὰ καταρρεῖ. ὥσπερ
γὰρ οἰκίας, οἶμαι, καὶ πλοίου καὶ τῶν ἄλλων τῶν
τοιούτων τὰ κάτωθεν ἰσχυρότατ' εἶναι δεῖ, οὕτω καὶ
τῶν πράξεων τὰς ἀρχὰς καὶ τὰς ὑποθέσεις ἀληθεῖς
καὶ δικαίας εἶναι προσήκει. τοῦτο δ' οὐκ ἔνι νῦν ἐν
τοῖς πεπραγμένοις Φιλίππῳ.

11 Φημὶ δὴ δεῖν ἡμᾶς τοῖς μὲν Ὀλυνθίοις βοηθεῖν,
καὶ ὅπως τις λέγει κάλλιστα καὶ τάχιστα, οὕτως
ἀρέσκει μοι πρὸς δὲ Θετταλοὺς πρεσβείαν πέμπειν,
ἣ τοὺς μὲν διδάξει ταῦτα, τοὺς δὲ παροξυνεῖ· καὶ γὰρ
νῦν εἰσιν ἐψηφισμένοι Παγασὰς ἀπαιτεῖν καὶ περὶ
12 Μαγνησίας λόγους ποιεῖσθαι. σκοπεῖσθε μέντοι
τοῦτ', ὦ ἄνδρες Ἀθηναῖοι, ὅπως μὴ λόγους ἐροῦσιν
μόνον οἱ παρ' ἡμῶν πρέσβεις, ἀλλὰ καὶ ἔργον τι
δεικνύειν ἕξουσιν, ἐξεληλυθότων ὑμῶν ἀξίως τῆς
πόλεως καὶ ὄντων ἐπὶ τοῖς πράγμασιν· ὡς ἅπας μὲν
λόγος, ἂν ἀπῇ τὰ πράγματα, μάταιόν τι φαίνεται
καὶ κενόν, μάλιστα δ' ὁ παρὰ τῆς ἡμετέρας πόλεως·

ὅσῳ γὰρ ἑτοιμότατ᾽ αὐτῷ δοκοῦμεν χρῆσθαι, τοσούτῳ
μᾶλλον ἀπιστοῦσι πάντες αὐτῷ. πολλὴν δὴ τὴν 13
μετάστασιν καὶ μεγάλην δεικτέον τὴν μεταβολήν,
εἰσφέροντας, ἐξιόντας, ἅπαντα ποιοῦντας ἑτοίμως,
εἴπερ τις ὑμῖν προσέξει τὸν νοῦν. κἂν ταῦτ᾽ ἐθελή-
σηθ᾽ ὡς προσήκει καὶ δεῖ περαίνειν, οὐ μόνον, ὦ
ἄνδρες Ἀθηναῖοι, τὰ συμμαχικὰ ἀσθενῶς καὶ ἀπίστως ἔχοντα φανήσεται Φιλίππῳ, ἀλλὰ καὶ τὰ τῆς
οἰκείας ἀρχῆς καὶ δυνάμεως κακῶς ἔχοντ᾽ ἐξελεγχθή-
σεται.

Ὅλως μὲν γὰρ ἡ Μακεδονικὴ δύναμις καὶ ἀρχὴ 14
ἐν μὲν προσθήκῃ μερίς ἐστίν τις οὐ μικρά, οἷον
ὑπῆρξέν ποθ᾽ ὑμῖν ἐπὶ Τιμοθέου πρὸς Ὀλυνθίους·
πάλιν αὖ πρὸς Ποτείδαιαν Ὀλυνθίοις ἐφάνη τι
τοῦτο συναμφότερον· νυνὶ δὲ Θετταλοῖς στασιάζουσι
καὶ τεταραγμένοις ἐπὶ τὴν τυραννικὴν οἰκίαν ἐβοή-
θησεν· καὶ ὅποι τις ἄν, οἶμαι, προσθῇ κἂν μικρὰν
δύναμιν, πάντ᾽ ὠφελεῖ· αὐτὴ δὲ καθ᾽ αὑτὴν ἀσθενὴς
καὶ πολλῶν κακῶν ἐστι μεστή. καὶ γὰρ οὗτος 15
ἅπασι τούτοις, οἷς ἄν τις μέγαν αὐτὸν ἡγήσαιτο,
τοῖς πολέμοις καὶ ταῖς στρατείαις, ἔτ᾽ ἐπισφαλεστέραν ἢ ὑπῆρχε φύσει κατεσκεύακεν αὑτῷ. μὴ γὰρ
οἴεσθ᾽, ὦ ἄνδρες Ἀθηναῖοι, τοῖς αὐτοῖς Φίλιππόν τε
χαίρειν καὶ τοὺς ἀρχομένους, ἀλλ᾽ ὁ μὲν δόξης ἐπιθυμεῖ καὶ τοῦτ᾽ ἐζήλωκε καὶ προῄρηται πράττων καὶ
κινδυνεύων, ἂν συμβῇ τι, παθεῖν, τὴν τοῦ διαπράξασθαι ταῦθ᾽ ἃ μηδεὶς πώποτ᾽ ἄλλος Μακεδόνων
βασιλεὺς δόξαν ἀντὶ τοῦ ζῆν ἀσφαλῶς ᾑρημένος·
τοῖς δὲ τῆς μὲν φιλοτιμίας τῆς ἀπὸ τούτων οὐ μέτ- 16
εστι, κοπτόμενοι δ᾽ ἀεὶ ταῖς στρατείαις ταύταις ταῖς
ἄνω κάτω λυποῦνται καὶ συνεχῶς ταλαιπωροῦσιν,

οὔτ᾽ ἐπὶ τοῖς ἔργοις οὔτ᾽ ἐπὶ τοῖς αὐτῶν ἰδίοις ἐώμενοι
διατρίβειν, οὔθ᾽ ὅσ᾽ ἂν ποιήσωσιν οὕτως ὅπως ἂν
δύνωνται, ταῦτ᾽ ἔχοντες διαθέσθαι, κεκλειμένων τῶν
17 ἐμπορίων τῶν ἐν τῇ χώρᾳ διὰ τὸν πόλεμον. οἱ μὲν
οὖν πολλοὶ Μακεδόνων πῶς ἔχουσι Φιλίππῳ, ἐκ
τούτων ἄν τις σκέψαιτ᾽ οὐ χαλεπῶς· οἱ δὲ δὴ περὶ
αὐτὸν ὄντες ξένοι καὶ πεζέταιροι δόξαν μὲν ἔχουσιν
ὡς εἰσὶ θαυμαστοὶ καὶ συγκεκροτημένοι τὰ τοῦ πολέμου, ὡς δ᾽ ἐγὼ τῶν ἐν αὐτῇ τῇ χώρᾳ γεγενημένων
τινὸς ἤκουον, ἀνδρὸς οὐδαμῶς οἵου τε ψεύδεσθαι,
18 οὐδένων εἰσὶν βελτίους. εἰ μὲν γάρ τις ἀνήρ ἐστιν
ἐν αὐτοῖς οἷος ἔμπειρος πολέμου καὶ ἀγώνων, τούτους
μὲν φιλοτιμίᾳ πάντας ἀπωθεῖν αὐτὸν ἔφη, βουλόμενον πάνθ᾽ αὑτοῦ δοκεῖν εἶναι τὰ ἔργα· πρὸς γὰρ
αὖ τοῖς ἄλλοις καὶ τὴν φιλοτιμίαν ἀνυπέρβλητον
εἶναι· εἰ δέ τις σώφρων ἢ δίκαιος ἄλλως, τὴν καθ᾽
ἡμέραν ἀκρασίαν τοῦ βίου καὶ μέθην καὶ κορδα-
κισμοὺς οὐ δυνάμενος φέρειν, παρεῶσθαι καὶ ἐν
19 οὐδενὸς εἶναι μέρει τὸν τοιοῦτον. λοιποὺς δὴ περὶ
αὐτὸν εἶναι λῃστὰς καὶ κόλακας καὶ τοιούτους ἀνθρώπους, οἵους μεθυσθέντας ὀρχεῖσθαι τοιαῦθ᾽ οἷ᾽ ἐγὼ
νῦν ὀκνῶ πρὸς ὑμᾶς ὀνομάσαι. δῆλον δ᾽ ὅτι ταῦτ᾽
ἐστὶν ἀληθῆ· καὶ γὰρ οὓς ἐνθένδε πάντες ἀπήλαυνον
ὡς πολὺ τῶν θαυματοποιῶν ἀσελγεστέρους ὄντας,
Καλλίαν ἐκεῖνον τὸν δημόσιον καὶ τοιούτους ἀνθρώπους, μίμους γελοίων καὶ ποιητὰς αἰσχρῶν ᾀσμάτων,
ὧν εἰς τοὺς συνόντας ποιοῦσιν ἕνεκα τοῦ γελασθῆναι,
20 τούτους ἀγαπᾷ καὶ περὶ αὑτὸν ἔχει. καίτοι ταῦτα,
καὶ εἰ μικρά τις ἡγεῖται, μεγάλ᾽, ὦ ἄνδρες Ἀθηναῖοι,
δείγματα τῆς ἐκείνου γνώμης καὶ κακοδαιμονιας ἐστὶν
τοῖς εὖ φρονοῦσιν. ἀλλ᾽, οἶμαι, νῦν μὲν ἐπισκοτεῖ

τούτοις τὸ κατορθοῦν· αἱ γὰρ εὐπραξίαι δειναὶ συγκρύψαι τὰ τοιαῦτ' ὀνείδη εἰ δέ τι πταίσει, τότ' ἀκριβῶς αὐτοῦ ταῦτ' ἐξετασθήσεται. δοκεῖ δ' ἔμοιγ'. ὦ ἄνδρες Ἀθηναῖοι, δείξειν οὐκ εἰς μακράν, ἂν οἵ τε θεοὶ θέλωσι καὶ ὑμεῖς βούλησθε. ὥσπερ γὰρ ἐν τοῖς 21 σώμασιν, τέως μὲν ἂν ἐρρωμένος ᾖ τις, οὐδὲν ἐπαισθάνεται, ἐπὰν δ' ἀρρώστημά τι συμβῇ, πάντα κινεῖται, κἂν ῥῆγμα κἂν στρέμμα κἂν ἄλλο τι τῶν ὑπαρχόντων σαθρὸν ᾖ, οὕτω καὶ τῶν πόλεων καὶ τῶν τυράννων, ἕως μὲν ἂν ἔξω πολεμῶσιν, ἀφανῆ τὰ κακὰ τοῖς πολλοῖς ἐστιν, ἐπειδὰν δ' ὅμορος πόλεμος συμπλακῇ, πάντ' ἐποίησεν ἔκδηλα.

Εἰ δέ τις ὑμῶν, ὦ ἄνδρες Ἀθηναῖοι, τὸν Φίλιππον 22 εὐτυχοῦνθ' ὁρῶν ταύτῃ φοβερὸν προσπολεμῆσαι νομίζει, σώφρονος μὲν ἀνθρώπου λογισμῷ χρῆται· μεγάλη γὰρ ῥοπή, μᾶλλον δὲ τὸ ὅλον ἡ τύχη παρὰ πάντ' ἐστὶ τὰ τῶν ἀνθρώπων πράγματα· οὐ μὴν ἀλλ' ἔγωγ', εἴ τις αἵρεσίν μοι δοίη, τὴν τῆς ἡμετέρας πόλεως τύχην ἂν ἑλοίμην, ἐθελόντων ἃ προσήκει ποιεῖν ὑμῶν αὐτῶν καὶ κατὰ μικρόν, ἢ τὴν ἐκείνου· πολὺ γὰρ πλείους ἀφορμὰς εἰς τὸ τὴν παρὰ τῶν θεῶν εὔνοιαν ἔχειν ὁρῶ ὑμῖν ἐνούσας ἢ 'κείνῳ. ἀλλ', 23 οἶμαι, καθήμεθ' οὐδὲν ποιοῦντες· οὐκ ἔνι δ' αὐτὸν ἀργοῦντ' οὐδὲ τοῖς φίλοις ἐπιτάττειν ὑπὲρ αὑτοῦ τι ποιεῖν, μή τί γε δὴ τοῖς θεοῖς. οὐ δὴ θαυμαστόν ἐστιν, εἰ στρατευόμενος καὶ πονῶν ἐκεῖνος αὐτὸς καὶ παρὼν ἐφ' ἅπασι καὶ μήτε καιρὸν μήθ' ὥραν παραλείπων ἡμῶν μελλόντων καὶ ψηφιζομένων καὶ πυνθανομένων περιγίγνεται οὐδὲ θαυμάζω τοῦτ' ἐγώ· τοὐναντίον γὰρ ἂν ἦν θαυμαστόν, εἰ μηδὲν ποιοῦντες ἡμεῖς ὧν τοῖς πολεμοῦσι προσήκει τοῦ

24 πάντα ποιοῦντος περιῆμεν. ἀλλ᾽ ἐκεῖνο θαυμάζω,
εἰ Λακεδαιμονίοις μέν ποτ᾽, ὦ ἄνδρες Ἀθηναῖοι, ὑπὲρ
τῶν Ἑλληνικῶν δικαίων ἀντήρατε, καὶ πόλλ᾽ ἰδίᾳ
πλεονεκτῆσαι πολλάκις ὑμῖν ἐξὸν οὐκ ἠθελήσατε,
ἀλλ᾽ ἵν᾽ οἱ ἄλλοι τύχωσι τῶν δικαίων, τὰ ὑμέτερ᾽
αὐτῶν ἀνηλίσκετ᾽ εἰσφέροντες καὶ προὐκινδυνεύετε
στρατευόμενοι, νυνὶ δ᾽ ὀκνεῖτ᾽ ἐξιέναι καὶ μέλλετ᾽
εἰσφέρειν ὑπὲρ τῶν ὑμετέρων αὐτῶν κτημάτων, καὶ
τοὺς μὲν ἄλλους σεσώκατε πολλάκις πάντας καὶ
καθ᾽ ἕν᾽ αὐτῶν ἐν μέρει, τὰ δ᾽ ὑμέτερ᾽ αὐτῶν ἀπολ-
25 ωλεκότες κάθησθε. ταῦτα θαυμάζω, κἄτι πρὸς
τούτοις, εἰ μηδεὶς ὑμῶν, ὦ ἄνδρες Ἀθηναῖοι, δύναται
λογίσασθαι, πόσον πολεμεῖτε χρόνον Φιλίππῳ καὶ
τί ποιούντων ὑμῶν ὁ χρόνος διελήλυθεν οὗτος. ἴστε
γὰρ δήπου τοῦθ᾽, ὅτι μελλόντων αὐτῶν, ἑτέρους τινὰς
ἐλπιζόντων πράξειν, αἰτιωμένων ἀλλήλους, κρινόντων, πάλιν ἐλπιζόντων, σχεδὸν ταῦθ᾽ ἅπερ νυνὶ
26 ποιούντων, ἅπας ὁ χρόνος διελήλυθεν. εἶθ᾽ οὕτως
ἀγνωμόνως ἔχετ᾽, ὦ ἄνδρες Ἀθηναῖοι, ὥστε δι᾽ ὧν ἐκ
χρηστῶν φαῦλα τὰ πράγματα τῆς πόλεως γέγονεν,
διὰ τούτων ἐλπίζετε τῶν αὐτῶν πράξεων ἐκ φαύλων
αὐτὰ χρηστὰ γενήσεσθαι; ἀλλ᾽ οὔτ᾽ εὔλογον οὔτ᾽
ἔχον ἐστὶ φύσιν τοῦτό γε· πολὺ γὰρ ῥᾷον ἔχοντας
φυλάττειν ἢ κτήσασθαι πάντα πέφυκεν. νῦν δ᾽ ὅ τι
μὲν φυλάξομεν, οὐδέν ἐστιν ὑπὸ τοῦ πολέμου λοιπὸν
τῶν πρότερον, κτήσασθαι δὲ δεῖ. αὐτῶν οὖν ἡμῶν
ἔργον τοῦτ᾽ ἤδη.

27 Φημὶ δὴ δεῖν εἰσφέρειν χρήματα, αὐτοὺς ἐξιέναι
προθύμως, μηδέν᾽ αἰτιᾶσθαι πρὶν ἂν τῶν πραγμάτων
κρατήσητε, τηνικαῦτα δ᾽ ἀπ᾽ αὐτῶν τῶν ἔργων κρί-
ναντας τοὺς μὲν ἀξίους ἐπαίνου τιμᾶν, τοὺς δ᾽ ἀδι-

κοῦντας κολάζειν, τὰς προφάσεις δ' ἀφελεῖν καὶ τὰ
καθ' ὑμᾶς ἐλλείμματα· οὐ γὰρ ἔστι πικρῶς ἐξετάσαι
τί πέπρακται τοῖς ἄλλοις, ἂν μὴ παρ' ὑμῶν αὐτῶν
πρῶτον ὑπάρξῃ τὰ δέοντα. τίνος γὰρ ἕνεκ', ὦ ἄνδρες 28
Ἀθηναῖοι, νομίζετε τοῦτον μὲν φεύγειν τὸν πόλεμον
πάντας ὅσους ἂν ἐκπέμψητε στρατηγούς, ἰδίους δ'
εὑρίσκειν πολέμους, εἰ δεῖ τι τῶν ὄντων καὶ περὶ τῶν
στρατηγῶν εἰπεῖν; ὅτι ἐνταῦθα μέν ἐστι τὰ ἆθλ'
ὑπὲρ ὧν ἐστιν ὁ πόλεμος ὑμέτερα ['Αμφίπολις] κἂν
ληφθῇ παραχρῆμ' ὑμεῖς κομιεῖσθε, οἱ δὲ κίνδυνοι
τῶν ἐφεστηκότων ἴδιοι, μισθὸς δ' οὐκ ἔστιν· ἐκεῖ δὲ
κίνδυνοι μὲν ἐλάττους, τὰ δὲ λήμματα τῶν ἐφεστηκότων καὶ τῶν στρατιωτῶν, Λάμψακος, Σίγειον, τὰ
πλοῖ' ἃ συλῶσιν. ἐπ' οὖν τὸ λυσιτελοῦν αὑτοῖς
ἕκαστοι χωροῦσιν. ὑμεῖς δ' ὅταν μὲν εἰς τὰ πράγ- 29
ματ' ἀποβλέψητε φαύλως ἔχοντα, τοὺς ἐφεστηκότας
κρίνετε, ὅταν δὲ δόντες λόγον τὰς ἀνάγκας ἀκούσητε
ταύτας, ἀφίετε. περίεστιν τοίνυν ὑμῖν ἀλλήλοις
ἐρίζειν καὶ διεστάναι, τοῖς μὲν ταῦτα πεπεισμένοις,
τοῖς δὲ ταῦτα, τὰ κοινὰ δ' ἔχειν φαύλως. πρότερον
μὲν γάρ, ὦ ἄνδρες Ἀθηναῖοι, εἰσεφέρετε κατὰ συμμορίας, νυνὶ δὲ πολιτεύεσθε κατὰ συμμορίας. ῥήτωρ
ἡγεμὼν ἑκατέρων καὶ στρατηγὸς ὑπὸ τούτῳ καὶ οἱ
βοησόμενοι τριακόσιοι· οἱ δ' ἄλλοι προσνενέμησθε,
οἱ μὲν ὡς τούτους, οἱ δ' ὡς ἐκείνους. δεῖ δὴ ταῦτ' 30
ἐπανέντας καὶ ὑμῶν αὐτῶν ἔτι καὶ νῦν γενομένους
κοινὸν καὶ τὸ βουλεύεσθαι καὶ τὸ λέγειν καὶ τὸ
πράττειν ποιῆσαι. εἰ δὲ τοῖς μὲν ὥσπερ ἐκ τυραννίδος ὑμῶν ἐπιτάττειν ἀποδώσετε, τοῖς δ' ἀναγκ-
άζεσθαι τριηραρχεῖν, εἰσφέρειν, στρατεύεσθαι, τοῖς
δὲ ψηφίζεσθαι κατὰ τούτων μόνον, ἄλλο δὲ μηδ'

2—2

ὁτιοῦν συμπονεῖν, οὐχὶ γενήσεται τῶν δεόντων ὑμῖν
οὐδὲν ἐν καιρῷ· τὸ γὰρ ἠδικημένον ἀεὶ μέρος
ἐλλείψει, εἶθ' ὑμῖν τούτους κολάζειν ἀντὶ τῶν
ἐχθρῶν ἐξέσται.

31 Λέγω δὴ κεφάλαιον, πάντας εἰσφέρειν ἀφ' ὅσων
ἕκαστος ἔχει τὸ ἴσον· πάντας ἐξιέναι κατὰ μέρος,
ἕως ἂν ἅπαντες στρατεύσησθε· πᾶσι τοῖς παριοῦσι
λόγον διδόναι, καὶ τὰ βέλτισθ' ὧν ἂν ἀκούσηθ'
αἱρεῖσθαι, μὴ ἂν ὁ δεῖν' ἢ ὁ δεῖν' εἴπῃ. κἂν ταῦτα
ποιῆτε, οὐ τὸν εἰπόντα μόνον παραχρῆμ' ἐπαινέ-
σεσθε, ἀλλὰ καὶ ὑμᾶς αὐτοὺς ὕστερον, βέλτιον τῶν
ὅλων πραγμάτων ὑμῖν ἐχόντων.

ΟΛΥΝΘΙΑΚΟΣ Γ

ΥΠΟΘΕΣΙΣ

Ἔπεμψαν βοήθειαν τοῖς Ὀλυνθίοις οἱ Ἀθηναῖοι, καί τι κατορθοῦν ἔδοξαν δι' αὐτῆς· καὶ ταῦτ' αὐτοῖς ἀπηγγέλλετο. ὁ δὲ δῆμος περιχαρής, οἵ τε ῥήτορες παρακαλοῦντες ἐπὶ τιμωρίαν Φιλίππου. ὁ δὲ Δημοσθένης δεδοικὼς μὴ θαρσήσαντες, ὡς τὰ πάντα νενικηκότες καὶ ἱκανὴν βοήθειαν πεποιημένοι τοῖς Ὀλυνθίοις, τῶν λοιπῶν ὀλιγωρήσωσι, διὰ τοῦτο παρελθὼν ἐπικόπτει τὴν ἀλαζονείαν αὐτῶν καὶ πρὸς εὐλάβειαν σώφρονα τὴν γνώμην μεθίστησι, λέγων οὐ περὶ τῆς Φιλίππου τιμωρίας νῦν αὐτοῖς εἶναι τὸν λόγον, ἀλλὰ περὶ τῆς τῶν συμμάχων σωτηρίας. οἶδεν γὰρ ὅτι καὶ Ἀθηναῖοι καὶ ἄλλοι πού τινες τοῦ μὲν μὴ τὰ οἰκεῖα προέσθαι ποιοῦνται φροντίδα, περὶ δὲ τὸ τιμωρήσασθαι τοὺς ἐναντίους ἧττον σπουδάζουσιν. ἐν 2 δὲ τούτῳ τῷ λόγῳ καὶ τῆς περὶ τῶν θεωρικῶν χρημάτων συμβουλῆς φανερώτερον ἅπτεται, καὶ ἀξιοῖ λυθῆναι τοὺς νόμους τοὺς ἐπιτιθέντας ζημίαν τοῖς γράψασιν αὐτὰ γενέσθαι στρατιωτικά, ἵν' ἀδεὲς ᾖ τὸ συμβουλεύειν τὰ βέλτιστα. παραινεῖ δὲ καὶ ὅλως πρὸς τὸν τῶν προγόνων ζῆλον ἀναστῆναι καὶ στρατεύεσθαι σώμασιν οἰκείοις, καὶ ἐπιτιμήσει πολλῇ κέχρηται κατὰ τοῦ δήμου θ' ὡς ἐκλελυμένου καὶ τῶν δημαγωγῶν ὡς οὐκ ὀρθῶς προϊσταμένων τῆς πόλεως.

Οὐχὶ ταὐτὰ παρίσταταί μοι γιγνώσκειν, ὦ ἄνδρες Ἀθηναῖοι, ὅταν τ' εἰς τὰ πράγματ' ἀποβλέψω καὶ

ὅταν πρὸς τοὺς λόγους οὓς ἀκούω· τοὺς μὲν γὰρ
λόγους περὶ τοῦ τιμωρήσασθαι Φίλιππον ὁρῶ γιγνομένους, τὰ δὲ πράγματ' εἰς τοῦτο προήκοντα, ὥσθ'
ὅπως μὴ πεισόμεθ' αὐτοὶ πρότερον κακῶς σκέψασθαι
δέον. οὐδὲν οὖν ἄλλο μοι δοκοῦσιν οἱ τὰ τοιαῦτα
λέγοντες ἢ τὴν ὑπόθεσιν, περὶ ἧς βουλεύεσθε, οὐχὶ
2 τὴν οὖσαν παριστάντες ὑμῖν ἁμαρτάνειν. ἐγὼ δ'
ὅτι μέν ποτ' ἐξῆν τῇ πόλει καὶ τὰ αὑτῆς ἔχειν
ἀσφαλῶς καὶ Φίλιππον τιμωρήσασθαι, καὶ μάλ'
ἀκριβῶς οἶδα· ἐπ' ἐμοῦ γάρ, οὐ πάλαι, γέγονε ταῦτ'
ἀμφότερα· νῦν μέντοι πέπεισμαι τοῦθ' ἱκανὸν προ-
λαβεῖν ἡμῖν εἶναι τὴν πρώτην, ὅπως τοὺς συμμάχους
σώσομεν. ἐὰν γὰρ τοῦτο βεβαίως ὑπάρξῃ, τότε καὶ
περὶ τοῦ τίνα τιμωρήσεταί τις καὶ ὃν τρόπον ἐξέσται
σκοπεῖν· πρὶν δὲ τὴν ἀρχὴν ὀρθῶς ὑποθέσθαι μάτ-
αιον ἡγοῦμαι περὶ τῆς τελευτῆς ὁντινοῦν ποιεῖσθαι
λόγον.

3   Ὁ μὲν οὖν παρὼν καιρός, εἴπερ ποτέ, πολλῆς
φροντίδος καὶ βουλῆς δεῖται· ἐγὼ δ' οὐχ ὅ τι χρὴ
περὶ τῶν παρόντων συμβουλεῦσαι χαλεπώτατον
ἡγοῦμαι, ἀλλ' ἐκεῖν' ἀπορῶ, τίνα χρὴ τρόπον, ὦ
ἄνδρες Ἀθηναῖοι, πρὸς ὑμᾶς περὶ αὐτῶν εἰπεῖν.
πέπεισμαι γὰρ ἐξ ὧν παρὼν καὶ ἀκούων σύνοιδα,
τὰ πλείω τῶν πραγμάτων ἡμᾶς ἐκπεφευγέναι τῷ μὴ
βούλεσθαι τὰ δέοντα ποιεῖν ἢ τῷ μὴ συνιέναι. ἀξιῶ
δ' ὑμᾶς, ἂν μετὰ παρρησίας ποιῶμαι τοὺς λόγους,
ὑπομένειν, τοῦτο θεωροῦντας, εἰ τἀληθῆ λέγω. καὶ
διὰ τοῦτο, ἵνα τὰ λοιπὰ βελτίω γένηται· ὁρᾶτε γὰρ
ὡς ἐκ τοῦ πρὸς χάριν δημηγορεῖν ἐνίους εἰς πᾶν προελήλυθε μοχθηρίας τὰ παρόντα.

4   Ἀναγκαῖον δ' ὑπολαμβάνω μικρὰ τῶν γεγενη-

μένων πρῶτον ὑμᾶς ὑπομνῆσαι. μέμνησθ', ὦ ἄνδρες
Ἀθηναῖοι, ὅτ' ἀπηγγέλθη Φίλιππος ὑμῖν ἐν Θρᾴκῃ
τρίτον ἢ τέταρτον ἔτος τουτὶ Ἡραῖον τεῖχος πολιορ-
κῶν. τότε τοίνυν μὴν μὲν ἦν μαιμακτηριών, πολλῶν
δὲ λόγων καὶ θορύβου γιγνομένου παρ' ὑμῖν ἐψηφί-
σασθε τετταράκοντα τριήρεις καθέλκειν καὶ τοὺς
μέχρι πέντε καὶ τετταράκοντ' ἐτῶν αὐτοὺς ἐμβαίνειν
καὶ τάλανθ' ἑξήκοντ' εἰσφέρειν. καὶ μετὰ ταῦτα 5
διελθόντος τοῦ ἐνιαυτοῦ τούτου, ἑκατομβαιών, μεταγειτνιών, βοηδρομιών—τούτου τοῦ μηνὸς μόγις μετὰ
τὰ μυστήρια δέκα ναῦς ἀπεστείλατ' ἔχοντα κενὰς
Χαρίδημον καὶ πέντε τάλαντ' ἀργυρίου. ὡς γὰρ
ἠγγέλθη Φίλιππος ἀσθενῶν ἢ τεθνεώς (ἦλθε γὰρ
ἀμφότερα), οὐκέτι καιρὸν οὐδένα τοῦ βοηθεῖν νομί-
σαντες ἀφεῖτ', ὦ ἄνδρες Ἀθηναῖοι, τὸν ἀπόστολον.
ἦν δ' οὗτος ὁ καιρὸς αὐτός· εἰ γὰρ τότ' ἐκεῖσ' ἐβοηθήσαμεν, ὥσπερ ἐψηφισάμεθα, προθύμως, οὐκ ἂν
ἠνώχλει νῦν ἡμῖν ὁ Φίλιππος σωθείς.
    Τὰ μὲν δὴ τότε πραχθέντ' οὐκ ἂν ἄλλως ἔχοι. 6
νῦν δ' ἑτέρου πολέμου καιρὸς ἥκει τις, δι' ὃν καὶ περὶ
τούτων ἐμνήσθην, ἵνα μὴ ταὐτὰ πάθητε. τί δὴ
χρησόμεθ', ὦ ἄνδρες Ἀθηναῖοι, τούτῳ· εἰ γὰρ μὴ
βοηθήσετε παντὶ σθένει κατὰ τὸ δυνατόν, θεάσασθ'
ὃν τρόπον ὑμεῖς ἐστρατηγηκότες πάντ' ἔσεσθ' ὑπὲρ
Φιλίππου. ὑπῆρχον Ὀλύνθιοι δύναμίν τινα κεκτη- 7
μένοι καὶ διέκειθ' οὕτω τὰ πράγματα· οὔτε Φίλιππος
ἐθάρρει τούτους οὔθ' οὗτοι Φίλιππον. ἐπράξαμεν
ἡμεῖς κἀκεῖνοι πρὸς ἡμᾶς εἰρήνην· ἦν τοῦθ' ὥσπερ
ἐμπόδισμά τι τῷ Φιλίππῳ καὶ δυσχερές, πόλιν
μεγάλην ἐφορμεῖν τοῖς ἑαυτοῦ καιροῖς διηλλαγμένην
πρὸς ἡμᾶς. ἐκπολεμῶσαι δεῖν ᾠόμεθα τοὺς ἀνθρώ-

πους ἐκ παντὸς τρόπου, καὶ ὃ ἅπαντες ἐθρύλουν,
8 πέπρακται νυνὶ τοῦθ᾽ ὁπωσδήποτε. τί οὖν ὑπό-
λοιπον, ὦ ἄνδρες Ἀθηναῖοι, πλὴν βοηθεῖν ἐρρωμένως
καὶ προθύμως; ἐγὼ μὲν οὐχ ὁρῶ· χωρὶς γὰρ τῆς
περιστάσης ἂν ἡμᾶς αἰσχύνης, εἰ καθυφείμεθά τι
τῶν πραγμάτων, οὐδὲ τὸι φόβον, ὦ ἄνδρες Ἀθηναῖοι,
μικρὸν ὁρῶ τὸν τῶν μετὰ ⁻αὗτα. ἐχόντων μὲν ὡς
ἔχουσι Θηβαίων ἡμῖν, ἀπειρηκότων δὲ χρήμασι
Φωκέων, μηδενὸς δ᾽ ἐμποδὼν ὄντος Φιλίππῳ τὰ
παρόντα καταστρεψαμένῳ πρὸς ταῦτ᾽ ἐπικλῖναι τὰ
9 πράγματα. ἀλλὰ μὴν εἴ τις ὑμῶν εἰς τοῦτ᾽ ἀναβάλλεται ποιήσειν τὰ δέοντα, ἰδεῖν ἐγγύθεν βούλεται
τὰ δεινά, ἐξὸν ἀκούειν ἄλλοθι γιγνόμενα, καὶ βοη-
θοὺς ἑαυτῷ ζητεῖν, ἐξὸν νῦν ἑτέροις αὐτὸν βοηθεῖν·
ὅτι γὰρ εἰς τοῦτο περιστήσεται τὰ πράγματα, ἐὰν
τὰ παρόντα προώμεθα, σχεδὸν ἴσμεν ἅπαντες δήπου.
10 Ἀλλ᾽ ὅτι μὲν δὴ δεῖ βοηθεῖν, εἴποι τις ἄν, πάντες
ἐγνώκαμεν, καὶ βοηθήσομεν· τὸ δ᾽ ὅπως, τοῦτο λέγε.
μὴ τοίνυν, ὦ ἄνδρες Ἀθηναῖοι, θαυμάσητε, ἂν παρά-
δοξον εἴπω τι τοῖς πολλοῖς. νομοθέτας καθίσατε.
ἐν δὲ τούτοις τοῖς νομοθέταις μὴ θῆσθε νόμον
μηδένα (εἰσὶ γὰρ ὑμῖν ἱκανοί), ἀλλὰ τοὺς εἰς τὸ
11 παρὸν βλάπτοντας ὑμᾶς λύσατε. λέγω τοὺς περὶ
τῶν θεωρικῶν, σαφῶς οὑτωσί, καὶ τοὺς περὶ τῶν
στρατευομένων ἐνίους, ὧν οἱ μὲν τὰ στρατιωτικὰ
τοῖς οἴκοι μένουσι διανέμουσι θεωρικά, οἱ δὲ τοὺς
ἀτακτοῦντας ἀθῴους καθιστᾶσιν, εἶτα καὶ τοὺς τὰ
δέοντα ποιεῖν βουλομένους ἀθυμοτέρους ποιοῦσιν.
ἐπειδὰν δὲ ταῦτα λύσητε καὶ τὴν τοῦ τὰ βέλτιστα
λέγειν ὁδὸν παράσχητ᾽ ἀσφαλῆ, τηνικαῦτα τὸν
γράψονθ᾽ ἃ πάντες ἴσθ᾽ ὅτι συμφέρει ζητεῖτε.

πρὶν δὲ ταῦτα πρᾶξαι μὴ σκοπεῖτε τίς εἰπὼν τὰ 12
βέλτισθ᾽ ὑπὲρ ὑμῶν ὑφ᾽ ὑμῶν ἀπολέσθαι βουλή-
σεται· οὐ γὰρ εὑρήσετε, ἄλλως τε καὶ τούτου μόνου
περιγίγνεσθαι μέλλοντος, παθεῖν ἀδίκως τι κακὸν
τὸν ταῦτ᾽ εἰπόντα καὶ γράψαντα, μηδὲν δ᾽ ὠφελῆσαι
τὰ πράγματα, ἀλλὰ καὶ εἰς τὸ λοιπὸν μᾶλλον ἔτ᾽
ἢ νῦν τὸ τὰ βέλτιστα λέγειν φοβερώτερον ποιῆσαι.
καὶ λύειν γ᾽, ὦ ἄνδρες Ἀθηναῖοι, τοὺς νόμους δεῖ
τούτους τοὺς αὐτοὺς ἀξιοῦν οἵπερ καὶ τεθήκασιν· οὐ 13
γάρ ἐστι δίκαιον, τὴν μὲν χάριν, ἣ πᾶσαν ἔβλαπτε
τὴν πόλιν, τοῖς τότε θεῖσιν ὑπάρχειν, τὴν δ᾽ ἀπέχθειαν, δι᾽ ἧς ἂν ἅπαντες ἄμεινον πράξαιμεν, τῷ νῦν
τὰ βέλτιστ᾽ εἰπόντι ζημίαν γενέσθαι. πρὶν δὲ ταῦτ᾽
εὐτρεπίσαι μηδαμῶς, ὦ ἄνδρες Ἀθηναῖοι, μηδέν᾽
ἀξιοῦτε τηλικοῦτον εἶναι παρ᾽ ὑμῖν, ὥστε τοὺς νόμους
τούτους παραβάντα μὴ δοῦναι δίκην, μηδ᾽ οὕτως
ἀνόητον, ὥστ᾽ εἰς πρόυπτον κακὸν αὑτὸν ἐμβαλεῖν.
Οὐ μὴν οὐδ᾽ ἐκεῖνό γ᾽ ὑμᾶς ἀγνοεῖν δεῖ, ὦ ἄνδρες 14
Ἀθηναῖοι, ὅτι ψήφισμ᾽ οὐδενὸς ἄξιόν ἐστιν, ἂν μὴ
προσγένηται τὸ ποιεῖν ἐθέλειν τά γε δόξαντα προθύμως ὑμᾶς. εἰ γὰρ αὐτάρκη τὰ ψηφίσματ᾽ ἦν ἢ
ὑμᾶς ἀναγκάζειν ἃ προσήκει πράττειν ἢ περὶ ὧν
γραφείη διαπράξασθαι, οὔτ᾽ ἂν ὑμεῖς πολλὰ ψηφιζόμενοι μικρά, μᾶλλον δ᾽ οὐδὲν ἐπράττετε τούτων, οὔτε
Φίλιππος τοσοῦτον ὑβρίκει χρόνον· πάλαι γὰρ ἂν
ἕνεκά γε ψηφισμάτων ἐδεδώκει δίκην. ἀλλ᾽ οὐχ 15
οὕτω ταῦτ᾽ ἔχει· τὸ γὰρ πράττειν τοῦ λέγειν καὶ
χειροτονεῖν ὕστερον ὂν τῇ τάξει πρότερον τῇ δυνάμει
καὶ κρεῖττόν ἐστιν. τοῦτ᾽ οὖν δεῖ προσεῖναι, τὰ δ᾽
ἄλλ᾽ ὑπάρχει. καὶ γὰρ εἰπεῖν τὰ δέοντα παρ᾽ ὑμῖν
εἰσιν, ὦ ἄνδρες Ἀθηναῖοι, δυνάμενοι, καὶ γνῶναι

πάντων ὑμεῖς ὀξύτατοι τὰ ῥηθέντα· καὶ πρᾶξαι δὲ
δυνήσεσθε νῦν, ἐὰν ὀρθῶς ποιῆτε.

16 Τίνα γὰρ χρόνον ἢ τίνα καιρόν, ὦ ἄνδρες
Ἀθηναῖοι, τοῦ παρόντος βελτίω ζητεῖτε; ἢ πόθ᾽ ἃ
δεῖ πράξετ᾽, εἰ μὴ νῦν; οὐχ ἅπαντα μὲν ἡμῶν προεί-
ληφε τὰ χωρί᾽ ἄνθρωπος, εἰ δὲ καὶ ταύτης κύριος τῆς
χώρας γενήσεται, πάντων αἴσχιστα πεισόμεθα; οὐχ
οὕς, εἰ πολεμήσαιεν, ἑτοίμως σώσειν ὑπισχνούμεθα,
οὗτοι νῦν πολεμοῦσιν; οὐκ ἐχθρός; οὐκ ἔχων τὰ
ἡμέτερα; οὐ βάρβαρος; οὐχ ὅ τι ἂν εἴποι τις;
17 ἀλλὰ πρὸς θεῶν πάντ᾽ ἐάσαντες καὶ μόνον οὐχὶ
συγκατασκευάσαντες αὐτῷ τότε τοὺς αἰτίους οἵτινες
τούτων ζητήσομεν; οὐ γὰρ αὐτοί γ᾽ αἴτιοι φήσομεν
εἶναι, σαφῶς οἶδα τοῦτ᾽ ἐγώ. οὐδὲ γὰρ ἐν τοῖς τοῦ
πολέμου κινδύνοις τῶν φυγόντων οὐδεὶς ἑαυτοῦ κατη-
γορεῖ, ἀλλὰ τοῦ στρατηγοῦ καὶ τῶν πλησίον καὶ
πάντων μᾶλλον, ἥττηται δ᾽ ὅμως διὰ πάντας τοὺς
φυγόντας δήπου· μένειν γὰρ ἐξῆν τῷ κατηγοροῦντι
τῶν ἄλλων, εἰ δ᾽ ἐποίει τοῦθ᾽ ἕκαστος, ἐνίκων ἄν.
18 καὶ νῦν, οὐ λέγει τις τὰ βέλτιστα· ἀναστὰς ἄλλος
εἰπάτω, μὴ τοῦτον αἰτιάσθω. ἕτερος λέγει τις βελτίω·
ταῦτα ποιεῖτ᾽ ἀγαθῇ τύχῃ. ἀλλ᾽ οὐχ ἡδέα ταῦτα·
οὐκέτι τοῦθ᾽ ὁ λέγων ἀδικεῖ, πλὴν εἰ δέον εὔξασθαι
παραλείπει. εὔξασθαι μὲν γάρ, ὦ ἄνδρες Ἀθηναῖοι,
ῥᾴδιον εἰς ταὐτὸ πάνθ᾽ ὅσα βούλεταί τις ἀθροίσαντ᾽
ἐν ὀλίγῳ, ἑλέσθαι δ᾽ ὅταν περὶ πραγμάτων προτεθῇ
σκοπεῖν, οὐκέθ᾽ ὁμοίως εὔπορον, ἀλλὰ δεῖ τὰ βέλτιστ᾽
ἀντὶ τῶν ἡδέων, ἂν μὴ συναμφότερ᾽ ἐξῇ, λαμβάνειν.

19 Εἰ δέ τις ἡμῖν ἔχει καὶ τὰ θεωρικὰ ἐᾶν καὶ
πόρους ἑτέρους λέγειν στρατιωτικούς, οὐχ οὗτος
κρείττων; εἴποι τις ἄν. φήμ᾽ ἔγωγε, εἴπερ ἔστιν,

ὦ ἄνδρες Ἀθηναῖοι· ἀλλὰ θαυμάζω, εἴ τῴ ποτ' ἀνθρώπων ἢ γέγονεν ἢ γενήσεται, ἂν τὰ παρόντ' ἀναλώσῃ πρὸς ἃ μὴ δεῖ, τῶν ἀπόντων εὐπορῆσαι πρὸς ἃ δεῖ. ἀλλ', οἶμαι, μέγα τοῖς τοιούτοις ὑπάρχει λόγοις ἡ παρ' ἑκάστου βούλησις, διόπερ ῥᾷστον ἁπάντων ἐστὶν αὑτὸν ἐξαπατῆσαι· ὃ γὰρ βούλεται, τοῦθ' ἕκαστος καὶ οἴεται, τὰ δὲ πράγματα πολλάκις οὐχ οὕτω πέφυκεν. ὁρᾶτ' οὖν, ὦ ἄνδρες Ἀθηναῖοι, 2c ταῦθ' οὕτως, ὅπως καὶ τὰ πράγματ' ἐνδέχεται καὶ δυνήσεσθ' ἐξιέναι καὶ μισθὸν ἕξετε. οὔ τοι σωφρόνων οὐδὲ γενναίων ἐστὶν ἀνθρώπων ἐλλείποντάς τι δι' ἔνδειαν χρημάτων τῶν τοῦ πολέμου εὐχερῶς τὰ τοιαῦτ' ὀνείδη φέρειν, οὐδ' ἐπὶ μὲν Κορινθίους καὶ Μεγαρέας ἁρπάσαντας τὰ ὅπλα πορεύεσθαι, Φίλιππον δ' ἐᾶν πόλεις Ἑλληνίδας ἀνδραποδίζεσθαι δι' ἀπορίαν ἐφοδίων τοῖς στρατευομένοις.

Καὶ ταῦτ' οὐχ ἵν' ἀπέχθωμαί τισιν ὑμῶν, τὴν 21 ἄλλως προῄρημαι λέγειν· οὐ γὰρ οὕτως ἄφρων οὐδ' ἀτυχής εἰμ' ἐγώ, ὥστ' ἀπεχθάνεσθαι βούλεσθαι μηδὲν ὠφελεῖν νομίζων· ἀλλὰ δικαίου πολίτου κρίνω τὴν τῶν πραγμάτων σωτηρίαν ἀντὶ τῆς ἐν τῷ λέγειν χάριτος αἱρεῖσθαι, καὶ τοὺς ἐπὶ τῶν προγόνων ἡμῶν λέγοντας ἀκούω, ὥσπερ ἴσως καὶ ὑμεῖς, οὓς ἐπαινοῦσι μὲν οἱ παριόντες ἅπαντες, μιμοῦνται δ' οὐ πάνυ, τούτῳ τῷ ἔθει καὶ τῷ τρόπῳ τῆς πολιτείας χρῆσθαι, τὸν Ἀριστείδην ἐκεῖνον, τὸν Νικίαν, τὸν ὁμώνυμον ἐμαυτῷ, τὸν Περικλέα. ἐξ οὗ δ' οἱ 22 διερωτῶντες ὑμᾶς οὗτοι πεφήνασι ῥήτορες, τί βούλεσθε; τί γράψω; τί ὑμῖν χαρίσωμαι; προπέποται τῆς παραυτίχ' ἡδονῆς καὶ χάριτος τὰ τῆς πόλεως πράγματα, καὶ τοιαυτὶ συμβαίνει, καὶ τὰ μὲν τούτων

23 πάντα καλῶς ἔχει, τὰ δ' ὑμέτερ' αἰσχρῶς. καίτοι
σκέψασθ' ὦ ἄνδρες Ἀθηναῖοι, ἅ τις ἂν κεφάλαι'
εἰπεῖν ἔχοι τῶν τ' ἐπὶ τῶν προγόνων ἔργων καὶ τῶν
ἐφ' ὑμῶν. ἔσται δὲ βραχὺς καὶ γνώριμος ὑμῖν ὁ
λόγος· οὐ γὰρ ἀλλοτρίοις ὑμῖν χρωμένοις παραδείγμασιν ἀλλ' οἰκείοις, ὦ ἄνδρες Ἀθηναῖοι, εὐδαίμοσιν
24 ἔξεστι γενέσθαι. ἐκεῖνοι τοίνυν, οἷς οὐκ ἐχαρίζονθ'
οἱ λέγοντες οὐδ' ἐφίλουν αὐτοὺς ὥσπερ ὑμᾶς οὗτοι
νῦν, πέντε μὲν καὶ τετταράκοντ' ἔτη τῶν Ἑλλήνων
ἦρξαν ἑκόντων, πλείω δ' ἢ μύρια τάλαντ' εἰς τὴν
ἀκρόπολιν ἀνήγαγον. ὑπήκουε δ' ὁ ταύτην τὴν χώραν
ἔχων αὐτοῖς βασιλεύς, ὥσπερ ἐστὶ προσῆκον βάρβαρον Ἕλλησι, πολλὰ δὲ καὶ καλὰ καὶ πεζῇ καὶ
ναυμαχοῦντες ἔστησαν τρόπαι' αὐτοὶ στρατευόμενοι,
μόνοι δ' ἀνθρώπων κρείττω τὴν ἐπὶ τοῖς ἔργοις δόξαν
25 τῶν φθονούντων κατέλιπον. ἐπὶ μὲν δὴ τῶν Ἑλληνικῶν ἦσαν τοιοῦτοι. ἐν δὲ τοῖς κατὰ τὴν πόλιν
αὐτὴν θεάσασθ' ὁποῖοι, ἔν τε τοῖς κοινοῖς καὶ ἐν τοῖς
ἰδίοις. δημοσίᾳ μὲν τοίνυν οἰκοδομήματα καὶ κάλλη
τοιαῦτα καὶ τοσαῦτα κατεσκεύασαν ἡμῖν ἱερῶν καὶ
τῶν ἐν τούτοις ἀναθημάτων, ὥστε μηδενὶ τῶν ἐπιγιγ-
νομένων ὑπερβολὴν λελεῖφθαι· ἰδίᾳ δ' οὕτω σώφρονες ἦσαν καὶ σφόδρ' ἐν τῷ τῆς πολιτείας ἤθει
26 μένοντες, ὥστε τὴν Ἀριστείδου καὶ τὴν Μιλτιάδου
καὶ τῶν τότε λαμπρῶν οἰκίαν εἴ τις ἄρ' οἶδεν ὑμῶν
ὁποία ποτ' ἐστίν, ὁρᾷ τῆς τοῦ γείτονος οὐδὲν σεμνοτέραν οὖσαν· οὐ γὰρ εἰς περιουσίαν ἐπράττετ' αὐτοῖς
τὰ τῆς πόλεως, ἀλλὰ τὸ κοινὸν αὔξειν ἕκαστος ᾤετο
δεῖν. ἐκ δὲ τοῦ τὰ μὲν Ἑλληνικὰ πιστῶς, τὰ δὲ
πρὸς τοὺς θεοὺς εὐσεβῶς, τὰ δ' ἐν αὐτοῖς ἴσως διοικεῖν μεγάλην εἰκότως ἐκτήσαντ' εὐδαιμονίαν.

Τότε μὲν δὴ τοῦτον τὸν τρόπον εἶχε τὰ πράγματ᾽ 27
ἐκείνοις, χρωμένοις οἷς εἶπον προστάταις. νυνὶ δὲ
πῶς ἡμῖν ὑπὸ τῶν χρηστῶν τῶν νῦν τὰ πράγματ᾽
ἔχει; ἆρά γ᾽ ὁμοίως καὶ παραπλησίως; οἷς—τὰ
μὲν ἄλλα σιωπῶ πόλλ᾽ ἂν ἔχων εἰπεῖν, ἀλλ᾽ ὅσης
ἅπαντες ὁρᾶτ᾽ ἐρημίας ἐπειλημμένοι, καὶ Λακεδαι-
μονίων μὲν ἀπολωλότων, Θηβαίων δ᾽ ἀσχόλων
ὄντων, τῶν δ᾽ ἄλλων οὐδενὸς ὄντος ἀξιόχρεω περὶ
τῶν πρωτείων ἡμῖν ἀντιτάξασθαι, ἐξὸν δ᾽ ἡμῖν καὶ
τὰ ἡμέτερ᾽ αὐτῶν ἀσφαλῶς ἔχειν καὶ τὰ τῶν ἄλλων
δίκαια βραβεύειν, ἀπεστερήμεθα μὲν χώρας οἰκείας, 28
πλείω δ᾽ ἢ χίλια καὶ πεντακόσια τάλαντ᾽ ἀνηλώ-
καμεν εἰς οὐδὲν δέον, οὓς δ᾽ ἐν τῷ πολέμῳ συμμάχους
ἐκτησάμεθα, εἰρήνης οὔσης ἀπολωλέκασιν οὗτοι,
ἐχθρὸν δ᾽ ἐφ᾽ ἡμᾶς αὐτοὺς τηλικοῦτον ἠσκήκαμεν.
ἢ φρασάτω τις ἐμοὶ παρελθών, πόθεν ἄλλοθεν ἰσχυ-
ρὸς γέγονεν ἢ παρ᾽ ἡμῶν αὐτῶν Φίλιππος. ἀλλ᾽, 29
ὧταν, εἰ ταῦτα φαύλως, τά γ᾽ ἐν αὐτῇ τῇ πόλει νῦν
ἄμεινον ἔχει. καὶ τί ἂν εἰπεῖν τις ἔχοι; τὰς ἐπάλξεις
ἃς κονιῶμεν, καὶ τὰς ὁδοὺς ἃς ἐπισκευάζομεν, καὶ
κρήνας, καὶ λήρους; ἀποβλέψατε δὴ πρὸς τοὺς
ταῦτα πολιτευομένους, ὧν οἱ μὲν ἐκ πτωχῶν πλούσιοι γεγόνασιν, οἱ δ᾽ ἐξ ἀδόξων ἔντιμοι, ἔνιοι δὲ τὰς
ἰδίας οἰκίας τῶν δημοσίων οἰκοδομημάτων σεμνοτέρας
εἰσὶ κατεσκευασμένοι· ὅσῳ δὲ τὰ τῆς πόλεως ἐλάττω
γέγονεν, τοσούτῳ τὰ τούτων ηὔξηται.
    Τί δὴ τὸ πάντων αἴτιον τούτων, καὶ τί δή ποθ᾽ 30
ἅπαντ᾽ εἶχε καλῶς τότε, καὶ νῦν οὐκ ὀρθῶς; ὅτι
τότε μὲν πράττειν καὶ στρατεύεσθαι τολμῶν αὐτὸς
ὁ δῆμος δεσπότης τῶν πολιτευομένων ἦν καὶ κύριος
αὐτὸς ἁπάντων τῶν ἀγαθῶν, καὶ ἀγαπητὸν ἦν παρὰ

τοῦ δήμου τῶν ἄλλων ἑκάστῳ καὶ τιμῆς καὶ ἀρχῆς
31 καὶ ἀγαθοῦ τινος μεταλαβεῖν· νῦν δὲ τοὐναντίον
κύριοι μὲν οἱ πολιτευόμενοι τῶν ἀγαθῶν καὶ διὰ
τούτων ἅπαντα πράττεται, ὑμεῖς δ' ὁ δῆμος ἐκνενευρισμένοι καὶ περιῃρημένοι χρήματα, συμμάχους, ἐν
ὑπηρέτου καὶ προσθήκης μέρει γεγένησθε, ἀγαπῶντες
ἐὰν μεταδιδῶσι θεωρικῶν ὑμῖν ἢ Βοηδρόμια πέμψωσιν οὗτοι, καὶ τὸ πάντων ἀνδρειότατον, τῶν ὑμετέρων
αὐτῶν χάριν προσοφείλετε. οἱ δ' ἐν αὐτῇ τῇ πόλει
καθείρξαντες ὑμᾶς ἐπάγουσιν ἐπὶ ταῦτα καὶ τιθα-
32 σεύουσι χειροήθεις αὐτοῖς ποιοῦντες. ἔστι δ' οὐδέποτ',
οἶμαι, μέγα καὶ νεανικὸν φρόνημα λαβεῖν μικρὰ καὶ
φαῦλα πράττοντας· ὁποῖ' ἄττα γὰρ ἂν τὰ ἐπιτηδεύματα τῶν ἀνθρώπων ᾖ, τοιοῦτον ἀνάγκη καὶ τὸ
φρόνημ' ἔχειν. ταῦτα μὰ τὴν Δήμητρ' οὐκ ἂν θαυ-
μάσαιμ' εἰ μείζων εἰπόντι ἐμοὶ γένοιτο παρ' ὑμῶν
βλάβη τῶν πεποιηκότων αὐτὰ γενέσθαι· οὐδὲ γὰρ
παρρησία περὶ πάντων ἀεὶ παρ' ἡμῖν ἐστιν, ἀλλ'
ἔγωγ' ὅτι καὶ νῦν γέγονε θαυμάζω.
33 Ἐὰν οὖν ἀλλὰ νῦν γ' ἔτ' ἀπαλλαγέντες τούτων
τῶν ἐθῶν ἐθελήσητε στρατεύεσθαί τε καὶ πράττειν
ἀξίως ὑμῶν αὐτῶν, καὶ ταῖς περιουσίαις ταῖς οἴκοι
ταύταις ἀφορμαῖς ἐπὶ τὰ ἔξω τῶν ἀγαθῶν χρήσησθε,
ἴσως ἄν, ἴσως, ὦ ἄνδρες Ἀθηναῖοι, τέλειόν τι καὶ
μέγα κτήσαισθ' ἀγαθὸν καὶ τῶν τοιούτων λημμάτων
ἀπαλλαγείητε, ἃ τοῖς ἀσθενοῦσι παρὰ τῶν ἰατρῶν
σιτίοις διδομένοις ἔοικε. καὶ γὰρ ἐκεῖν' οὔτ' ἰσχὺν
ἐντίθησιν οὔτ' ἀποθνῄσκειν ἐᾷ· καὶ ταῦθ' ἃ νέμεσθε
νῦν ὑμεῖς, οὔτε τοσαῦτ' ἐστίν, ὥστ' ὠφέλειαν ἔχειν
τινὰ διαρκῆ, οὔτ' ἀπογνόντας ἄλλο τι πράττειν ἐᾷ,
ἀλλ' ἔστι ταῦτα τὴν ἑκάστου ῥᾳθυμίαν ἡμῶν ἐπαυξάν-

οντα. οὐκοῦν σὺ μισθοφορὰν λέγεις; φήσει τις. 34
καὶ παραχρῆμά γε τὴν αὐτὴν σύνταξιν ἁπάντων,
ὦ ἄνδρες Ἀθηναῖοι, ἵνα τῶν κοινῶν ἕκαστος τὸ μέρος
λαμβάνων, ὅτου δέοιθ' ἡ πόλις, τοῦθ' ὑπάρχοι.
ἔξεστιν ἄγειν ἡσυχίαν· οἴκοι μένων βελτίων, τοῦ
δι' ἔνδειαν ἀνάγκῃ τι ποιεῖν αἰσχρὸν ἀπηλλαγμένος.
συμβαίνει τι τοιοῦτον οἷον καὶ τὰ νῦν· στρατιώτης
αὐτὸς ὑπάρχων ἀπὸ τῶν αὐτῶν τούτων λημμάτων,
ὥσπερ ἐστὶ δίκαιον ὑπὲρ τῆς πατρίδος. ἔστι τις ἔξω
τῆς ἡλικίας ἡμῶν· ὅσ' οὗτος ἀτάκτως νῦν λαμβάνων
οὐκ ὠφελεῖ, ταῦτ' ἐν ἴσῃ τάξει λαμβάνων, πάντ'
ἐφορῶν καὶ διοικῶν ἃ χρὴ πράττεσθαι. ὅλως δ' οὔτ' 35
ἀφελὼν οὔτε προσθεὶς πλὴν μικρῶν, τὴν ἀταξίαν
ἀνελὼν εἰς τάξιν ἤγαγον τὴν πόλιν τὴν αὐτὴν τοῦ
λαβεῖν, τοῦ στρατεύεσθαι, τοῦ δικάζειν, τοῦ ποιεῖν
τοῦθ' ὅ τι καθ' ἡλικίαν ἕκαστος ἔχοι καὶ ὅτου καιρὸς
εἴη [τάξιν ποιήσας]. οὐκ ἔστιν ὅπου μηδὲν ἐγὼ
ποιοῦσι τὰ τῶν ποιούντων εἶπον ὡς δεῖ νέμειν, οὐδ'
αὐτοὺς μὲν ἀργεῖν καὶ σχολάζειν καὶ ἀπορεῖν, ὅ τι δ'
οἱ τοῦ δεῖνος νικῶσιν ξένοι, ταῦτα πυνθάνεσθαι·
ταῦτα γὰρ νυνὶ γίγνεται. καὶ οὐχὶ μέμφομαι τὸν 36
ποιοῦντά τι τῶν δεόντων ὑπὲρ ὑμῶν, ἀλλὰ καὶ ὑμᾶς
ὑπὲρ ὑμῶν αὐτῶν ἀξιῶ πράττειν ταῦτ' ἐφ' οἷς ἑτέρους τιμᾶτε, καὶ μὴ παραχωρεῖν, ὦ ἄνδρες Ἀθηναῖοι,
τῆς τάξεως, ἣν ὑμῖν οἱ πρόγονοι τῆς ἀρετῆς μετὰ
πολλῶν καὶ καλῶν κινδύνων κτησάμενοι κατέλιπον.
    Σχεδὸν εἴρηχ' ἃ νομίζω συμφέρειν· ὑμεῖς δ'
ἕλοισθ' ὅ τι καὶ τῇ πόλει καὶ ἅπασι συνοίσειν ὑμῖν
μέλλει.

NOTES

The argument (ὑπόθεσις) is due to Libanius (*vide* Introd. p. lii), a voluminous author who flourished at Antioch in the fourth century A.D. His works include rhetorical treatises, declamations, and a number of letters, some of which are addressed to the most prominent men of his day.

I

The exordium is parodied by Lucian, Ζεὺς Τραγῳδός, 15.

1. περὶ ὧν νυνὶ σκοπεῖτε. 'In regard to what you are now considering.' ὧν = ἐκείνων ἅ.

ὅτε...ἔχει. The conjunction has a causal force = 'as.' Cf. Plato *Protag.* 354 C ὅτε δὴ τοῦτο οὕτως ἔχει.

προθύμως. To be taken with ἀκούειν. Cf. Lucian, Ζεὺς Τραγῳδός 15, προσήκει προθύμως ἀκροᾶσθαι; *contra Aristocratem* 4, προθύμως ἀκούσητε. The adverb is here thrown for emphasis to the beginning of the sentence, as in iii. 5, εἰ γὰρ τότ' ἐκεῖσ' ἐβοηθήσαμεν, ὥσπερ ἐψηφισάμεθα, προθύμως, it is, for the same reason, placed at the end. Cf. also iii. 8.

εἴ τι χρήσιμον ἐσκεμμένος ἥκει τις. Observe the tense of the participle upon which τι χρήσιμον depends. 'If a man has come with (i.e. has brought with him) some profitable result of his reflections.' For Demosthenes' own practice in regard to the preparation of his speeches cf. Introd. pp. xiii—xiv.

τῆς ὑμετέρας τύχης ὑπολαμβάνω. 'I conceive it part of your fortune that' etc. For the genitive τύχης cf. *infra*, i. 10 τῆς ἡμετέρας ἀμελείας. Demosthenes consistently represents the Athenians as the favourites of Fortune, whose blessings they nevertheless persist in neglecting. Cf. *infra* 10; ii. *ad init.*; *Phil.* i. 12 τῆς τύχης ἥπερ ἀεὶ βέλτιον ἢ ἡμεῖς ἡμῶν αὐτῶν ἐπιμελούμεθα.

2. ὁ μὲν οὖν παρὼν καιρός. οὖν marks the transition from the brief introduction to the body of the speech. μέν is antithetic to δέ in the following sentence (ἡμεῖς δ'...πρὸς αὐτά), the urgency of the crisis being contrasted with the indifference of the Athenians towards it. Cf. iii. 3.

λέγει φωνὴν ἀφιείς. An instance of the figure προσωποποιία, i.e. personification. Cf. Quintilian ix. 2, fictiones personarum, quae προσωποποιίαι dicuntur; Cicero, *in Catilinam* i. 7. 18, quae (sc. patria) tecum, Catilina, sic agit et quodam modo tacita loquitur. Similarly Aeschines, *contra Ctesiphontem* 130 οὐ προεσήμαινον ἡμῖν οἱ θεοὶ φυλάξασθαι, μόνον οὐκ ἀνθρώπων φωνὰς προσκτησάμενοι;

τῶν πραγμάτων ὑμῖν ἐκείνων αὐτοῖς ἀντιληπτέον ἐστίν, 'you must grapple with the situation yonder' (i.e. the affair of Olynthus) *yourselves.* For the phrase cf. *infr.* 14 ἀντιληπτέον ἐρρωμένως τῶν πραγμάτων. In the emphatic pronoun αὐτοῖς is struck the key-note of Demosthenes' policy, *viz.* the demand from the Athenians of *personal* interest and service. Cf. *infr.* 6 αὐτοὺς ἐξιόντας, 9 ἐβοηθήσαμεν αὐτοί, 24 στρατευομένους αὐτούς, iii. 4 αὐτοὺς ἐμβαίνειν.

εἴπερ ὑπὲρ σωτηρίας αὐτῶν φροντίζετε. εἴπερ, an emphatic 'if'; cf. ii. 13 εἴπερ τις ὑμῖν προσέξει τὸν νοῦν. αὐτῶν (neuter)=τῶν πραγμάτων ἐκείνων.

οὐκ οἶδ' ὅντινα. To be taken closely together, 'We seem to me to take with regard to it I know not what attitude.' The expression is a euphemism. Demosthenes holds that the Athenians are criminally indifferent.

δή (cf. *infr.* 17 φημὶ δὴ διχῇ βοηθητέον εἶναι, ii. 27 φημὶ δὴ δεῖν εἰσφέρειν χρήματα κ.τ.λ.) serves to introduce the definite proposals of Demosthenes, which fall into two parts; (i) the immediate voting and speedy preparation of the relief force desired by the Olynthians (τὴν βοήθειαν): (ii) the despatch of an embassy to bear news of the vote and the coming aid (ταῦτα) and to watch the course of events (παρέσται τοῖς πράγμασιν).

ἤδη. Emphatic, 'now,' 'straightway.'

παρασκευάσασθαι, sc. τὴν βοήθειαν. Others, reading βοηθήσετε with the Palatine MS., make the ὅπως clause the object of παρασκευάσασθαι. For the combination of the fut. indic. (βοηθήσετε) and aor. subj. (πάθητε) they compare e.g. Plato, *Timaeus* 18 E μηχανᾶσθαι...ὅπως ἑκάτεροι ξυλλήξονται καὶ μή τις αὐτοῖς ἔχθρα γίγνηται. Some, adopting βοηθήσετε, prefer to regard καὶ μὴ πάθητε ταὐτὸν ὅπερ καὶ πρότερον as a parenthetic injunction addressed by Demosthenes to his audience.

τὴν ταχίστην. Adverbial, 'in the speediest way,' 'as soon as possible.' Cf. iii. 2 τὴν πρώτην.

ἐνθένδε, i.e. from Athens. The word is emphatic and equivalent in effect to αὐτοί—an Athenian, *not* a mercenary force. Vide Index B s.v. αὐτός.

μὴ πάθητε ταὐτὸν ὅπερ καὶ πρότερον, 'and not have the same experience as before,' i.e. fail to intervene while the opportunity is ripe. Cf. *infr.* 8 οὐδὲ παθεῖν ταὐτὸν ὅπερ ἤδη πολλάκις πρότερον πεπόνθατε. καί enforces the possible parallel between the past and present.

3. πανοῦργος, 'unscrupulous' (πᾶν ἔργον). Cf. Latin improbus. ἄνθρωπος = ὁ ἄνθρωπος, i.e. Philip. Cf. *infr.* 23. The MSS. in both places give ἄνθρωπος.

πράγμασι χρῆσθαι. The infinitive is explanatory of δεινός (epexegetic infinitive) 'clever at dealing with a situation.' For a similar recognition of Philip's ability cf. Aesch. *cont. Ctes.* 148 οὐ γὰρ ἦν ἀσύνετος.

τὰ μὲν εἴκων...τὰ δ' ἀπειλῶν...τὰ δ' ἡμᾶς διαβάλλων καὶ τὴν ἀπουσίαν τὴν ἡμετέραν, 'partly by yielding...partly by threatening... partly by disparaging us and our absence,' i.e. failure to take an active part against Philip.

ἡνίκ' ἂν τύχῃ, sc. εἴκων, 'whenever he happens to yield,' i.e. 'now and again,' 'at this, that, and the other time.' Cf. *de Fals. Leg.* 136 κῦμ' ἀκατάστατον, ὡς ἂν τύχῃ, κινούμενον, 'moving as it happens to move,' i.e. 'haphazard.'

τρέψηται καὶ παρασπάσηταί τι τῶν ὅλων πραγμάτων. So MSS. Some bracket τρέψηται καί and translate παρασπάσηται 'detach to his own side,' 'wrest to his own use.' Others render τρέψηται 'turn to his own advantage' or 'overturn'; but neither translation is satisfactory. Perhaps we should read στρέψῃ τε καὶ παρασπάσῃ τι τῶν ὅλων πραγμάτων, 'may bring about strain and rupture in some point of supreme importance.' For the medical metaphor cf. ii. 21 κἂν ῥῆγμα κἂν στρέμμα κἂν ἄλλο τι τῶν ὑπαρχόντων σαθρὸν ᾖ, *de Cor.* 198 ὥσπερ τὰ ῥήγματα καὶ τὰ σπάσματα, ὅταν τι κακὸν τὸ σῶμα λάβῃ, τότε κινεῖται.

τὰ ὅλα πράγματα (cf. summa res), things which make all the difference, which are of supreme importance. Cf. *de Cor.* 28 τὰ μικρὰ συμφέροντα τῆς πόλεως ἔδει με φυλάττειν, τὰ δ' ὅλα, ὥσπερ οὗτοι, πεπρακέναι;

4. οὐ μὴν ἀλλ' = 'not but what,' 'yet for all that.' Cf. ii. 22; *Philippics* i. 38 ἀληθῆ μέν ἐστι τὰ πολλά, ὡς οὐκ ἔδει, οὐ μὴν ἀλλ' ἴσως οὐχ ἡδέ' ἀκούειν.

ἐπιεικῶς. Emphatic by its position; 'it is probably (there is good ground for believing that) that which is the most impregnable point in Philip's position, which is at the same time (καί) of greatest advantage to you.'

τὸ γὰρ εἶναι...τῷ στρατεύματι. The whole phrase stands as subject to the predicates προέχει and ἔχει. Cf. Sonn. *Gk Gr.* §§ 316, 309. For Philip's sole control cf. *de Cor.* 235 ἁπλῶς αὐτὸς δεσπότης, ἡγεμών, κύριος πάντων, where the advantage which this gave him is strongly enforced.

καὶ ῥητῶν καὶ ἀπορρήτων = 'both what is public and what is private.' The antithesis is only for rhetorical effect, as in *de Cor.* 122 βοᾷς ῥητὰ καὶ ἄρρητ' ὀνομάζων, where however the adjectives have a different meaning.

κατὰ καιρόν = Latin tempore, 'seasonably,' 'opportunely.'

ποιήσαιθ'. Observe that the middle voice is naturally used in speaking of the conclusion by Philip of an agreement to which he himself was a party.

5. δῆλον γάρ...ὅτι. An iambic senarius. Aristotle (*Rhet.* iii. 8) declares ῥυθμὸν δεῖ ἔχειν τὸν λόγον, μέτρον δὲ μή· ποίημα γὰρ ἔσται· but he adds that the iambic enters largely into ordinary speech (ὁ δὲ ἴαμβος αὐτή ἐστιν ἡ λέξις ἡ τῶν πολλῶν· διὸ μάλιστα πάντων τῶν μέτρων ἰαμβεῖα φθέγγονται λέγοντες. Cf. *Poet.* xxii. 18) and Cicero, *Orat.* 189 makes the same observation (senarios uero et Hipponacteos effugere uix possumus; magnam enim partem ex iambis constat nostra oratio). Hexameters, pentameters and other species of verse have been detected in Demosthenes as in other authors, e.g. Livy and Tacitus.

οὐδ' ὑπὲρ μέρους χώρας κινδυνεύουσιν. οὐδὲ marks a step upward in the series of perils, 'now danger threatens not reputation, *not even* a portion of territory.' κινδυνεύειν is followed by περὶ (or ὑπέρ) with genit. (*a*) of what is threatened by the danger, e.g. κινδυνεύειν περὶ τῆς ψυχῆς (so here δόξης, μέρους χώρας), (*b*) of the danger which threatens, e.g. Isocrates, *de Pace* 37 οὐδὲν ἀλλ' ἢ συμβουλεύουσιν ἡμῖν πάλιν περὶ ἀνδραποδισμοῦ κινδυνεύειν (so here ἀναστάσεως καὶ ἀνδραποδισμοῦ).

ἀναστάσεως, sc. πέρι, = 'subversion,' 'utter destruction.' Cf. Aesch. *Pers.* 107 πόλεων τ' ἀναστάσεις and the use of the adjective ἀνάστατος and the verb ἀνίστημι e.g. Eurip. *Hecuba* 494 καὶ νῦν πόλις μὲν πᾶσ' ἀνέστηκεν δορί.

ἅ τ' Ἀμφιπολιτῶν ἐποίησε τοὺς παραδόντας αὐτῷ τὴν πόλιν καὶ Πυδναίων τοὺς ὑποδεξαμένους, 'both what he did to those of the people of Amphipolis who placed their city in his hands, and (what he did to) those of the people of Pydna who welcomed him.' Notice the double accusative after ποιεῖν as in the phrase κακὰ ποιεῖν τινά, to do evil to a man. By the regular Greek idiom the relative pronoun is not repeated in the second clause, while the verb ἐποίησε also is naturally left to be supplied. Cf. ii. 4 καὶ μεγάλα...φαίνοιτ᾽ ἂν ὀνείδη, n.

Amphipolis, an important city on the Strymon, commanding the approach to Thrace and the Chersonese, fell into the hands of Philip in 357 B.C. Pydna, on the Thermaic gulf, met a similar fate a short time afterwards (vide Introduction, p. xviii).

ἄπιστον. Note the gender, 'an object of mistrust.' Similarly Aeschines, contra Timarchum 84 οὕτως ἰσχυρόν ἐστιν ἡ ἀλήθεια, Eurip. Hipp. 109-10 τερπνὸν ἐκ κυναγίας | τράπεζα πλήρης, Verg. Aen. iv. 569-70 uarium et mutabile semper | femina.

ταῖς πολιτείαις, 'constitutional governments,' as contrasted with ἡ τυραννίς ='unconstitutional power,' 'despotism.' Cf. Phil. ii. 21 οὐ γὰρ ἀσφαλῶς ταῖς πολιτείαις αἱ πρὸς τυράννους αὗται ὁμιλίαι, ibid. 25 βασιλεὺς γὰρ καὶ τύραννος ἅπας ἐχθρὸς ἐλευθερίᾳ καὶ νόμοις ἐναντίος. Dorothy Temple, Letter to her husband (Oct. 31st, 1670), 'I have a letter from P. who says...that it were to be wished our politicians at home would consider well that there is no trust to be put in alliances with ambitious kings, especially such as make it their fundamental maxim to be base.'

6. ἐθελῆσαι. Mark the ingressive force of the aorist, 'make up your minds.' Cf. ii. 13, iii. 33 ἐθελήσητε. Similarly παροξυνθῆναι, 'bestir yourselves.'

εἰσφέροντας. The word is specially used for the payment of extra-ordinary taxes levied owing to the financial strain of military operations.

αὐτοὺς ἐξιόντας. Cf. supr. 2 τῶν πραγμάτων ὑμῖν ἐκείνων αὐτοῖς ἀντιληπτέον ἐστίν n.

μηδὲν ἐλλείποντας. The sentence δεῖν ἐθελῆσαι...ἐλλείποντας is an indirect command. Hence the imperatival nature of the participle ἐλλείποντας demands the negative μή.

οὐδὲ γὰρ λόγος οὐδὲ σκῆψις...ὑπολείπεται. The negatives must be given their proper force. 'For indeed there is not a reason, no nor an excuse remaining.'

7. ἐκπολεμῶσαι. Observe the tense, 'to set the Olynthians at war with Philip,' 'to start a war between the O. and P.' Cf. supr. 6 ἐθελῆσαι.

αὐτόματον, 'of itself,' 'naturally,' 'without interference.' Cf. *infr.*
9 τὰ δὲ μέλλοντ' αὐτόμαт' οἰόμενοι σχήσειν καλῶς.

καὶ ταῦθ', 'and that too,' used, generally with a participle, to add emphatically a further factor in the situation.

μέχρι του ταῦτ' ἂν ἐγνωκότες ἦσαν ἴσως. Observe the tense of the participle ἐγνωκότες and the emphatic position of the phrase μέχρι του, 'they would perhaps be unreliable allies (σφαλεροὶ σύμμαχοι) and of their present temper (ταῦτ' ἐγνωκότες) *only* up to a point.'

ἐκ τῶν πρὸς αὐτοὺς ἐγκλημάτων = 'because of grievances concerning them themselves,' 'because of what they themselves complain of' (ἐξ ὧν αὐτοὶ ἐγκαλοῦσι). πρὸς αὐτούς is here equivalent to a subjective genitive, the phrase being more euphonious than with ἑαυτῶν. Cf. *Phil.* ii. 3 τὴν πρὸς ὑμᾶς ἀπέχθειαν (your hatred) ὀκνοῦντες, *de Cor.* 36 (συνέβη) τὴν μὲν ἀπέχθειαν τὴν πρὸς Θηβαίους καὶ Θετταλοὺς τῇ πόλει γενέσθαι. With words which in their nature involve the action of one party with another (e.g. φιλία, ἔχθρα, φθόνος κ.τ.λ.) πρός with the acc. may denote either the one *from* whom or the one *to* whom the action proceeds.

βεβαίαν. The position of the adjective shows that it is used predicatively. 'It is natural for them to cherish an enduring hatred.' Cf. ii. 1 τοιαύτην *n.*

ὑπὲρ ὧν φοβοῦνται, 'in regard to what they fear.' In Demosthenes ὑπέρ with gen. is frequently equivalent in meaning to περί. ὧν = ἐκείνων ἅ. Cf. *supr.* 1 περὶ ὧν νυνὶ σκοπεῖτε.

8. οὐδὲ παθεῖν ταὐτὸν κ.τ.λ. Cf. *supr.* 2.

ὅθ' ἥκομεν Εὐβοεῦσιν βεβοηθηκότες, 'when we had returned after having lent aid to the Euboeans.' Observe the force of ἥκομεν. The date to which reference is made is 357 B.C. (Introd. p. xix).

Ἱέραξ καὶ Στρατοκλῆς. Stratocles was banished from Amphipolis, probably after Philip's capture of the city. The decree recording his banishment is still extant (Hicks, *Hist. Greek Inscriptions,* 98).

παρῆσαν...ἐπὶ τουτὶ τὸ βῆμα. παρῆσαν, Dobree; cf. ii. 8 παρελθών *n.* and Index B s.v. παριέναι. The MSS. give παρῆσαν, for the use of which with ἐπί and Acc. cf. ii. 8 πρὸς τοῦτο πάρεστι *n.* and Thuc. ii. 34 καὶ γυναῖκες πάρεισιν αἱ προσήκουσαι ἐπὶ τὸν τάφον ὀλοφυρόμεναι.

εἰ γὰρ...παρειχόμεθ'...εἴχετ' ἂν Ἀμφίπολιν τότε. A hypothetical sentence referring to *past* time, the condition being one which, it is implied, was unfulfilled and the action in the case of either verb being extended through a period of time; hence the imperfect tenses. 'If we

had exhibited...you would have held possession of Amphipolis then';
not 'you would have *gained* possession' which would require the aorist
ἔσχετ' ἄν.

ἡμεῖς ὑπὲρ ἡμῶν αὐτῶν. Observe the emphasis of the repeated
pronoun 'on behalf of *ourselves*.' Cf. Soph. *Oed. Col.* 1356 τὸν αὐτὸς
αὐτοῦ πατέρα τόνδ' ἀπήλασας.

9. Πύδνα. Cf. *supr.* 5 *n.*

Ποτείδαια, an important Athenian possession on the isthmus
connecting the peninsula of Pallene with the mainland, was seized by
Philip in 356 B.C. and handed over by him to the Olynthians. *Vide*
Introd. p. xviii.

Μεθώνη, an Athenian port on the Thermaic Gulf north of Pydna,
was captured by Philip in 353 B.C. In the course of the siege Philip
was deprived of the sight of one eye through a wound inflicted by an
arrow. *Vide* Introd. p. xxi.

Παγασαί, a port at the northern end of the Pagasaean Gulf and an
important strategic point in regard to both Thessaly and Boeotia, was
taken by Philip in 352 B.C. and occupied by a Macedonian garrison.
Vide Introd. p. xxi.

καθ' ἕκαστα λέγων, 'enumerating them severally.'

τούτων ἐνὶ τῷ πρώτῳ. ἐνί indefinite, 'any one of them, the first.'

ἐβοηθήσαμεν αὐτοί. For the pronoun, cf. *supr.* 2 τῶν πραγμάτων
ὑμῖν ἐκείνων αὐτοῖς ἀντιληπτέον ἐστὶν *n.*

ῥάονι...τῷ Φιλίππῳ, 'we should find Philip more amenable and
far more humble now.' For this use of χρῆσθαι cf. uti in Latin.

νῦν δέ, 'but as it is'; nunc vero.

ἡμεῖς. Notice the insertion and position of the emphatic pronoun;
'We *ourselves*.' For this view of Philip's advance, cf. *Phil.* i. 11 οὐδὲ
γὰρ οὗτος παρὰ τὴν αὐτοῦ ῥώμην τοσοῦτον ἐπηύξηται ὅσον παρὰ τὴν
ἡμετέραν ἀμέλειαν.

Μακεδονίας. Mark the emphatic position of the word at the end
of the sentence. For Demosthenes' contemptuous opinion of Macedonia
cf. ii. 14 αὐτὴ δὲ καθ' αὑτὴν ἀσθενὴς καὶ πολλῶν κακῶν ἐστι μεστή: for
his view of the Macedonians, cf. *Phil.* iii. 31 ὀλέθρου Μακέδονος ὅθεν
οὐδ' ἀνδράποδον πρίαιτό τις ἄν ποτε, *Phil.* i. 10, Introd. p. xx. *n.* 2.

10. τῶν παρὰ τῶν θεῶν ἡμῖν ὑπηργμένων, 'what has been done
for us by the gods.' Cf. *supr.* 1 τῆς ὑμετέρας τύχης κ.τ.λ. *n.*

καίπερ οὐκ ἐχόντων ὡς δεῖ πολλῶν. A rhetorical euphemism.

τὸ μὲν γάρ...τὸν πόλεμον. Object of ἂν...θείη and antithetic to τὸ δὲ...χρῆσθαι, which is object of ἂν θείην and is divided into two parts coupled by μήτε...τε, *viz.* (i) μήτε πάλαι τοῦτο πεπονθέναι, (ii) πεφηνέναι τέ τιν' ἡμῖν συμμαχίαν τούτων ἀντίρροπον, ἂν βουλώμεθα χρῆσθαι. τούτων refers to πολλά, the many losses incurred during the war. With χρῆσθαι supply αὐτῇ, i.e. τῇ συμμαχίᾳ.

τῆς ἡμετέρας ἀμελείας ἄν τις θείη δικαίως, 'one would rightly ascribe to (lit. put down as part of) our neglect.' Cf. *supr.* 1 τῆς ὑμετέρας τύχης ὑπολαμβάνω *n.*

11. παρόμοιόν ἐστιν ὅπερ...κτήσεως, sc. ἐστίν. For the construction, cf. Xen. *Anab.* v. 4. 34 μόνοι τε ὄντες ὅμοια ἔπραττον, ἅπερ ἂν μετ' ἄλλων ὄντες (sc. ἄνθρωποι ποιήσειαν), ἔν τε ὄχλῳ ὄντες ἐποίουν ἅπερ ἂν ἄνθρωποι ἐν ἐρημίᾳ ποιήσειαν.

καὶ περὶ τῆς τῶν χρημάτων κτήσεως = 'in the acquisition of wealth also.' καί emphasizes the parallel. Cf. *supr.* 2 μὴ πάθητε ταὐτὸν ὅπερ καὶ πρότερον.

ἂν μὲν γάρ κ.τ.λ. γάρ, as usual, serves to introduce the *detailed* comparison.

ὅσ' ἄν τις λάβῃ, καὶ σώσῃ, 'if a man keeps as much as he gets.' καί marks that the action of keeping is *additional* to that of getting.

μεγάλην ἔχει τῇ τύχῃ τὴν χάριν, 'the gratitude which he has to Fortune is great.' For the position of the adjective μεγάλην, cf. *supr.* 7 βεβαίαν εἰκὸς τὴν ἔχθραν αὐτοὺς...ἔχειν *n.*

συνανήλωσε. Gnomic aorist, used of a general truth. Cf. *infr.* 15 ἀπέστησαν. The contemporaneous expenditure of the wealth and the memory thereof is emphasized by the use of the compound συνανήλωσε.

οἱ μὴ χρησάμενοι. The expression is a generic one 'such as do not employ'; hence the negative μή.

πρὸς τὸ τελευταῖον ἐκβάν = 'by that which issues last,' i.e. 'the final result.' πρός is used with the accusative case to express the standard. Cf. ad in Latin. τελευταῖον is, in effect, adverbial.

καὶ σφόδρα δεῖ, 'there is a very urgent need.' καί emphasizes the adverb σφόδρα.

ταῦτα, sc. τὰ λοιπά.

ἀποτριψόμεθα. ἀποτρίβεσθαι (middle voice) is a *vox propria* for ridding oneself of defilement, and is then used metaphorically in reference to disgrace, slander and the like. Cf. Aeschines, *contra Timarchum* 120

αἰσχύνομαι γάρ...εἰ Τίμαρχος...μὴ τὸ πρᾶγμα ὅλον ἀποτρίψασθαι ἐπι-
χειρήσει.

**12. εἰ δὲ προησόμεθ᾽, ὦ ἄνδρες Ἀθηναῖοι, καὶ τούτους τοὺς
ἀνθρώπους,** 'if we persist in abandoning these men as well,' i.e. in
addition to (καὶ) the citizens of Amphipolis and the other places which
they had failed to save from Philip. For *προησόμεθα,* cf. *supr.* 9
προιέμενοι. The future indicative with εἰ imparts a minatory or monitory tone to the condition. Cf. *infr.* 15 εἰ τοῦτο γενήσεται.

τί τὸ κωλῦον ἔτ᾽ αὐτὸν ἔσται, 'what will be left to prevent him?'
κωλύειν, when used negatively, or (as here) in a question equivalent
in force to a negative, omits before the following infinitive the negatives
μὴ οὐ, which are generally inserted in such a case after other verbs and
phrases signifying prevention. Cf. Sonn. *Gk Gr.* § 369 c.

βαδίζειν. Cf. *infr.* 25 τίς αὐτὸν κωλύσει δεῦρο βαδίζειν;

τὸ κατ᾽ ἀρχάς, together='originally.' The neuter article, both in
the singular and plural number, is often inserted with adverbs and
adverbial phrases. Cf. iii. 34 τὰ νῦν.

Ἀμφίπολιν...Πύδναν...Ποτείδαιαν, Μεθώνην, *vide supr.* 5 *n.,* 9 *n.*

Θετταλίας. Thessaly, an important district of Northern Greece,
lay south of Macedonia and north of Boeotia. It contained several
important cities, among them Φεραί and Παγασαί (cf. *supr.* 9). The
district of Μαγνησία (*infr.* 13) stretched along the Thracian sea on the
eastern side of Thessaly. *Vide* Introd. p. xxi.

13. ὃν ἐβούλετ᾽...τρόπον, 'in the way in which he wished.'
Observe that the antecedent τρόπον, being placed in the relative clause,
has no article (τόν) accompanying it. Sonn. *Gk Gr.* § 363 (3). Cf.
iii. 27 χρωμένοις οἷς εἶπον προστάταις *n.*

Θρᾴκην. Thrace, to the east of Macedonia, was laid open to
Philip's aggression by his capture of Amphipolis (cf. *supr.* 5). He
invaded the country in the latter half of 352 B.C., when he threatened
the Chersonese and caused great alarm at Athens, as he thus en-
dangered the supplies of corn brought to the city by ships from the
Euxine ports. Introd. p. xxi.

τῶν βασιλέων, 'the princes' or 'chieftains' who controlled the
various tribes inhabiting Thrace.

ἠσθένησεν. Observe the tense, 'fell sick.' Cf. *supr.* 6 ἐθελῆσαι *n.*

τὰς δ᾽ ἐπ᾽ Ἰλλυριοὺς κ.τ.λ., 'or his marches upon the Illyrians and Paeonians, against Arybbas, and to the places which (ὅποι) one might mention, I say nothing.' The Illyrians and Paeonians lay to the west and north of Macedonia. Philip had turned his arms against these tribes first as early as 358 B.C. (Introd. p. xvii.) Arybbas was a chief of the Molossi, a people of Epirus, and uncle to Philip's wife Olympias. He was probably attacked in 352–351 B.C. Later he was driven from his kingdom. (Introd. p. xxx.)

14. νῦν. Mark the emphatic position.

καὶ τὸ προΐεσθαι καθ᾽ ἕκαστον ἀεί τι τῶν πραγμάτων ὡς ἀλυσιτελές, 'both how unprofitable is the neglect of each point as it occurs in the course of events.' The prepositional phrase καθ᾽ ἕκαστόν τι forms the object of προΐεσθαι. Cf. Thuc. iv. 30 ἐμπρήσαντός τινος κατὰ μικρὸν τῆς ὕλης. For προΐεσθαι, cf. *supr.* 9, and for the use of ἀεί ii. 7.

ᾗ χρῆται καὶ συζῇ Φίλιππος. A strong phrase, 'which is Philip's habit and nature.'

ὁ μὲν...ἐγνωκὼς ἔσται. Observe the full force of the future perfect, 'shall have made up his mind.'

ἀντιληπτέον ἐρρωμένως. Cf. *supr.* 2.

εἰς τί ποτ᾽ ἐλπὶς ταῦτα τελευτῆσαι, 'where, pray, is it to be expected this will end.' ποτέ (cf. *tandem* in Latin) imparts an eager tone to the question. Cf. iii. 30 τί δὴ ποθ᾽ ἅπαντ᾽ εἶχε καλῶς τότε καὶ νῦν οὐκ ὀρθῶς ; For the aorist τελευτῆσαι following an expression denoting hope, cf. *Phil.* iii. 5 εἰ πάνθ᾽ ἃ προσῆκε πραττόντων οὕτως διέκειτο, οὐδ᾽ ἂν ἐλπὶς ἦν αὐτὰ γενέσθαι βελτίω, Plato, *Phaedo* 67 B πολλὴ ἐλπὶς ἀφικομένῳ οἷ ἐγὼ πορεύομαι ἐκεῖ ἱκανῶς, εἴπερ που ἄλλοθι, κτήσασθαι τοῦτο κ.τ.λ., Eur. *Herc. Furens* 745–6 ἃ πάρος οὔποτε διὰ φρενὸς ἤλπισε παθεῖν.

15. ὅστις ἀγνοεῖ = ὥστε ἀγνοεῖν. 'So simple as not to know.'

τὸν ἐκεῖθεν πόλεμον, 'the war yonder,' i.e. in Chalcidice. Observe the form of the adverb ἐκεῖθεν, which, although used attributively with τὸν πόλεμον, is influenced by the force of the verb ἥξοντα. Cf. *contra Aristocratem* 31 τὸν ἐκ τῆς ἐκκλησίας πέρυσι πάντες ἑωρᾶθ᾽ ὑπ᾽ ἐκείνων ἀπαχθέντα, Thuc. i. 63 ὅπως εἴργωσι τοὺς ἐκεῖθεν ἐπιβοηθεῖν.

εἰ τοῦτο γενήσεται. Cf. *supr.* 12 εἰ δὲ προησόμεθα κ.τ.λ. *n.*

μὴ τὸν αὐτὸν τρόπον ὥσπερ οἱ δανειζόμενοι ῥᾳδίως, 'lest in the same manner as those who borrow lightly.' δανείζειν, to lend > < δανείζεσθαι, to borrow. The Athenians, declares Demosthenes, may prove to have borrowed their ease in not interfering with Philip at a great price. Like those who borrow money at a high rate of interest they may enjoy peace for a time (cf. μικρὸν εὐπορήσαντες χρόνον in the simile) on the strength of their present position. But in the end (ὕστερον) they may have to pay heavy interest in a hard struggle with the Macedonian (πολλὰ καὶ χαλεπὰ ποιεῖν), a struggle which may imperil their position—strong enough at present to secure them freedom from attack—as an independent state (κινδυνεύσωμεν περὶ τῶν ἐν αὑτῇ τῇ χώρᾳ). Cf. in the simile καὶ τῶν ἀρχαίων ἀπέστησαν.

ἐπὶ τοῖς μεγάλοις=‘at a high rate of interest.’ So ἐπὶ πολλῷ below, ‘at a great cost.’ Cf. de Fals. Leg. 96 ἦν (sc. εἰρήνην) δέδοικα...μὴ λελήθαμεν ὥσπερ οἱ δανειζόμενοι ἐπὶ πολλῷ ἄγοντες.

καὶ τῶν ἀρχαίων ἀπέστησαν, ‘be deprived of the capital as well.’ For the tense of ἀπέστησαν cf. supr. 11 συνανήλωσε. τὰ ἀρχαῖα = the capital on the strength of which the loan is made, and which in the end is lost as well as (καὶ) the interest paid.

φανῶμεν ἐρρᾳθυμηκότες, ‘may prove to have enjoyed our leisure.’ Mark carefully the difference between φαίνεσθαι with a participle and with an infinitive. Thus φαίνεσθαι ἐρρᾳθυμηκώς, to have plainly or obviously enjoyed leisure ; φαίνεσθαι ἐρρᾳθυμηκέναι, to appear to have enjoyed leisure.

ζητοῦντες, sc. ποιεῖν.

ὧν. An instance of the (so-called) partitive genitive.

16. τὸ μὲν οὖν ἐπιτιμᾶν...τὸ δ’ ὑπὲρ τῶν παρόντων κ.τ.λ. Cf. supr. 2 ὁ μὲν οὖν παρὼν καιρὸς...ἡμεῖς δ’ κ.τ.λ. For ὑπέρ cf. supr. 7 ὑπὲρ ὧν φοβοῦνται καὶ πεπόνθασιν n.

παντός=‘the part of any one,’ ‘in any one’s power.’ Cf. infr. συμβούλου, ‘the part of a counsellor or statesman.’

ἐγὼ δ’ οὐκ ἀγνοῶ κ.τ.λ. Mark the emphatic pronoun, ‘for my part.’ To μέν the antithetic particle is μήν below (οὐ μὴν οἶμαι). ‘I am not ignorant...yet I think.’

κατὰ γνώμην, ‘according to your mind,’ ‘as you look for it to do.’ Contrast infr. 21 παρὰ γνώμην.

περὶ ὧν...ἡγοῦμαι. ὧν = ἐκείνων ἅ. Cf. supr. 1 περὶ ὧν νυνὶ σκοπεῖτε. ὑποστείλασθαι, ‘to prevaricate,’ ‘to dissemble’; lit. ‘shorten sail.’

17. φημὶ δή κ.τ.λ. Cf. ii. 11 φημὶ δὴ δεῖν ἡμᾶς τοῖς μὲν Ὀλυνθίοις βοηθεῖν, ii. 27 φημὶ δὴ δεῖν εἰσφέρειν χρήματα.

βοηθητέον εἶναι τοῖς πράγμασιν ὑμῖν, ‘you must try to save the situation.' Observe the different relation to the verb of the two words in the dative case; τοῖς πράγμασιν, object of βοηθητέον; ὑμῖν, dative of the agent. (Sonn. *Gk Gr.* § 423.)

τῷ τε...ἐκπέμπειν καὶ τῷ...ἐτέροις, 'both by...and by,' explanatory of διχῇ, 'in two ways.'

ἐκείνου, Philip.

στρατιώταις ἐτέροις, 'a second body of troops,' i.e. in addition to those sent to succour the cities for the Olynthians (τοὺς τοῦτο ποιήσοντας στρατιώτας).

εἰ δὲ θατέρου τούτων ὀλιγωρήσετε, 'if you persist in neglecting either (τοῦ ἐτέρου) of these projects,' i.e. succouring Olynthus and attacking Macedonia (τὴν ἐκείνου χώραν). On the tense of ὀλιγωρήσετε cf. *supr.* 12 εἰ δὲ προησόμεθα *n.*

18. εἴτε γὰρ...παραστήσεται. This clause puts the first alternative, *viz.* if the Athenians ravage Macedonia but leave Philip to reduce Olynthus. The second alternative, *viz.* assisting Olynthus only (μόνον) and leaving Macedonia unassailed, is given in the clause εἴτε βοηθησάντων...τοῖς πράγμασι.

τὴν ἐκείνου, sc. χώραν, which is inserted *supr.* 17. Cf. *infr.* τὴν οἰκείαν.

ὑπομείνας τοῦτ' "Ολυνθον παραστήσεται, 'he shall submit to this and reduce Olynthus.' τοῦτο = τὸ ὑμᾶς κακῶς τὴν χώραν ποιεῖν.

προσκαθεδεῖται καὶ προσεδρεύσει τοῖς πράγμασι, 'he shall sit by and keep a watch upon events.'

δή, marking the inference, 'therefore.'

19. ὅσ' οὐδενὶ τῶν ἄλλων ἀνθρώπων στρατιωτικά, sc. ἐστι. 'As much as no one of the rest of mankind has for warlike purposes,' i.e. you have a sum larger than the military funds of any one else. Many editors follow Madvig and Cobet in deleting στρατιωτικά, on the ground that it is implied in the following sentence (εἰ μὲν οὖν ταῦτα τοῖς στρατευομένοις ἀποδώσετε) that the Athenian monies are *not* allocated to military purposes. But the adjective's force may well be limited to the relative clause only. For the Theoric Fund, to which Demosthenes here alludes, see App. B.

ταῦτα δ' ὑμεῖς...λαμβάνετε. Observe the insertion of the pronoun; 'This money *you* receive in such a way as you desire.' Cf. *infr.* 20 λαμβάνειν εἰς τὰς ἑορτάς.

εἰ μὲν οὖν ταῦτα τοῖς στρατευομένοις ἀποδώσετε, 'if then you mean to pay it to those who serve as soldiers.' For μὲν οὖν cf. *supr.* 2 *n.* οὖν introduces the two alternatives; μέν contrasts this sentence with εἰ δὲ μή. For the tense of ἀποδώσετε cf. *supr.* 12 εἰ δὲ προησόμεθα *n.*

οὐδενὸς ὑμῖν προσδεῖ πόρου. Mark the compound verb: 'you have no need of an *additional* (προς) supply.' Cf. *infr.* 27 προσδεῖν, iii. 31 προσοφείλετε.

προσδεῖ, μᾶλλον δ' ἅπαντος ἐνδεῖ τοῦ πόρου. μᾶλλον δέ corrective (cf. Latin vel potius, immo vero). 'You have need of an additional supply, or rather of the whole supply.' Cf. ii. 22 μεγάλη γὰρ ῥοπή, μᾶλλον δὲ τὸ ὅλον ἡ τύχη, iii. 14 μικρά, μᾶλλον δ' οὐδέν.

20. ἐγὼ μὲν γὰρ ἡγοῦμαι κ.τ.λ. This sentence states Demosthenes' *personal* view (cf. the emphatic ἐγὼ μέν). The opposite view of the Athenians is given in the sentence ὑμεῖς δέ κ.τ.λ.

σύνταξιν, 'system,' ' arrangement.'

τοῦ τε λαμβάνειν, sc. τὰ χρήματα, ' for the receipt of money.'

ὑμεῖς δ', sc. ἡγεῖσθε δεῖν.

οὕτω πως ἄνευ πραγμάτων, ' in some such unlaborious way as the present.' ἄνευ πραγμάτων, 'without working for it.'

δή. Cf. *supr.* 18 *n.*

εἰσφέρειν. Cf. *supr.* 6 *n.*

ἔστι. Mark the accent, ' is possible.'

λέγουσι δὲ καὶ ἄλλους τινὰς ἄλλοι πόρους. Observe the repetition ἄλλους ἄλλοι: ' They speak of other ways and means besides this (καί), one party of these, another party of those.' καί marks that the πόροι spoken of are different from and above and beyond that proposed by Demosthenes.

ἀντιλάβεσθε τῶν πραγμάτων. Cf. *supr.* 14.

21. ἄξιον, sc. ἐστί=operae pretium est, ' it is worth while.'

τὰ πράγματ', explained by the words added at the end of the sentence, τὰ Φιλίππου, 'the position of Philip.' Observe that in Greek these words are made the object of the verbs ἐνθυμηθῆναι καὶ λογίσασθαι, whereas in English they would naturally form the subject of καθέστηκεν, ' how the position of P. now stands.' Cf. iii. 17 τότε τοὺς αἰτίους οἵτινες τούτων ζητήσομεν *n.*

μὴ σκοπῶν ἀκριβῶς, 'without careful examination.' The participle is hypothetical, hence the negative μή.

οὐδ' ὡς ἄν κάλλιστ', sc. ἔχοι. Observe that οὔτε γάρ...ἔχει corresponds to οὔτ' ἂν ἐξήνεγκε. οὐδ' ὡς ἂν κάλλιστα amplifies emphatically οὔτε...εὐτρεπῶς. 'For the present position is neither...easy for him, nay it is not at all as favourable as might be, nor would he ever have launched (ἐξήνεγκε) this war.'

ὡς ἐπιών (sc. ἀναιρεῖταί τις τὰ πράγματα), placed for emphasis at the beginning of the sentence. Cf. *supr.* 7 μέχρι του *n.* 'By his mere approach.'

τότ' with ἤλπιζε, 'then,' i.e. at the time when he started his campaign; 'but he hoped then to carry everything away with him by his mere advance.'

παρὰ γνώμην, 'contrary to his expectation.' *Vide supr.* 16 κατὰ γνώμην.

τὰ τῶν Θετταλῶν, 'the attitude of the Thessalians,' a periphrasis for οἱ Θετταλοί. Cf. *infr.* 25 τὰ τῶν Ὀλυνθίων.

22. ταῦτα γὰρ κ.τ.λ., 'for this (i.e. τὰ τῶν Θετταλῶν) has been (ἦν), I suppose, always and naturally faithless to all men, and, just as it has been, it is also (καί) now to him,' i.e. Philip. μέν...δέ contrast the past behaviour in general of the Thessalians with the present particular instance of it towards Philip. καί marks the parallel between the two. Thessalian faithlessness is dwelt on in *cont. Aristoc.* 112 ὑμεῖς μὲν... οὐδένα προὐδώκατε πώποτε τῶν φίλων, Θετταλοὶ δ' οὐδένα πώποθ' ὄντιν' οὔ.

Παγασάς, *supr.* 13, 9.

αὐτόν. Mark that verbs of 'asking' may be followed both by an accusative of the request made and an accusative of the person of whom it is made. Sonnenschein, *Gk Gr.* § 330.

Μαγνησίαν, *supr.* 13.

δώσοιεν. Future optative representing future indicative of the direct speech. This is the only use of the future optative.

καρποῦσθαι. Epexegetic or explanatory infinitive.

δέοι. The optative, since the sentence is part of the rumour (ἤκουον). The word must be supplied in the next sentence to govern the infinitive λαμβάνειν.

εἰ δὲ τούτων ἀποστερήσεται τῶν χρημάτων, 'but if he is to be deprived of this money.' Observe the middle voice of the future tense used in a passive signification. For the tense cf. *supr.* 12 εἰ δὲ προησόμεθα *n.*

εἰς στενὸν κομιδῇ...καταστήσεται, 'the means of maintenance for his mercenaries will be reduced to very narrow limits.' κομιδῇ (adverb)

with στενόν.   τὰ τῆς τροφῆς, a periphrasis for ἡ τροφή.   Cf. *supr.* 21
τὰ τῶν Θετταλῶν, *infr.* 25 τὰ τῶν Ὀλυνθίων.

23.   τόν γε Παίονα καὶ τὸν Ἰλλυριόν.   The singular number is
used collectively for the peoples.   For the situation of these cf. *supr.*
13 *n.*   Weil prefers to refer the words to the princes of these races.

ἁπλῶς, 'in a word.'

ἄνθρωπος.   Cf. *supr.* 3, 'the fellow,' i.e. Philip.

οὐδὲν ἄπιστον ἴσως, a rhetorical understatement.

τὸ γὰρ εὖ πράττειν...γίγνεται, 'for to be successful beyond one's
deserts is to the unwise the beginning of foolishness.'   Cf. *contra
Aristocratem* 113 where a similar sentiment is expressed at greater
length.   For παρὰ τὴν ἀξίαν cf. ii. 3 ὑπὲρ τὴν ἀξίαν, ii. 8 παρὰ τὴν
αὐτῶν ἀξίαν.

πολλάκις δοκεῖ τὸ φυλάξαι τἀγαθὰ τοῦ κτήσασθαι χαλεπώτερον
εἶναι.   Contrast ii. 26 πολὺ γὰρ ῥᾷον ἔχοντας φυλάττειν ἢ κτήσασθαι
πάντα πέφυκεν.

24.   τὴν ἀκαιρίαν τὴν ἐκείνου καιρὸν ὑμέτερον νομίσαντας, 'concluding his (i.e. Philip's) difficulty to be your opportunity.'

συνάρασθαι τὰ πράγματα, 'to join in taking up the burden of the
trouble.'   The meaning of the infinitive συνάρασθαι is defined by the
three participles which follow (καὶ πρεσβευομένους...καὶ στρατευομένους
...καὶ παροξύνοντας...).

πρεσβευομένους ἐφ' ἃ δεῖ.   In full, πρεσβευομένους ἐπ' ἐκεῖνα (= for
those objects) ἐφ' ἃ δεῖ πρεσβεύεσθαι.

στρατευομένους αὐτούς.   The pronoun looks forward to τοὺς ἄλλους
ἅπαντας, 'serving *yourselves* as well as exhorting all the rest to do so.'
Cf. ii. 12 σκοπεῖσθε μέντοι τοῦτο...ὅπως μὴ λόγους ἐροῦσιν μόνον οἱ παρ'
ἡμῶν πρέσβεις ἀλλὰ καὶ ἔργον τι δεικνύειν ἕξουσιν.

λογιζομένους...πῶς ἂν αὐτὸν οἴεσθ'...ἐλθεῖν;   The participle λογιζομένους is resumed after the long hypothetical sentence in the question,
πῶς οἴεσθε;—a natural anacoluthon; 'considering that, if Philip were to
secure such an opportunity against us and war were to occur in the
neighbourhood of our land—how readily, think you, would Philip come
against you?' ἂν ἐλθεῖν represents ἂν ἔλθοι in oratio recta.   Cf. *contra
Meidiam* 209 ἐνθυμεῖσθε...εἰ γένοιντο...οὗτοι κύριοι...τίνος συγγνώμης
τυχεῖν ἂν οἴεσθε;

πρὸς τῇ χώρᾳ, 'in the neighbourhood of our land,' i.e. Attica.

εἶτ', introducing an indignant question. Cf. et in Latin, e.g. Cic. *pro Milone* 91 et sunt qui de uia Appia querantur, taceant de Curia?

εἰ μηδ' ἃ πάθοιτ' ἄν...οὐ τολμήσετε; After verbs expressing wonder, emotion and the like, the dependent clause is frequently in Greek introduced by εἰ (cf. Sonnenschein, *Gk Gram.* § 368 E). The apodosis to the hypothetical clause, εἰ δύναιτ' ἐκεῖνος, is to be found in the relative clause, ἃ πάθοιτ' ἄν. The construction is broken, and after the intervening clauses, ἃ πάθοιτ' ἄν, εἰ δύναιτ' ἐκεῖνος, the orator abandons the subordinate clause which εἰ μηδέ was to introduce, and finishes with an independent question— ταῦτα ποιῆσαι καιρὸν ἔχοντες οὐ τολμήσετε; 'Then are you not ashamed that even what would be done to you, if he should have the power—will you not dare to do this, when you have an opportunity?' For the anacoluthon cf. iii. 27 οἷς...τὰ μὲν ἄλλα σιωπῶ κ.τ.λ.

25. μηδὲ τοῦθ' ὑμᾶς λανθανέτω. Mark the force of the negative: 'this *also* must not escape your attention.'

ἐὰν μὲν γὰρ ἀντέχῃ τὰ τῶν Ὀλυνθίων. The opposite hypothesis is given below, ἂν δ' ἐκεῖνα Φίλιππος λάβῃ. τὰ τῶν Ὀλυνθίων = the power of the Olynthians. Cf. *supr.* 21 τὰ τῶν Θετταλῶν n.

τὴν ἐκείνου, sc. χώραν. Cf. *supr.* 17 and τὴν ὑπάρχουσαν καὶ οἰκείαν ταύτην below.

τίς αὐτὸν κωλύσει δεῦρο βαδίζειν; 'Who will stop him from marching hither?' (i.e. to Attica). Cf. *supr.* 12 τί τὸ κωλῦον ἔτ' αὐτὸν ἔσται βαδίζειν n. βαδίζειν is the reading of the MSS. Others (from quotation) read here the participle βαδίζοντα.

26. Θηβαῖοι; A supposed answer to the question τίς αὐτὸν κωλύσει δεῦρο βαδίζειν; The rhetorical figure by which an opponent's argument is thus anticipated and countered is known as ὑποφορά or προκατάληψις.

μὴ λίαν πικρὸν εἰπεῖν ᾖ, 'I am afraid it is a very bitter thing to say.' The words refer to the remark which follows, apologizing for its offensiveness, but implying that it is true all the same. The subjunctive with μή is also used in Plato in a hesitating assertion. Cf. Goodwin, *M. and T.* § 265.

καὶ συνεισβαλοῦσιν ἑτοίμως, 'they will actually join readily in an invasion.' Observe the compound with συν and the force of καί, equivalent to *ultro* in Latin. In the 5th cent. B.C. when Xerxes entered Boeotia the Thebans went over to the Persian side and their conduct on that occasion was not readily forgotten. Distrust of Thebes was a marked feature in Athenian political sentiment in the 4th cent. B.C. Cf. iii. 8 ἐχόντων μὲν ὡς ἔχουσι Θηβαίων ἡμῖν, *Phil.* ii. 9 τοὺς δὲ Θηβαίους ἡγεῖθ' (sc. ὁ Φίλιππος), ὅπερ συνέβη, ἀντὶ τῶν ἑαυτοῖς γιγνομένων τὰ λοιπὰ ἐάσειν ὅπως βούλεται πράττειν ἑαυτόν, καὶ οὐχ ὅπως ἀντιπράξειν καὶ διακωλύσειν, ἀλλὰ καὶ συστρατεύσειν, ἂν αὐτοὺς κελεύῃ. Cf. Introd. p. xxxiv.

ἀλλὰ Φωκεῖς; Another suggestion supposed to be made by one of the orator's audience. Since 355 B.C. the Phocians had been engaged in war with Thessaly and Thebes. (*Vide* Introd. p. xx f.) Cf. ii. 7, iii. 27.

οἱ τὴν οἰκείαν...ἄλλος τις. For τὴν οἰκείαν cf. *supr.* 25. In 352 B.C. Philip, supporting the Thessalians and Thebans, defeated the Phocian leader, Onomarchus, near Pagasae in Thessaly. But on advancing southwards to enter Phocis, he found the pass of Thermopylae barred against him by the Athenians, who in alarm at the news of his victory had despatched a body of troops with a fleet in support to the aid of the Phocians. *Vide* Introd. p. xxi.

ἀλλ᾽, ὅταν, οὐχὶ βουλήσεται, sc. ὁ Φίλιππος δεῦρο βαδίζειν. A third supposed objection against Demosthenes' views. Cf. iii. 29 ἀλλ᾽ ὅταν, εἰ ταῦτα φαύλως, τά γ᾽ ἐν αὐτῇ τῇ πόλει νῦν ἄμεινον ἔχει.

τῶν ἀτοπωτάτων. For the genitive cf. ii. 2 τῶν αἰσχρῶν.

27. τὰ διάφορ'...ἤ. διάφορος (and other expressions involving a comparison) may be followed by ἤ. Cf. *contra Androt.* 55 εἰ θέλετε σκέψασθαι τί δοῦλον ἢ ἐλεύθερον εἶναι διαφέρει.

οὐδὲ λόγου προσδεῖν ἡγοῦμαι, 'I do not think even requires the addition of an explanation.' For προσδεῖν cf. *supr.* 19; Aeschines, *contra Timarchum* 78 οὐδὲν γάρ, οἶμαι, δοκεῖ προσδεῖσθαι ὑμῖν λόγου οὐδὲ μαρτυρίας, ὅσα τις σαφῶς οἶδεν αὐτός.

αὐτούς, 'by yourselves' (μόνους), without an army of opponents in the country as well.

ἔξω, 'outside the city,' i.e. in the surrounding country of Attica.

ὅσ' ἀνάγκη στρατοπέδῳ χρωμένους τῶν ἐκ τῆς χώρας λαμβάνειν, 'to take as much of the products of the country as it is necessary to do when in camp.' The verb λαμβάνειν is governed by δεήσειεν. It must be supplied again in the relative clause ὅσ' ἀνάγκη...χρωμένους where it depends upon ἀνάγκη, sc. ἐστί. The preposition in the phrase τῶν (neut.) ἐκ τῆς χώρας is due to the influence of the verb λαμβάνειν. Cf.

Thuc. i. 8 οἱ γὰρ ἐκ τῶν νήσων κακοῦργοι ἀνέστησαν ὑπ' αὐτοῦ, and *supr.*
15 τὸν ἐκεῖθεν πόλεμον *n.*

μηδενὸς ὄντος ἐν αὐτῇ πολεμίου λέγω. λέγω = 'I mean.' The gen.
abs. is conditional; hence negative μή. Cf. *supr.* 21 μὴ σκοπῶν ἀκριβῶς.

τοὺς γεωργοῦντας ὑμῶν, 'those of you who have farms.' Observe
that the (so-called) partitive genitive is not placed between the word
upon which it depends and the article belonging to that word. Cf.
Sonn. *Gk Gram.* § 390. Those who had farms would naturally suffer
much by such a condition of affairs as is here suggested, and still more
by the invasion of any enemy. Hence the farmers were not as a rule in
favour of war. So in the *Peace* of Aristophanes (421 B.C.) they
compose the chorus of the play and are opposed to the continuance of
hostilities with Sparta.

πρὸ τοῦ = 'before this,' i.e. 'up to now.' Observe the survival of
the use of the article as a demonstrative pronoun. The phrase is used
attributively with τὸν χρόνον.

ἥξει, minatory future '*shall* have come.'

ζημιώσεσθαι. The future middle is used, as is often the case with
verbs in -άω, -έω, -όω, in a passive sense. Cf. *supr.* 22 ἀποστερήσεται.

πρόσεσθ', 'there is *besides*' (πρός). Cf. *supr.* 19 προσδεῖ.

οὐδεμιᾶς ἐλάττων ζημία. An instance of litotes. Cf. *supr.* 9
καιρὸς...ὃς οὐδενός ἐστιν ἐλάττων.

τοῖς γε σώφροσιν, 'at least in the opinion of the wise.' An instance
of the so-called dativus judicantis. Cf. Sonn. *Gk Gram.* § 424.

28. δή, introducing the general conclusion. Cf. *supr.* 18 *ad fin.*

ἐκεῖσε, 'yonder,' i.e. to the neighbourhood of Macedonia. Cf
supr. 25 ἐκεῖ...ἢ παρ' ὑμῖν.

τῶν πολλῶν ὧν...ἔχουσι. τῶν πολλῶν is neuter in gender; the
relative ὧν is attracted into the case of its antecedent.

καλῶς ποιοῦντες, 'I am glad to say.' The phrase καλῶς ποιῶν in
the appropriate number, gender and case, is added to a verb to mark
appreciation of the action thereof. Cf. *de Cor.* 231 ὑμεῖς καλῶς ποιοῦντες
τοὺς καρποὺς κεκόμισθε, Aristoph. *Plutus* 863 καλῶς ποιῶν ἀπόλλυται.

τοὺς δ' ἐν ἡλικίᾳ, 'those of an age for military service,' i.e. between
the ages of 20 and 60. Cf. iii. 34 ἔξω τῆς ἡλικίας *n.*

φοβεροὶ φύλακες τῆς οἰκείας ἀκεραίου γένωνται, 'may prove formidable guardians to keep their land free from harm.' For τῆς οἰκείας
cf. *supr.* 25 τὴν ὑπάρχουσαν καὶ τὴν οἰκείαν ταύτην. ἀκεραίου is used

predicatively, i.e. to complete the meaning of the verbal phrase φοβεροὶ φύλακες γένωνται.

αὐτοῖς. Dative of the agent after the perfect passive participle πεπολιτευμένων; so below after πεπραγμένων. In both cases the pronoun refers to τοὺς λέγοντας ('statesmen').

εὔθυναι. The holder of a public office at Athens had at the conclusion of his tenure of it to submit to a formal examination before a board (εὔθυνα) of his conduct therein. Here the word is extended to the account which the citizens generally would demand from those who took part in the debates in the Assembly (τοὺς λέγοντας) for the results of the policies which they had advocated.

ὡς...τοιοῦτοι κριταὶ καὶ τῶν πεπραγμένων αὐτοῖς ἔσεσθε. καί marks the parallel between the circumstances which surround the Athenians, and their judgment of the actions of their statesmen, 'since of whatever kind are the circumstances that surround you, such judges likewise (καί) will you be of what they have done.'

χρηστὰ δ' εἴη παντὸς εἴνεκα, sc. τὰ πράγματα. 'Happy may they be on every account.' For the prayer of good omen concluding the speech cf. iii. *ad fin., n.*

II

1. ἐπὶ πολλῶν, 'on many occasions.' Cf. *contra Meidiam*, 183 ἐπὶ πάντων ὁμοίως, 'on all occasions alike.'

ἄν...ἰδεῖν. The particle belongs to the infinitive which depends on δοκεῖ.

τὴν παρὰ τῶν θεῶν εὔνοιαν. Cf. i. 10, *de Cor.* 253 ἐγὼ τὴν τῆς πόλεως τύχην ἀγαθὴν ἡγοῦμαι, Aesch. *cont. Ctes.* 130 οὐδεμίαν τοι πώποτε ἔγωγε μᾶλλον πόλιν ἑώρακα ὑπὸ μὲν τῶν θεῶν σωζομένην.

φανερὰν γιγνομένην τῇ πόλει. The adjective is used predicatively with the participle and in translation becomes equivalent to an adverb; 'being plainly bestowed upon the city.'

οὐχ ἥκιστα δ', 'and not least,' i.e. 'and especially,' 'and most of all.' Cf. i. 27 οὐδεμιᾶς ἐλάττων ζημία.

τὸ γάρ...ἀνάστασιν forms the subject of the verb ἔοικεν. 'For the fact that,' etc.

τοὺς πολεμήσοντας Φιλίππῳ, 'those who are going to make war upon Philip,' i.e. the Olynthians. This phrase forms the subject of γεγενῆσθαι ('have arisen') and also (after ὥστε) of νομίζειν.

καὶ χώραν ὅμορον καὶ δύναμίν τινα κεκτημένους. The conjunctions belong to the substantives. For χώραν ὅμορον cf. i. 5. For the use of τινά cf. Thuc. viii. 3, στρατῷ τινι, 'with a considerable army.' According to Dem. *de Fals. Leg.* 230 the Olynthians had more than 10,000 hoplites and nearly 1000 horse.

καὶ τὸ μέγιστον ἀπάντων...ἔχοντας. καί couples ἔχοντας to κεκτημένους. τὸ μέγιστον ἀπάντων is in apposition with the whole clause τὴν ὑπὲρ τοῦ πολέμου γνώμην...ἀνάστασιν. Cf. iii. 31, τὸ πάντων ἀνδρειότατον.

τοιαύτην. Observe that the adjective is really part of the predicate; 'holding their opinion concerning the war such as to' (ὥστε), i.e. 'holding such *an* opinion concerning the war as to.' Cf. i. 7 βεβαίαν *n.* For the use of ὑπέρ, cf. i. 7, 16.

εἶτα. This conjunction (and ἔπειτα) respond alone, without δέ, to πρῶτον μέν. Cf. *de Cor. ad init.* πρῶτον μὲν...εὔχομαι...ὅσην εὔνοιαν ἔχων ἐγὼ διατελῶ...τοσαύτην ὑπάρξαι μοι...ἔπειθ' ὅπερ ἐστὶ μάλισθ' ὑπὲρ ὑμῶν...τοῦτο παραστῆσαι τοὺς θεοὺς ὑμῖν κ.τ.λ.

ἀνάστασιν. Cf. i. 5 *n.* The sentiment of the two passages is similar.

δαιμονίᾳ τινὶ καὶ θείᾳ παντάπασιν ἔοικεν εὐεργεσίᾳ = 'resembles in every way a blessing from heaven, as it were, and the gods.' τις appended to an adjective widens that adjective's sphere of application. Cf. Aesch. *Prom. Vinct.* 696 φόβου πλέα τις εἶ = ' thou art full, as 'twere, of fear.'

2. αὐτούς. Emphatic, 'for ourselves.'

ὅπως μή...δόξομεν. Verbs denoting effort, attention, and the like (here σκοπεῖν) are followed by ὅπως with future indicative. Cf. Sonn. *Gk Gr.* § 369 a.

τῶν ὑπαρχόντων. Gen. of comparison. 'We must then see to it now for ourselves that we shall not be thought to treat ourselves more hardly (χείρους περὶ ἡμᾶς αὐτοὺς εἶναι) than circumstances do.'

τῶν αἰσχρῶν, μᾶλλον δὲ τῶν αἰσχίστων. For the genitive cf. i. 26 τῶν ἀτοπωτάτων. For μᾶλλον δέ in a corrective sense cf. i. 19 μᾶλλον δ' ἅπαντος ἐνδεῖ τοῦ πόρου.

πόλεων καὶ τόπων ὧν ἦμέν ποτε κύριοι. The antecedents πόλεων

καὶ τόπων are attracted into the case of the relative pronoun ὧν.   Cf.
Plato, *Meno* 96 A, ἔχεις οὖν εἰπεῖν ἄλλου ὁτουοῦν πράγματος, οὗ οἱ μὲν
φάσκοντες διδάσκαλοι εἶναι οὐχ ὅπως ἄλλων διδάσκαλοι ὁμολογοῦνται, ἀλλ'
οὐδὲ αὐτοὶ ἐπίστασθαι, Verg. *Aen.* i. 573 urbem quam statuo uestra
est.   For the places lost by the Athenians *vide* i. 8 *ad fin.*; 9 *ad init.*;
12 *ad fin.*

τῶν...συμμάχων καὶ καιρῶν.   In the genitive to correspond with
the balancing words (πόλεων καὶ τόπων) in the parallel clause.

3. τὸ μὲν οὖν κ.τ.λ.   οὖν marks the transition.   Cf. i. 2; *infr.* 5.
μὲν οὖν are repeated below (4 *ad init.* ταῦτα μὲν οὖν παραλείψω), the
intervening sentences being explanatory of οὐχὶ καλῶς ἔχειν ἡγοῦμαι.
The antithetic clause (introduced by δέ > < μέν) is ἃ δὲ καὶ χωρὶς
τούτων...ταῦτ' εἰπεῖν πειράσομαι.

ὑπὲρ τούτων, 'on this subject,' i.e. the power of Philip and the
necessity of the Athenians doing what they ought to do.   For ὑπέρ
cf. *supr.* 1 τὴν ὑπὲρ τοῦ πολέμου γνώμην τοιαύτην ἔχοντας.

ἐκείνῳ μὲν ἔχειν φιλοτιμίαν, 'to involve distinction for him' (i.e.
Philip, as ἐκεῖνον *supr.* 1).   For the sense of φιλοτιμία cf. *de Fals. Leg.*
223 ἀπεστέρημαι καὶ τῶν ἰδίων φιλοτιμιῶν.

οὐχὶ καλῶς.   A litotes (cf. above where οὐχὶ καλῶς ἔχειν = to be
wrong).   *Vide* i. 27 and *supr.* 1 οὐχ ἥκιστα.   That the phrase is here
equivalent to αἰσχρῶς is shown by πλεῖον' αἰσχύνην ὠφλήκατε below.

ὅσῳ...τοσούτῳ = Latin quanto...tanto; English the...the.

ὑπὲρ τὴν ἀξίαν...τὴν αὐτοῦ, 'over and above his deserts.'   Cf. i. 23
παρὰ τὴν ἀξίαν.

παρὰ πᾶσι = apud omnes, 'in the opinion of all.'

ὑμεῖς δ' ὅσῳ...ὠφλήκατε, 'but the more disastrous *your* (note
ὁ μέν > < ὑμεῖς δέ) fortunes have been than they should have been, the
more disgrace have you incurred.'

4. ἐνθένδ', 'from here,' i.e. the Assembly at Athens.   Cf. *infr.*
τοῖς ὑπὲρ αὐτοῦ πεπολιτευμένοις.

ὧν.   In gender neuter, the antecedent being ταῦτα, supplied as the
object of λέγειν; the case is dependent upon χάριν and δίκην.

τοῖς ὑπὲρ αὐτοῦ πεπολιτευμένοις, 'to those whose public acts
have been directed to serve him' (*viz.* Philip).   The allusion is to the
party at Athens favourable to Macedon and staunchly opposed by

Demosthenes. Among the leaders of this party were Philocrates and, subsequently, Aeschines.

ὑμῖν δὲ δίκην προσήκει λαβεῖν, sc. παρὰ τῶν ὑπὲρ αὐτοῦ πεπολιτευμένων. 'Those matters therefore for which *he* (ἐκεῖνος μέν) owes thanks to those whose public acts have been directed to serve him, while *you* (ὑμῖν δέ) should exact punishment for them, I do not now see the occasion to relate.'

ἃ δὲ καὶ χωρὶς τούτων ἔνι, sc. λέγειν. The relative pronoun is in the accusative case governed by λέγειν (understood) and ἀκηκοέναι.

ἀκηκοέναι. A full perfect, 'to have heard,' 'to have been told of.'

καὶ μεγάλ'...φαίνοιτ' ἂν ὄνειδη. The subject of φαίνοιτο is ἃ, the relative in the nominative case being supplied from the preceding relative in the accusative case. When two or more relative clauses refer to the same antecedent (here ταῦτ') and the second relative differs in case from the first, it is in Greek either omitted (as here), or replaced, in the appropriate case, by a personal pronoun. Cf. iii. 24 οἷς οὐκ ἐχαρίζονθ' οἱ λέγοντες οὐδ' ἐφίλουν αὐτούς, Sonn. *Gk Gram.* §§ 563, 5.

βουλομένοις ὀρθῶς δοκιμάζειν. 'To men wishing rightly to appraise them' (sc. Philip's misdeeds as recounted by Demosthenes). For the use of the participle without the article cf. iii. 35 οὐκ ἔστιν ὅπου μηδὲν ἐγὼ ποιοῦσιν τὰ τῶν ποιούντων εἶπον ὡς δεῖ νέμειν.

5. τὸ μὲν οὖν...δεικνύναι. Cf. *supr.* 3.

δικαίως. Observe the emphatic position of this word.

ὅπερ καὶ ἀληθὲς ὑπάρχει = 'as is true too in fact.' The antecedent to ὅπερ is the clause τοῦ ἐκείνον φλαῦρον φαίνεσθαι. καὶ marks the parallel between the revelation of Philip's character and the real state of the case.

τοὺς ὑπερεκπεπληγμένους...τὸν Φίλιππον, 'those aghast with dismay at Philip as invincible.' ὑπερεκπεπληγμένους —a strong expression—is followed, although passive in voice, by an object in the accusative, owing to its analogy to a verb of fearing. Cf. Thuc. iii. 82, 5 τοὺς ἐναντίους ἐκπεπληγμένος, and iii. 7 ἐθάρρει τούτους n.

οἷς πρότερον παρακρουόμενος μέγας ηὐξήθη, 'whereby previously he fraudulently rose to greatness.' The antecedent to οἷς is πάντα = 'every means.' παρακρουόμενος = cheating, here equivalent in force to an adverb. The sense of the word is said to be derived from the practice of fraudulent tradesmen, who in selling to their customers knocked off (παρακρούεσθαι) the top of the contents of a measure. Cf. the verb κρουσιμετρεῖν and L. & S. s. v.   Notice that the adjective μέγας is used predicatively with ηὐξήθη.

πρὸς αὐτὴν ἥκει τὴν τελευτὴν τὰ πράγματ' αὐτοῦ. Observe the emphatic position of αὐτήν, 'his activities have reached their uttermost limit.'

6. σφόδρ', with φοβερὸν...καὶ θαυμαστόν.
νῦν δέ = 'but as it is.' Cf. i. 9.

6-7. εὑρίσκω κ.τ.λ. The object of εὑρίσκω is (ἐκεῖνον) προσαγαγόμενον. προσαγαγόμενον itself is followed by three objects: (a) τὴν μὲν ἡμετέραν εὐήθειαν, (b) τὴν δ' Ὀλυνθίων φιλίαν, (c) Θετταλοὺς δέ; is modified in point of time by (a) τὸ κατ' ἀρχάς, ὅτ' Ὀλυνθίους...διαλεχθῆναι, (b) μετὰ ταῦτα, (c) νῦν τὰ τελευταῖα; and has added to it the means by which it worked in three phrases, (a) τῷ τὴν Ἀμφίπολιν... κατασκευάσαι, (b) τῷ Ποτείδαιαν...ἐκείνοις, (c) τῷ Μαγνησίαν...ἀναδέξασθαι.

6. εὐήθειαν, 'simplicity,' 'stupidity.' Cf. i. 15 εὐήθης. Literally the word = 'good nature.'

τὸ κατ' ἀρχάς, 'in the first place.' Cf. i. 12.

6-7. ὅτ' Ὀλυνθίους ἀπήλαυνόν τινες κ.τ.λ. In 357 B.C. Philip established himself in possession of Amphipolis. This event alarmed the Olynthians, who made overtures to Athens for an alliance against Philip. Such a combination however was prevented by Philip through his supporters at Athens (τινές, cf. *supr.* 4 τοῖς ὑπὲρ αὐτοῦ πεπολιτευμένοις). These maintained that he would hand over Amphipolis to the Athenians, and a secret arrangement (τὸ θρυλούμενόν ποτ' ἀπόρρητον ἐκεῖνο) was concluded that in return for Amphipolis Athens should abandon to him the town of Pydna (i. 5) on the Thermaic Gulf. Rejected by the Athenians the Olynthians made terms with Philip, who, while keeping Amphipolis and seizing Pydna for himself, secured the estrangement of the Olynthians from Athens by capturing and placing in their possession the Athenian colony of Poteidaea (i. 9). Introd. p. xviii.

6. ἐνθένδε. Cf. *supr.* 4.

βουλομένους...διαλεχθῆναι, 'desirous of conversations' (in the diplomatic sense). Cf. *de Cor.* 28 ἀλλὰ τί ἐχρῆν με ποιεῖν; μὴ προσάγειν γράψαι τοὺς ἐπὶ τοῦθ' ἥκοντας, ἵν' ὑμῖν διαλεχθῶσιν;

τὴν Ἀμφίπολιν. Cf. i. 5.

φάσκειν is frequently used, like the Latin verb *dictitare*, of saying *what is not true*, professing, pretending.

τὸ θρυλούμενόν ποτ' ἀπόρρητον ἐκεῖνο, 'that great secret once on everybody's lips.' Notice the oxymoron in θρυλούμενον ἀπόρρητον. For θρυλεῖν cf. i. 7 δ πάντες ἐθρυλεῖτε.

προσαγαγόμενον, 'drew over to his side,' and so, 'availed himself of,' 'profited by.' Cf. *infr.* 7 προσλαμβάνων.

7. τοὺς μὲν πρότερον συμμάχους, the people of Poteidaea.

ἐκείνοις, sc. τοῖς Ὀλυνθίοις.

Θετταλούς, i. 12.

Μαγνησίαν, i. 13.

τὸν Φωκικὸν πόλεμον. The struggle against Phocis, sometimes called The Sacred War, in which Thessaly, in conjunction with Thebes, had been engaged since 356 B.C. Cf. i. 26 *n.*; iii. 27; Introd. p. xx.

ὅλως = 'altogether,' 'in a word,' summarizing the behaviour of Philip. Cf. i. 5 καὶ ὅλως ἄπιστον οἶμαι ταῖς πολιτείαις ἡ τυραννίς, *infr.* 14, iii. 35.

τὴν γὰρ ἑκάστων ἄνοιαν...οὕτως ηὐξήθη, 'for through deceiving and profiting by the foolishness of each people, one after another (ἀεί), that did not know him, in this way he has grown great.'

ἑκάστων. Observe the plural number. ἕκαστος = each individual > < ἕκαστοι = each *group of* individuals.

ἀεί = 'from time to time,' i.e. according as the ignorance of one people after another offered Philip his chance. Cf. i. 14 τὸ προΐεσθαι καθ' ἕκαστον ἀεί τι τῶν πραγμάτων ὡς ἀλυσιτελές.

προσλαμβάνων. Cf. Plato, *Phaedrus* 272 A προσλαβόντι καιροὺς τοῦ πότε λεκτέον καὶ ἐπισχετέον, Aeschines, *contra Ctesiphontem* 126 προσλαβὼν τὴν τοῦ γράψαντος ἀπειρίαν.

8. ἤρθη μέγας. Cf. *supr.* 5 οἷς πρότερον παρακρουόμενος μέγας ηὐξήθη *n.*

καὶ καθαιρεθῆναι = 'likewise to be pulled down.' καί marks the correspondence between καθαιρεθῆναι and ἤρθη.

καιροῦ. The gen. case depends upon τοῦτο. Cf. Sonn. *Gk Gram.* § 391.

μὲν δή. This combination of particles is employed to introduce a conclusion which has been reached before passing to a new point.

πρὸς τοῦτο πάρεστι. Observe the accusative case with πρός, due to the suggestion in πάρεστι, itself a verb denoting rest, of the *progression* of affairs to their present *position*. Cf. i. 8 παρῆσαν ἐπὶ τουτὶ τὸ βῆμα *n*.

παρελθών. παριέναι (aor. παρελθεῖν) is the regular word for coming forward to address the assembly. Cf. iii. 28 ἢ φρασάτω τις ἐμοὶ παρελθών κ.τ.λ.

μᾶλλον δ' ὑμῖν = 'or rather to you.' For the corrective use of μᾶλλον δέ cf. *infr.* 22; i. 19.

ὡς οὐκ ἀληθῆ ταῦτ' ἐγὼ λέγω. ἀληθῆ is used predicatively, and is emphasized by its position.

ὡς οἱ τὰ πρῶτ' ἐξηπατημένοι τὰ λοιπὰ πιστεύσουσιν, 'that those who have been deceived at first will believe thereafter.' So our proverbial philosophy assures us, 'once bitten, twice shy' and 'a burnt child dreads the fire.' τὰ πρῶτα and τὰ λοιπά are correlative; both are adverbial accusatives.

παρὰ τὴν αὐτῶν ἀξίαν, 'contrary to their own deserts,' 'undeservedly.' Cf. i. 23.

ἄσμενοι. Emphatic by its position, 'with all their hearts.'

9. καὶ μήν, used regularly to introduce a further development in the argument.

βίᾳ καθέξειν...τὰ πράγματα, 'will maintain his position by *force*.'

τὰ χωρία = 'the positions of importance,' e.g. Amphipolis and Pagasae.

ἰσχύσῃ. For the tense cf. i. 13 ἠσθένησεν *n*.

ἀνεχαίτισε. Gnomic aorist, used in a statement applicable in all nstances, past, present and future. Cf. διέλυσεν and i. 11 συναγήλωσε, i. 15 ἀπέστησαν. The word is used here metaphorically, being applied literally to the throwing by a horse of its rider.

10. ἀλλὰ τὰ τοιαῦτ' κ.τ.λ. 'But such things persist, indeed, once in a way and for a brief period, and, it may be, blossom fair with hope, yet in time they are found out and drop and fall of themselves.' The metaphor is from an unhealthy plant which flourishes for a time, perhaps blossoms, yet soon the blossom fades and falls.

ἀντέχει. Cf. i. 25 ἐὰν μὲν γὰρ ἀντέχῃ τὰ τῶν Ὀλυνθίων.

καὶ σφόδρα γ' ἤνθησεν. For καί...γε cf. iii. 34 καὶ παραχρῆμά γε τὴν αὐτὴν σύνταξιν ἀπάντων n.

ἤνθησεν. Gnomic aorist. Cf. *supr.* 9 ἀνεχαίτισε n.

ἂν τύχῃ, sc. ἀνθήσαντα. Cf. i. 3 ἡνίκ' ἂν τύχῃ.

περὶ αὐτὰ καταρρεῖ. The metaphor is drawn from the falling flower. περὶ αὐτά implies that the collapse is due to internal unsoundness and not to external force. Cf. Thuc. vi. 18 νομίσατε...τὴν πόλιν, ἂν μὲν ἡσυχάζῃ, τρίψεσθαί τε αὐτὴν περὶ αὐτήν, ὥσπερ καὶ ἄλλο τι κ.τ.λ.

ὥσπερ γὰρ κ.τ.λ. Cf. for the lofty moral tone of the whole passage, *Phil.* iii. 16 τὸ δ' εὐσεβὲς καὶ τὸ δίκαιον, ἄν τ' ἐπὶ μικροῦ τις ἄν τ' ἐπὶ μείζονος παραβαίνῃ, τὴν αὐτὴν ἔχει δύναμιν.

οὕτω καὶ τῶν πράξεων...προσήκει, 'so likewise the beginnings and foundations of action must be genuine and honest.' καί marks the application of the principle in the moral (πράξεων) *as well as* in the material sphere (οἰκίας καί...πλοίου καὶ τῶν ἄλλων τῶν τοιούτων).

11. Φημὶ δὴ δεῖν...βοηθεῖν. Cf. i. 17 φημὶ δὴ διχῇ βοηθητέον εἶναι.

καὶ ὅπως...ἀρέσκει μοι, 'and the best and speediest way which is proposed has my approval.'

πρὸς δὲ Θετταλοὺς πρεσβείαν πέμπειν. The Thessalians, according to Demosthenes, were disaffected towards Philip. Cf. *supr.* 8; i. 22.

ταῦτα, i.e. the assistance we are sending to Olynthus; according to others it = the weakness of Philip's position, upon which Demosthenes has been dwelling.

παροξυνεῖ. Cf. i. 24 παροξύνοντας τοὺς ἄλλους ἅπαντας.

καὶ γὰρ νῦν εἰσιν ἐψηφισμένοι Παγασὰς ἀπαιτεῖν καὶ περὶ Μαγνησίας λόγους ποιεῖσθαι. Cf. i. 22. περὶ Μαγνησίας λόγους ποιεῖσθαι = 'to raise the question of Magnesia.'

12. ἀλλὰ καὶ ἔργον τι δεικνύειν ἕξουσιν, 'but shall also have some deed to point to.' δεικνύειν epexegetic infinitive. Cf. i. 3 χρῆσθαι, i. 22 καρποῦσθαι.

ἐξεληλυθότων...πράγμασιν, 'owing to your having taken the field in a manner worthy of the city and a hand in the course of events.' For ἐξεληλυθότων cf. i. 6 ἐξιόντας; with ὄντων ἐπὶ τοῖς πράγμασιν may be compared i. 2 πάρεσται τοῖς πράγμασιν.

ὅσῳ γὰρ κ.τ.λ. 'For in so far as we are thought to use it (αὐτῷ = τῷ λόγῳ) most readily, the more do all mistrust it.' Cf. *supr.* 3 ὅσῳ χεῖρον

ἢ προσῆκε κέχρησθε τοῖς πράγμασιν, τοσούτῳ πλεῖον' αἰσχύνην ὠφλήκατε.
Observe that we have a superlative in one clause (ἑτοιμότατα) and
a comparative (μᾶλλον) in the other. Cf. *in Polyclem* 15 ὅσῳ γὰρ
ἄμεινον ἐπληρωσάμην τὴν ναῦν, τοσούτῳ μοι πλείστη ἀπόλειψις ἐγένετο.
The fondness of the Athenians for fair-seeming speeches and high-
sounding propɔsals, and their failure to follow these up with efficient
action, are a commonplace in Demosthenes. The character of the
nation had changed since the days when the Corinthians declared that
the Athenians were 'swift to devise, and to carry out in deed whatever
they decided' (Thuc. i. 70).

13. πολλὴν δὴ τὴν μετάστασιν καὶ μεγάλην δεικτέον τὴν μεταβολήν, 'you must then show a great change and a vast alteration.'
Both adjectives are used predicatively. Cf. *supr.* 1 τὴν ὑπὲρ τοῦ πολέμου
γνώμην τοιαύτην ἔχοντας *n.*

εἰσφέροντας, ἐξιόντας, ἅπαντα ποιοῦντας ἑτοίμως. Supply ὑμᾶς
with which the participles agree. For the accusative of the agent after
the neuter verbal adjective used impersonally, cf. Xen. *Mem.* iii. 11. 1
ἰτέον ἂν εἴη θεασομένους (sc. ἡμᾶς), Plat. *Crit.* 49 A οὐδενὶ τρόπῳ φαμὲν
ἑκόντας ἀδικητέον εἶναι, Sonn. *Gk Gram.* § 542. With this passage
compare i. 6 χρήματ' εἰσφέροντας προθύμως καὶ αὐτοὺς ἐξιόντας καὶ μηδὲν
ἐλλείποντας.

εἴπερ τις ὑμῖν προσέξει τὸν νοῦν, 'if, that is to say, any one is
to pay attention to you.' For the emphatic εἴπερ, cf. i. 2 εἴπερ ὑπὲρ
σωτηρίας αὐτῶν φροντίζετε.

ἐθελήσηθ'. Cf. i. 6 ἐθελῆσαι *n.*

ἀσθενῶς καὶ ἀπίστως ἔχοντα φανήσεται Φιλίππῳ. For φαίνεσθαι
with participle cf. i. 15 φανῶμεν ἐρρᾳθυμηκότες *n.* The dative Φιλίππῳ
is to be taken with ἀσθενῶς καὶ ἀπίστως ἔχοντα. Cf. *supr.* 8 καιροῦ μὲν
δή,...πρὸς τοῦτο πάρεστι Φιλίππῳ τὰ πράγματα.

τὰ τῆς οἰκείας ἀρχῆς καὶ δυνάμεως. Cf. i. 21 τὰ τῶν Θετταλῶν.

14. ὅλως μὲν γάρ. For ὅλως cf. *supr.* 7 ὅλως δ' οὐδείς ἐστιν, i. 5
καὶ ὅλως ἄπιστον, οἶμαι, ταῖς πολιτείαις ἡ τυραννίς. μέν which has here no
answering conjunction (μέν solitarium) simply emphasizes ὅλως. Cf.
iii. 8 ἐγὼ μὲν οὐχ ὁρῶ.

ἐν μὲν προσθήκῃ μερίς ἐστίν τις οὐ μικρά, 'as an accessory is a not
unimportant factor.' Others read ἐν μὲν προσθήκης μέρει (cf. *infr.* 18
ἐν οὐδενὸς μέρει, iii. 31 ἐν ὑπηρέτου καὶ προσθήκης μέρει). προσθήκη has

a contemptuous note. Cf. *additamentum* in Cic. *pro Sestio* 31, 68 intercessit Ligus iste nescio qui, additamentum inimicorum meorum.

ἐπὶ Τιμοθέου. Timotheus was the son of Conon, the Athenian admiral, and himself a distinguished naval commander. Assisted by Perdiccas III of Macedon he captured Torone and Poteidaea in 364 B.C. A eulogy of him is to be found in Isocrates xv. 107–113.

πρὸς Ποτείδαιαν Ὀλυνθίοις, sc. *ὑπῆρξεν.* The combination of Philip with the Olynthians and his handing over to them of the captured Athenian dependency Poteidaea took place in 356 B.C. Cf. i. 9; *supr.* 6–7 ὅτ᾽ Ὀλυνθίους ἀπήλαυνόν τινες κ.τ.λ.

ἐφάνη τι. For the force of τι cf. the use of τις *supr.* 1 χώραν ὅμορον καὶ δύναμίν τινα κεκτημένους *n.*

συναμφότερον, 'in conjunction with another power.'

νυνὶ δὲ Θετταλοῖς στασιάζουσι. This is the reading of the Paris MS. S. Most MSS. insert after Θετταλοῖς the words νοσοῦσι καί. νοσεῖν is a *vox propria* of the political troubles of states. Cf. *Phil.* iii. 9 ὑφ᾽ ὧν ἀπόλωλε καὶ νενόσηκεν ἡ Ἑλλάς, *ibidem* 12 πυνθάνεσθαι γὰρ αὐτοὺς ὡς νοσοῦσι καὶ στασιάζουσιν.

ἐπὶ τὴν τυραννικὴν οἰκίαν ἐβοήθησεν. The royal house is that of the tyrants of Pherae (Lycophron and Peitholaus) whom Philip expelled in 352 B.C. (*νυνί*) and so secured a footing for himself in Thessaly.

πάντ᾽ ὠφελεῖ, 'it is of the utmost benefit.'

15. ἐπισφαλεστέραν, 'more unstable,' 'more insecure.'

δόξης ἐπιθυμεῖ. Verbs signifying desire (with the exception of ποθεῖν) are followed by the gen. case.

τοῦτ᾽ ἐζήλωκε, 'has made this his ambition.'

προῄρηται, 'has deliberately elected.' προαιρεῖσθαι (cf. προαίρεσις) is regularly applied to the conscious selection of one out of two or more possibilities of choice.

ἃ μηδεὶς πώποτ᾽ ἄλλος Μακεδόνων βασιλεὺς sc. διεπράξατο. The clause is a *generic* relative one; hence the negative μηδείς, not οὐδείς.

16. τῆς μὲν φιλοτιμίας τῆς ἀπὸ τούτων. φιλοτιμία = 'glory,' 'distinction.' Cf. *supr.* 3 ἐκείνῳ μὲν ἔχειν φιλοτιμίαν.

ταῖς ἄνω κάτω. Observe the asyndeton and homoioteleuton, suggestive of the ceaseless succession of campaigns. Cf. Aristoph. *Birds*, 3 τί, ὦ πονήρ᾽, ἄνω κάτω πλανύττομεν;

οὕτως ὅπως ἂν δύνωνται, 'in such ever way as they can.'

κεκλειμένων τῶν ἐμπορίων...διὰ τὸν πόλεμον.   Athens was still in command of the sea, and the inability of the Macedonians to protect their maritime commerce led to the closing of their harbours, and the cessation of the export even of such articles as their constant military expeditions still permitted them to produce.

17. Φιλίππῳ. Cf. *supr.* 13 ἀσθενῶς καὶ ἀπίστως ἔχοντα φανήσεται Φιλίππῳ.

ἐκ τούτων (neut.) = 'from these considerations.'

οἱ δὲ δὴ...θαυμαστοί.   δή adds an ironical note to the sentence. 'Of course the mercenaries and footguards attendant upon his person are *reputed* (note the force of μέν) to be wonderful men.'

συγκεκροτημένοι τὰ τοῦ πολέμου = lit. 'welded together in matters of war,' i.e. 'a compact, well-drilled, fighting force.' The word is used (*contra Meidiam* 17) of 'knocking into shape' a chorus, Τηλεφάνης ὁ αὐλητὴς...αὐτὸς συγκροτεῖν καὶ διδάσκειν ᾤετο δεῖν τὸν χορόν.

οὐδένων...βελτίους = 'better than none,' a litotes for 'as inefficient as any troops.'

18. ἔμπειρος πολέμου καὶ ἀγώνων.   Adjectives denoting the presence or absence of knowledge, skill and the like, are followed by the gen. case.

φιλοτιμίᾳ, 'through ambition.' Cf. φιλοτιμίαν below.

αὐτόν (sc. τὸν Φίλιππον), subj. of ἀπωθεῖν.

ἔφη, sc. Demosthenes' anonymous informant, whose account is continued in the oratio obliqua which follows.

πρὸς γὰρ αὖ τοῖς ἄλλοις...εἶναι.   Supply αὐτόν (i.e. τὸν Φίλιππον) as subject of εἶναι ἀνυπέρβλητον. τὴν φιλοτιμίαν is an accusative of respect. 'For he declared that, moreover, in addition to the rest, in ambition also (καί) he (i.e. Philip) was not to be surpassed.'

εἰ δέ τις σώφρων ἢ δίκαιος ἄλλως, sc. ἐστί. 'If there was a modest man or again an upright one.' The adverb ἄλλως marks the adjective δίκαιος as an alternative additional to σώφρων.

τὴν καθ' ἡμέραν ἀκρασίαν τοῦ βίου καὶ μέθην καὶ κορδακισμούς. ἀκρασίαν τοῦ βίου are to be taken closely together. The phrase καθ' ἡμέραν applies not only to ἀκρασίαν τοῦ βίου but to μέθην and κορδακισμούς also. The word κορδακισμός is applied to an extravagant dance of a vulgar character.   It is a mark of the 'reckless' man that he performs such a dance when sober ; Theophrastus, *Char.* vi. ἀμέλει δυνατὸς (sc. ὁ ἀπονενοημένος) καὶ ὀρχεῖσθαι νήφων τὸν κόρδακα καὶ προσωπεῖον μὴ ἔχων ἐν κωμικῷ χορῷ. Cf. Cic. *pro Murena*, vi. 13 nemo fere saltat sobrius, nisi forte insanit, neque in solitudine neque in conuiuio moderato atque honesto.

οὐ δυνάμενος. If we retain the nominative case of the participle, we must regard it as forming part of the protasis, the apodosis beginning at παρεῶσθαι. The negative οὐ (instead of μή) is to be explained by its close association with δυνάμενος, the two together being equivalent to ἀδυνατῶν = being *un*able.

ἐν οὐδενὸς...μέρει, 'of no account,' lit. 'in the portion of nothing.' Cf. iii. 31 ἐν ὑπηρέτου καὶ προσθήκης μέρει.

19. δή, 'therefore,' 'accordingly.' Cf. i. 18.

οἵους μεθυσθέντας ὀρχεῖσθαι. For οἷος followed by the infinitive cf. Goodwin, *M. and T.* § 759. Observe the tense of μεθυσθέντας which goes closely with the infinitive; 'men of a kind to get drunk and dance.' Dancing among the Greeks and Romans was closely associated with drunkenness. Cf. Aristoph. *Wasps*, 1476-8 ὁ γὰρ γέρων ὡς ἔπιε διὰ πολλοῦ χρόνου | ἤκουσέ τ' αὐλοῦ, περιχαρὴς τῷ πράγματι | ὀρχούμενος τῆς νυκτὸς οὐδὲν παύεται. Alexis, 222, says ἅπαντες ὀρχοῦντ' εὐθὺς ἂν οἴνου μόνον | ὀσμὴν ἴδωσιν. In Theophrastus (*Char.* xiii.) the unseasonable man's way is ὀρχησάμενος ἅψασθαι ἑτέρου μηδέπω μεθύοντος. Cf. also Athenaeus xiv. 629 and Horace, *Satires* ii. 1. 24-5 saltat Milonius, ut semel icto | accessit feruor capiti numerusque lucernis.

τοιαῦθ' κ.τ.λ. Particular kinds of the κορδακισμός mentioned above. Lucian, περὶ ὀρχήσεως, suggests the unseemly character of such mimetic dances.

ἐνθένδε, 'from here,' i.e. Athens. Cf. i. 2.

θαυματοποιῶν, 'jugglers.' Cf. Plato, *Soph.* 235 B.

ἐκεῖνον, 'the notorious.'

τὸν δημόσιον, sc. δοῦλον, 'the public slave.' That such persons, though sometimes wealthy, were held in low repute is shown by Aeschines, *contra Timarchum* 54. Of Kallias nothing further is known.

ὧν, attracted into the case of its antecedent ἀσμάτων. Cf. i. 28 ὧν καλῶς ποιοῦντες ἔχουσι, Aeschines, *contra Timarchum* 136 περὶ δὲ τῶν ποιημάτων ὧν φασιν οὗτοί με πεποιηκέναι.

20. τῆς ἐκείνου γνώμης καὶ κακοδαιμονίας, 'of his disposition and delusion.' For κακοδαιμονία cf. Aristoph. *Pl.* 501 μανίαν κακοδαιμονίαν τε.

τοῖς εὖ φρονοῦσιν, 'to men of understanding.' Cf. i. 27 τοῖς γε σώφροσιν *n*.

αἱ γὰρ εὐπραξίαι δειναὶ συγκρύψαι τὰ τοιαῦτ' ὀνείδη, 'for successes are apt to cover up scandals like these.' For the epexegetic infinitive συγκρύψαι cf. i. 3, δεινὸς...πράγμασι χρῆσθαι.

εἰ δέ τι πταίσει. Monitory future. With πταίειν cf. *supr.* 9 ἡ πρώτη πρόφασις καὶ μικρὸν πταῖσμ' ἅπαντ' ἀνεχαίτισε καὶ διέλυσεν.

αὐτοῦ ταῦτ', 'these things belonging to him,' i.e. 'these defects in his condition.'

δείξειν οὐκ εἰς μακράν, 'matters will be made clear before long,' 'we shall not have long to wait to see.' For δείξει used impersonally in this sense, cf. Aristoph. *Frogs* 1261 δείξει δὴ τάχα.

21. ὥσπερ γὰρ ἐν τοῖς σώμασιν κ.τ.λ. Cf. *de Cor.* 198 ὥσπερ τὰ ῥήγματα καὶ τὰ σπάσματα, ὅταν τι κακὸν τὸ σῶμα λάβῃ, τότε κινεῖται, Plato, *Rep.* 556 E ὥσπερ σῶμα νοσῶδες μικρᾶς ῥοπῆς ἔξωθεν δεῖται προσλαβέσθαι πρὸς τὸ κάμνειν.

κἂν ῥῆγμα κἂν στρέμμα κἂν ἄλλο τι τῶν ὑπαρχόντων σαθρὸν ᾖ, 'whether it be a rupture or a sprain or some other weakness in the system.'

ἐπειδὰν δ' ὅμορος πόλεμος συμπλακῇ, 'but when war grapples with them on their own frontiers.' ὅμορος is emphatic. The word συμπλέκεσθαι is often used of wrestlers coming to grips. After συμπλακῇ must be supplied ταῖς πόλεσι καὶ τοῖς τυράννοις.

ἐποίησεν, a gnomic aorist. Cf. *supr.* 9 ἀνεχαίτισε.

22. φοβερὸν προσπολεμῆσαι. The infinitive is epexegetic of the adjective; 'formidable to engage in war with,' 'a redoubtable opponent.'

σώφρονος μὲν ἀνθρώπου λογισμῷ χρῆται. The antithetic sentence is introduced by οὐ μὴν ἀλλὰ below. Cf. i. 4.

μᾶλλον δὲ τὸ ὅλον, 'or rather, everything.' Cf. i. 19 προσδεῖ, μᾶλλον δ' ἅπαντος ἐνδεῖ τοῦ πόρου.

παρὰ πάντ'...τὰ τῶν ἀνθρώπων πράγματα, 'throughout all human affairs.'

τὴν τῆς ἡμετέρας πόλεως τύχην. Cf. i. 1 τῆς ὑμετέρας τύχης ὑπολαμβάνω *n.*

αὐτῶν. Cf. i. 2 τῶν πραγμάτων ὑμῖν ἐκείνων αὐτοῖς ἀντιληπτέον ἐστίν *n.*

ἢ τὴν ἐκείνου, sc. τύχην. ἢ (= than) is due to the comparison implied in the verb ἂν ἑλοίμην. Cf. < Lysias > *Epitaphios*, 62, θάνατον

μετ' ἐλευθερίας αἱρούμενοι ἢ βίον μετὰ δουλείας, i. 27 τὰ διάφορα...
ἢ n.

πολὺ γὰρ πλείους ἀφορμὰς εἰς τὸ τὴν παρὰ τῶν θεῶν εὔνοιαν ἔχειν.
ἀφορμαί = ' starting-places ' and so ' ways to,' ' reasons for possessing
the goodwill of Heaven.' For the favour of the gods bestowed upon
Athens cf. *supr.* 1.

23. καθήμεθ', 'we sit idle.' καθῆσθαι in Demosthenes is often
applied to a listless inactivity. Cf. *infr.* 24 *ad fin.* κάθησθε.

οὐκ ἔνι δ' αὐτὸν ἀργοῦντ' οὐδὲ τοῖς φίλοις ἐπιτάττειν κ.τ.λ., ' but
it is not possible for a man while remaining idle himself to order even
his friends to do something on his behalf, much less indeed the gods.'
αὐτόν, with the participle ἀργοῦντα and agreeing with the understood
subject (τινά) of ἐπιτάττειν. For the force of μή τί γε cf. *contra
Meidiam* 148 ἀλλ' οὐδὲ καθ' αὑτὸν στρατιώτης οὗτος οὐδενός ἐστ' ἄξιος,
μή τί γε τῶν ἄλλων ἡγεμών.

οὐδὲ θαυμάζω τοῦτ' ἐγώ. Mark the position of the emphatic pronoun, 'no, nor do *I* wonder at this.'

πυνθανομένων. Cf. iii. 35 ὅ τι δ' οἱ τοῦ δεῖνος νικῶσιν ξένοι, ταῦτα
πυνθάνεσθαι n.

ὧν τοῖς πολεμοῦσι προσήκει. ὧν = ἐκείνων ἅ. Cf. i. 1 περὶ ὧν
νυνὶ σκοπεῖτε.

24. ἐκεῖνο. Used (cf. illud in Latin) at the beginning of the
sentence to sum up the object of θαυμάζω, *viz. the contrast* between the
past and present behaviour of the Athenians, which is expressed by
the antithetic sentences, εἰ Λακεδαιμονίοις μέν ποτ'...προὐκινδυνεύετε
στρατευόμενοι > <νυνὶ δ' ὀκνεῖτ' ἐξιέναι...κτημάτων, and τοὺς μὲν ἄλλους...
ἐν μέρει> <τὰ δ' ὑμέτερ' αὐτῶν ἀπολωλεκότες κάθησθε. Cf. iii. 3 ἀλλ'
ἐκεῖν' ἀπορῶ, τίνα χρὴ τρόπον, ὦ ἄνδρες Ἀθηναῖοι, πρὸς ὑμᾶς περὶ αὐτῶν
εἰπεῖν, where ἐκεῖνο is explained by the dependent question τίνα χρὴ
τρόπον κ.τ.λ.

ἐξόν. Absolute use of the *accusative* of the participle, as is regular
with *impersonal* verbs. Cf. iii. 9.

εἰ...οὐκ ἠθελήσατε, when a clause introduced by εἰ is no longer
regarded as hypothetical, but εἰ = ὅτι, e.g. after θαυμάζω, δεινόν and the
like, the negative οὐ replaces μή. Contrast *infr.* 25 θαυμάζω...εἰ
μηδείς...δύναται λογίσασθαι, where the clause introduced by εἰ is regarded
as stating a *hypothesis*, not (as in εἰ...οὐκ ἠθελήσατε) a historical fact.

πάντας καὶ καθ' ἕν αὐτῶν ἐν μέρει, 'all together and individually in turn.' The reference is to the part played in the Persian Wars and against Sparta by Athens, as well as to efforts on behalf of individual states such as are alluded to in the speech *pro Megalopol.* 14 τῶν πάντων οὐδέν' ἂν ἀντειπεῖν οἴομαι ὡς οὐ καὶ Λακεδαιμονίους καὶ πρότερον Θηβαίους καὶ τὸ τελευταῖον Εὐβοέας ἔσωσεν ἡ πόλις. Cf. i. 8 ἥκομεν Εὐβοεῦσιν βεβοηθηκότες.

κάθησθε. Ct. *supr.* 23 καθήμεθα.

25. λογίσασθαι. Observe the tense; 'realize' as the result of calculations.

πόσον πολεμεῖτε χρόνον, 'how long you have been at war.' Observe that Greek employs the present tense to denote an action begun in the past and still continued in the present.

τί ποιούντων ὑμῶν ὁ χρόνος διελήλυθεν οὗτος. The emphasis is on the genitive absolute, 'what you have been doing while this time has passed.'

μελλόντων, sc. ὑμῶν. As in the previous sentence the emphasis falls upon the participial phrases.

αὐτῶν, emphatic, in contrast with the following ἑτέρους τινάς. Cf. *Phil.* i. 7 αὐτὸς μὲν οὐδὲν ἕκαστος ποιήσειν ἐλπίζων, τὸν δὲ πλήσιον πάνθ' ὑπὲρ αὐτοῦ πράξειν.

κρινόντων, 'instituting prosecutions.' Cf. *infr.* 29 κρίνετε, *de Cor.* 197 τοὺς Ἀθηναίων κρίνουσι φίλους.

26. εἶθ' οὕτως ἀγνωμόνως ἔχετ'; For εἶτα introducing an indignant question cf. i. 24 εἶτ' οὐκ αἰσχύνεσθε;

πολὺ γὰρ ῥᾷον ἔχοντας φυλάττειν ἢ κτήσασθαι πάντα πέφυκεν. The infinitives are the subjects of πέφυκεν. πάντα, which is obj. of the infinitives, = 'in every case.' 'For with everything it is naturally much easier for men to keep possession than acquire it.' Contrast i. 23 πολλάκις δοκεῖ τὸ φυλάξαι τἀγαθὰ τοῦ κτήσασθαι χαλεπώτερον εἶναι.

ὅ τι μὲν φυλάξομεν. A final relative clause = 'for us to keep.'

αὐτῶν οὖν ἡμῶν ἔργον τοῦτ' ἤδη. Again the emphatic αὐτῶν. Cf. 1. 2 τῶν πραγμάτων ὑμῖν ἐκείνων αὐτοῖς ἀντιληπτέον ἐστιν and note. For ἤδη = 'forthwith' cf. i. 2 ψηφίσασθαι μὲν ἤδη. The stress laid upon the word is marked by its position in the sentence.

27. φημὶ δὴ δεῖν. For the expression cf. *supr.* 11; i. 17 φημὶ δὴ διχῇ βοηθητέον εἶναι τοῖς πράγμασιν ὑμῖν.

εἰσφέρειν χρήματα, αὐτοὺς ἐξιέναι προθύμως. Cf. i. 6 χρήματ' εἰσφέροντας προθύμως καὶ αὐτοὺς ἐξιόντας *n.* ; *supr.* 13 εἰσφέροντας, ἐξιόντας.

τὰ καθ' ὑμᾶς ἐλλείμματα, ' failings on your part.'

28. καὶ περὶ τῶν στρατηγῶν, 'about the generals too,' i.e. as well
as about the other topics dealt with in the speech.

τῶν ἐφεστηκότων ἴδιοι, ' peculiar to those in command.'

λήμματα. The word seems to have an invidious connotation,
quasi 'pickings.' Cf. *de Chers.* 25 quoted below and Aesch. *cont.*
Ctes. 149.

Λάμψακος. A city of Asia Minor situated near the north-east end
of the Hellespont.

Σίγειον. A city of the Troad situated at the entrance into the
Hellespont from the Aegaean Sea. It seems that Chares, a leader of
mercenaries in Athenian employ, abandoning the war against Athens'
revolted allies and transferring his services to the Persian satrap
Artabazus, had occupied these towns in 356 B.C.

τὰ πλοῖ' ἃ συλῶσιν. For war directed against commerce cf.
de Chers. 25 καὶ διδόασιν οἱ διδόντες οὔτε τὰ μίκρ' οὔτε τὰ πόλλ' ἀντ'
οὐδενός...ἀλλ' ὠνούμενοι μὴ ἀδικεῖσθαι τοὺς παρ' αὐτῶν ἐκπλέοντας ἐμπόρ-
ους, μὴ συλᾶσθαι, παραπέμπεσθαι τὰ πλοῖα τὰ αὐτῶν, τὰ τοιαῦτα.
φασὶ δ' εὐνοίας ('benevolences') διδόναι καὶ τοὔνομ' ἔχει τὰ λήμματα
ταῦτα.

ἕκαστοι. Observe the number. 'Each force.' Cf. *supr.* 7 ἑκάστων *n.*

29. κρίνετε, 'put upon trial,' 'arraign.' Cf. *supr.* 25 κρινόντων.

δόντες λόγον. λόγον διδόναι = 'to grant a hearing to,' 'to allow to
speak.' Cf. *infr.* 31 λόγον διδόναι. As the passive λόγου τυχεῖν is
used. Cf. *de Cor.* 13 ; *cont. Aristocr.* 62.

εἰσεφέρετε κατὰ συμμορίας, ' you paid the war tax by symmories.'
For the payment of the εἰσφορὰ the Athenians were grouped in boards
(συμμορίαι). Each board had a chairman (ἡγεμών) and manager
(ἐπιμελήτης). The 300 wealthiest citizens were distributed among the
various boards, and formed in the case of each one of these the chief
supporters of the ἡγεμὼν and ἐπιμελητής. The sum due from a συμμορία
was paid by the members of 'the three hundred' included in it (οἱ
προεισφέροντες), and these subsequently recovered from the other
members their proportion of the tax.

In the 5th century B.C. the functions of speaker in the Assembly and general in the field were usually combined in the person of the same individual, e.g. Themistocles, Pericles, Nicias, Alcibiades. But in the 4th century the political and military spheres became separated, except in the case of a few men like Phocion, and Demosthenes here compares the organization of a political party with that of a symmory —the orator corresponding to the ἡγεμών and having the support of a general, i.e. an executive officer, and a band of associates—equivalent to the members of ' the three hundred ' rich citizens in the symmory— whose function it is to support his proposals in the Assembly with shouts of approval.

30. ὑμῶν αὐτῶν ἔτι καὶ νῦν γενομένους, 'becoming even now, late as it is, your own masters.' ὑμῶν αὐτῶν = lit. ' of yourselves,' a possessive genitive. For the submissiveness of the Athenians of Demosthenes' day to their statesmen cf. *contra Aristocratem*, 209 τότε μὲν γὰρ ὁ δῆμος ἦν δεσπότης τῶν πολιτευομένων, νῦν δ' ὑπηρέτης, and the picture in iii. 30—1, with note there. Aeschines makes the same complaint as Demosthenes. Cf. *contra Ctesiphontem* 235 οὐχ ὑφ' ὑμῖν αὐτοῖς ἔξετε τοὺς πολιτευομένους;

ἐκ τυραννίδος ὑμῶν. ὑμῶν is an objective genitive depending upon τυραννίδος.

κατὰ τούτων, sc. τῶν ἀναγκαζομένων τριηραρχεῖν, εἰσφέρειν, στρατεύεσθαι.

ἐν καιρῷ = Latin tempore, 'at the proper time.' Observe the emphatic position of the phrase at the end of the sentence.

31. λέγω δὴ κεφάλαιον, ' I propose then in brief.'

τὸ ἴσον, ' what is fair,' ' their due proportion.'

πάντας ἐξιέναι κατὰ μέρος, ἕως ἂν ἅπαντες στρατεύσησθε, 'that all shall take the field in turn, until every one has done service.' The names of Athenians liable to serve in war were kept on a roll. From this list individuals were called upon for military duties in regular succession. But the system was abused ; laws permitting exemption in certain cases were passed (cf. iii. 11) ; and men contrived to have the position of their names on the list altered, so that it should appear that they had performed military service, when they had in reality not done so. Cf. Aristoph. *Knights*, 1369—71

> ἔπειθ' ὁπλίτης ἐντεθεὶς ἐν καταλόγῳ
> οὐδεὶς κατὰ σπουδὰς μετεγγραφήσεται,
> ἀλλ' ὥσπερ ἦν τὸ πρῶτον ἐγγεγράψεται.

Peace, 1180—1

      τοὺς μὲν ἐγγράφοντες ἡμῶν, τοὺς δ' ἄνω τε καὶ κάτω
      ἐξαλείφοντες δὶς ἢ τρίς.

τοῖς παριοῦσι. Cf. *supr.* 8 παρελθών *n.*

λόγον διδόναι. Cf. *supr.* 29 δόντες λόγον.

βέλτιον τῶν ὅλων πραγμάτων ὑμῖν ἐχόντων. The note of optimism upon which this speech ends corresponds to the prayers for prosperity with which the first and third orations conclude.

III

1. The opening passage (οὐχὶ ταὐτὰ...δέον) is parodied by Lucian, Δὶς κατηγορούμενος 26.

οὐχὶ ταὐτὰ παρίσταταί μοι γιγνώσκειν. οὐχὶ ταὐτὰ, a litotes = 'very different.' The infinitive is epexegetic of παρίσταται, 'very different thoughts occur to my mind' (lit. 'to me to know').

πρὸς τοὺς λόγους, οὓς ἀκούω, sc. ἀποβλέψω. ἀποβλέπειν, 'to gaze at,' used properly of physical sight, comes to mean simply 'to consider carefully,' 'to pay attention to.' Observe the rhetorical variation of the preposition in the phrases εἰς τὰ πράγματα and πρὸς τοὺς λόγους.

τοὺς μὲν γὰρ λόγους περὶ τοῦ τιμωρήσασθαι Φίλιππον ὁρῶ γιγνομένους. λόγος γίγνεται is the regular passive of λόγον ποιοῦμαι. Notice the ingressive force of the tense of τιμωρήσασθαι ('about *taking steps* to punish'). Cf. i. 6 ἐθελῆσαι *n.*

ὅπως μὴ πεισόμεθ' αὐτοὶ πρότερον κακῶς. κακῶς belongs to πεισόμεθα, but gains emphasis from its position at the end of its clause ; evil, unless we take care, will be for *us*, not for Philip. Verbs denoting care, precaution, effort and the like, as here σκέψασθαι, complete their construction by ὅπως with the future indicative (neg. μή). Cf. ii. 2 ὅπως μὴ...δόξομεν *n.*

δέον. The construction in the clause introduced by ὥστε is made to correspond with that of the clause upon which it depends (γιγνομένους ...προήκοντα...δέον) Goodwin, *M. and T.* §607 *a.* Cf. < *Phil.* > iv. 40 οὐδὲ γὰρ...ὁρῶ τὸν ἐν ἡλικίᾳ πρὸς τοὺς πρεσβυτέρους οὕτω διακείμενον...ὥστε, εἰ μὴ ποιήσουσιν ἅπαντες ὅσ' ἂν αὐτός, οὐ φάσκοντα ποιήσειν οὐδὲν οὐδ' αὐτόν. Isoc. *Paneg.* 64 φαίνονται δ' ἡμῶν οἱ πρόγονοι τοσοῦτον ἁπάντων διενεγκόντες, ὥστε...Θηβαίοις ἐπιτάττοντες.

τὰ τοιαῦτα = περὶ τοῦ τιμωρήσασθαι Φίλιππον.

οὐχὶ τὴν οὖσαν together = ' not the real,' ' a quite false.'

παριστάντες ὑμῖν ἁμαρτάνειν, ' to make the mistake of putting before you.' For ἁμαρτάνειν with the participle cf. Sonn. *Gk Gram.* § 549 C.

2.   ἐπ' ἐμοῦ, 'in my own time.' Cf. *infr.* 21 ἐπὶ τῶν προγόνων ἡμῶν. γέγονε, ' have been possible.'

τὴν πρώτην. Adverbial, ' at first,' ' to begin with.' Cf. i. 2 τὴν ταχίστην.

ὅπως τοὺς συμμάχους σώσομεν. Cf. *supr.* 1 ὅπως μὴ πείσομεθ' αὐτοὶ πρότερον κακῶς *n.*

καὶ περὶ τοῦ τίνα τιμωρήσεταί τις καὶ ὃν τρόπον. The article τοῦ belongs to the whole succeeding phrase, which stands to it in the same relation as a noun. Observe that the *relative* pronoun (ὃν τρόπον) is sometimes used instead of the interrogative to introduce a *dependent* (*indirect*) question. καὶ = ' also,' ' further,' marking that these questions are *secondary* to the question of saving Olynthus.

3.   ὁ μὲν οὖν παρὼν καιρός. Cf. i. 2 *ad init.*

ἐκεῖν' ἀπορῶ. The pronoun ἐκεῖνο anticipates, with emphasis, the dependent question (τίνα χρὴ τρόπον...εἰπεῖν) which follows. Cf. ii. 24 ἀλλ' ἐκεῖνο θαυμάζω *n.*

ἐξ ὧν, by brachylogy for ἐξ ἐκείνων ἅ. Cf. i. 1 περὶ ὧν νυνὶ σκοπεῖτε *n.*

τὰ πλείω τῶν πραγμάτων. The genitive of the divided whole (partitive genitive) is not placed between the word on which it depends and the article belonging to that word.

ποιῶμαι τοὺς λόγους, ' say what I have to say.' Observe that the *middle* voice is used in combination with a noun to form a periphrasis equivalent to a simple verb. Thus λόγους ποιεῖσθαι = λέγειν, πλοῦν ποιεῖσθαι = πλεῖν, πόλεμον ποιεῖσθαι = πολεμεῖν.

ἐκ τοῦ πρὸς χάριν δημηγορεῖν ἐνίους, ' because some speak only to please.' πρὸς χάριν (cf. πρὸς βίαν = ' violently ') is emphatic. Demosthenes attributes the evil position of Athens' affairs to those statesmen who sought only to keep the people self-satisfied and amused. Cf. *infr.* 31. Similarly Aeschines in *contra Ctesiphontem* 127 says τὸ γὰρ ἀεὶ πρὸς ἡδονὴν λεγόμενον οὑτωσὶ τὴν πόλιν διατέθηκεν.

εἰς πᾶν προελήλυθε μοχθηρίας, ' has reached the uttermost limit of wretchedness.' We might have expected rather εἰς πᾶσαν...μοχθηρίαν, but the genitive familiarly used after such expressions as εἰs τοῦτο, εἰs τοσοῦτο (e.g. εἰs τοσοῦτο προελήλυθε μοχθηρίαs), is here employed after εἰs πᾶν. Cf. Aeschines, *contra Timarchum* 62 ἐν παντὶ δὲ κακοῦ γενόμενοs ὁ Πιττάλακοs προσπίπτει ἀνδρὶ καὶ μάλα χρηστῷ, Thuc. vii. 55 ἐν παντὶ δὴ ἀθυμίαs ἦσαν.

4. ὅτ' ἀπηγγέλθη Φίλιπποs ὑμῖν ἐν Θράκῃ, 'when news was brought to you of Philip in Thrace.' For the personal subject with ἀπηγγέλθη cf. *infr.* 5 ὡs γὰρ ἠγγέλθη Φίλιπποs ἀσθενῶν ἢ τεθνεώs, i. 9 Πύδνα, Ποτείδαια, Μεθώνη, Παγασαί, τἄλλα...πολιορκούμεν' ἀπηγγέλλετο.

τρίτον ἢ τέταρτον ἔτοs τουτί, 'two or three years ago.' The invasion of Thrace by Philip took place in 352 B.C. Cf. i. 13 *n.*

Ἡραῖον τεῖχοs. A fortified position in Thrace, generally identified with Heraeum, on the shore of the Propontis.

μαιμακτηριών. An Attic month corresponding roughly with November.

τοὺs μέχρι πέντε καὶ τετταράκοντ' ἐτῶν, i.e. those between the ages of 20 and 45 years. Cf. *infr.* 34 ἔξω τῆs ἡλικίαs *n.* These would form about three quarters of the total number available for foreign service.

αὐτοὺs ἐμβαίνειν. A citizen, not a mercenary, force. Contrast *infr.* 5 κενάs, and cf. i. 2 ἐνθένδε *n.*

τάλανθ' ἑξήκοντ', sc. χρυσοῦ. Contrast *infr.* 5 ἀργυρίου *n.* The amount actually raised was less than $\frac{1}{180}$th part of that proposed.

5. διελθόντοs τοῦ ἐνιαυτοῦ τούτου, ἑκατομβαιών, μεταγειτνιών, βοηδρομιών—τούτου τοῦ μηνὸs κ.τ.λ. The orator, after the genitive absolute, begins an enumeration of the months that had elapsed in the *new* year, the Attic year beginning with the month ἑκατομβαιών. With βοηδρομιὼν he reaches the point when the Athenians at last began to act and continues with τούτου τοῦ μηνόs. The months mentioned extend roughly from mid-July to mid-October.

μετὰ τὰ μυστήρια. The Eleusinian Mysteries were celebrated at Eleusis from the 20th to the 23rd of Boedromion in honour of Demeter and Persephone. The solemn proclamation of the Mysteries was made by the Archon Basileus in the Stoa Poikilé at Athens on the 16th of the month, and this was followed by purificatory ceremonies and sacrifices culminating in the procession along the Sacred Way from Athens to Eleusis on the 19th—20th.

κενάς, 'without crews'> <πλήρης 'with full complement.' The ships were left to be manned by mercenaries. Contrast *supr.* 4 αὐτοὺς ἐμβαίνειν.

Χαρίδημον. A leader of mercenary troops who received the gift of Athenian citizenship. A native of Oreus in Euboea he not only bore arms in the Athenian service, but fought also for the revolted satrap Artabazus against Artaxerxes III of Persia, and for the Thracian prince, Cotys, who conferred upon him the hand of his daughter in marriage. When Cotys was killed, Charidemus lent his support to his son Cersobleptes, on whose behalf he contended with the Athenians for possession of the Thracian Chersonese.

ἀργυρίου. The word is emphatic. A talent of silver was worth about $\frac{1}{12}$ of a talent of gold.

ὡς γὰρ ἠγγέλθη Φίλιππος ἀσθενῶν ἢ τεθνεώς. Cf. *supr.* 4 ὅτ' ἀπηγγέλθη Φίλιππος ὑμῖν ἐν Θρᾴκῃ *n.* For the illness of Philip in Thrace cf. i. 13.

ἐκεῖσ', i.e. to Thrace.

εἰ γάρ...ἐβοηθήσαμεν, ὥσπερ ἐψηφισάμεθα, προθύμως, οὐκ ἂν ἠνώχλει νῦν ἡμῖν ὁ Φίλιππος σωθείς. Mark the change of tense, the aorist referring to the condition which was not fulfilled in the *past*, the imperfect referring to the result, which, if the condition had been fulfilled, would not exist in the *present*. Observe the emphatic position in their clauses of προθύμως and σωθείς. 'If we had sent aid with the zeal with which we voted it, Philip would not have escaped to trouble us to-day.'

6. **τὰ μὲν δὴ τότε πραχθέντ' οὐκ ἂν ἄλλως ἔχοι,** 'well, what was done then cannot be altered.' For μὲν δή dismissing a topic from consideration cf. ii. 8.

δι' ὃν καὶ περὶ τούτων ἐμνήσθην. καί marks that the mention of past events (§§ 4, 5) is *an addition to* his discussion of the present crisis. 'Because of which I have inserted a reference to these events.'

βοηθήσετε. For the monitory use of the future indicative in the protasis of a conditional sentence cf. i. 12 εἰ δὲ προησόμεθ', ὦ ἄνδρες Ἀθηναῖοι, καὶ τούτους τοὺς ἀνθρώπους *n.*

παντὶ σθένει κατὰ τὸ δυνατόν. A formal phrase, quoted here by Demosthenes as is shown by (i) the use of σθένος, a poetical word, (ii) the collocation of five short syllables in κατὰ τὸ δυνατόν.

θεάσασθ' ὃν τρόπον. For the use of the *relative* to introduce a dependent question cf. *supr.* 2 περὶ τοῦ τίνα τιμωρήσεταί τις καὶ ὃν τρόπον.

ὑμεῖς ἐστρατηγηκότες πάντ' ἔσεσθ' ὑπὲρ Φιλίππου, 'you will prove to have managed all *your* operations in the interest of *Philip.*' Observe the full force of the future perfect verbal form. Mark the insertion of the pronoun ὑμεῖς and the position of Φιλίππου.

7. ὑπῆρχον κ.τ.λ. Note the absence of conjunction, the sentence beginning in detail the survey proposed in the last sentence of the preceding paragraph (θεάσασθ' ὃν τρόπον...Φιλίππου). Such passages are sometimes called asyndetic explanations, i.e. explanations without any introductory conjunctions. So below the asyndetic sentences from οὔτε Φίλιππος ἐθάρρει κ.τ.λ. to the end of the paragraph are explanations of the sentence διέκειθ' οὕτω τὰ πράγματα.

δύναμίν τινα κεκτημένοι. Cf. ii. 1 καὶ χώραν ὅμορον καὶ δύναμίν τινα κεκτημένους *n.*

ἐθάρρει τούτους. θαρρεῖν, properly an intransitive verb, is followed by a direct object in the accusative case since οὐκ ἐθάρρει = ἐφοβεῖτο. Cf. the use of a direct object after ἐκπλήττεσθαι, 'to be struck with terror' (= φοβεῖσθαι), e.g. Thuc. vi. 11 ἡμᾶς δ' ἂν οἱ ἐκεῖ Ἕλληνες μάλιστα μὲν ἐκπεπληγμένοι εἶεν, *supr.* ii. 5 τοὺς ὑπερεκπεπληγμένους ὡς ἄμαχόν τινα τὸν Φίλιππον *n.*

πόλιν μεγάλην, sc. Olynthus.

ἐφορμεῖν τοῖς ἑαυτοῦ καιροῖς. A nautical metaphor, ἐφορμεῖν being properly used of a blockading vessel. For a similar metaphorical use cf. Soph. *Oed. Col.* 812 μηδέ με | φύλασσ' ἐφορμῶν. 'For a large city on friendly terms with us to lie waiting for the chances which he offers.'

ἐκπολεμῶσαι δεῖν ᾠόμεθα κ.τ.λ. Cf. i. 7 νυνὶ γὰρ ὃ πάντες ἐθρυλεῖτε, ὡς Ὀλυνθίους ἐκπολεμῶσαι δεῖ Φιλίππῳ, γέγονεν αὐτόματον.

ὁπωσδήποτε, lit. 'in whatever way it has been done,' i.e. 'somehow or other.' Cf. *de Cor.* 146 τοὺς ὁποιουσδήποθ' ὑμεῖς ἐξεπέμπετε στρατηγούς, 'generals of some kind or other.' Demosthenes employs these expressions when he does not wish to stay to discuss the subject in detail. So he adds frequently, as in the passage quoted from *de Cor.*, the words ἐῶ γὰρ τοῦτό γε, 'for of *this* I say nothing now.'

8. ἐγὼ μὲν οὐχ ὁρῶ. μέν is sometimes employed, without any answering conjunction (μέν *solitarium*), simply to add emphasis, '*I* do

not see.' Cf. *contra Aristocratem* 137 ἐγὼ μὲν οὐχ ὁρῶ, ii. 14 ὅλως μὲν γάρ *n.*

οὐδὲ τὸν φόβον...μικρὸν ὁρῶ τὸν τῶν μετὰ ταῦτα, 'I see in the sequel no small peril either.' *οὐδέ* implies a reference to *τῆς αἰσχύνης.* The disgrace would be a great one, but, apart from that, the peril *too* is not small.' Observe that *μικρὸν* is used predicatively.

ἐχόντων μὲν ὡς ἔχουσι Θηβαίων ἡμῖν, 'the attitude of the Thebans to us being what it is.' A euphemistic expression. Cf. i. 26 *ad init.* with notes.

ἀπειρηκότων δὲ χρήμασι Φωκέων, 'the finances of the Phocians being exhausted.' In 356 B.C. the Phocians had seized Delphi with its vast temple-treasures, but seven years of warfare had now exhausted even these. For the position of Phocis cf. i. 26; Introd. pp. xx—xxi.

μηδενὸς δ' ἐμποδὼν ὄντος κ.τ.λ. Cf. i. 12 εἰ δὲ προησόμεθ', ὦ ἄνδρες Ἀθηναῖοι, καὶ τούτους τοὺς ἀνθρώπους, εἶτ' Ὄλυνθον ἐκεῖνος καταστρέψεται, φρασάτω τις ἐμοὶ τί τὸ κωλῦον ἔτ' αὐτὸν ἔσται βαδίζειν ὅποι βούλεται, with note on construction with κωλύειν, and i. 25 ἂν δ' ἐκεῖνα Φίλιππος λάβῃ, τίς αὐτὸν κωλύσει δεῦρο βαδίζειν;

πρὸς ταῦτ'...τὰ πράγματα i.e. to the situation in Attica.

9. εἰς τοῦτ', 'up to that point,' 'until then,' *viz.* when Philip is ready to attack us.

ἀναβάλλεται ποιήσειν. The idea of *procrastination* is emphasized by the use of the *future* infinitive.

ἐξόν. Accusative absolute. Cf. ii. 24.

περιστήσεται. With passive force (cf. i. 22 καταστήσεται), 'matters will come round to this.' The verb is regularly used of the 'reversals' or 'changes' of fortune, usually connoting that these are for the worse.

σχεδὸν ἴσμεν ἅπαντες δήπου, 'we are all, I presume (δήπου), pretty sure.' An ironical understatement of the fact.

10. ἀλλ' ὅτι μὲν δὴ δεῖ βοηθεῖν. For the use of μὲν δή in dismissing a topic from consideration cf. *supr.* 6 τὰ μὲν δὴ τότε πραχθέντ' οὐκ ἂν ἄλλως ἔχοι.

τὸ δ' ὅπως, sc. βοηθήσομεν. For the use of the article cf. *supr.* 2 καὶ περὶ τοῦ τίνα τιμωρήσεταί τις καὶ ὃν τρόπον *n.*

νομοθέτας, 'legislative commissioners.' At the first ordinary meeting of the Assembly on the 11th of Hecatombaeon in each year the existing laws of the State were submitted to scrutiny. If the Assembly decided in favour of amending them in any particulars, definite proposals were drafted, posted in public by the statues of the twelve ἐπώνυμοι, and handed to the clerk of the Council to be read to the Assembly. The proposals were considered by the Council, and the Assembly at its fourth ordinary meeting voted the appointment of νομοθέται, who were usually one thousand in number and were chosen from the dicasts by lot. Over them presided an ἐπιστάτης and five πρόεδροι chosen by lot from the Council. Five advocates (σύνδικοι) were also appointed by the Assembly to defend the law or laws attacked, and the νομοθέται after hearing the arguments on both sides decided by a majority in favour of one or the other. Even if the amendment was passed, its author was still liable to prosecution under a γραφὴ παρανόμων on the ground that his proposal conflicted with some already existing law, or even that it was generally inexpedient. Demosthenes here suggests an extraordinary application of this regular procedure to deal with the present crisis.

ἐν δὲ τούτοις τοῖς νομοθέταις, 'at this legislative commission.' For the use of ἐν cf. ἐν τοῖς δικασταῖς.

11. λέγω τοὺς περὶ τῶν θεωρικῶν. For the Theoric Fund cf. i. 19, Appendix B. Contrast this undisguised reference (σαφῶς οὑτωσί) with the veiled language of i. 19 ἔστιν, ὦ ἄνδρες Ἀθηναῖοι, χρήμαθ' ὑμῖν κ.τ.λ.

τοὺς περὶ τῶν στρατευομένων ἐνίους. Cf. ii. 31 πάντας ἐξιέναι κατὰ μέρος, ἔως ἂν ἅπαντες στρατεύσησθε ν.

θεωρικά, predicative = 'as festival money.' Cf. i. 20 ὑμεῖς δ' (ἡγεῖσθε δεῖν) οὕτω πως ἄνευ πραγμάτων λαμβάνειν εἰς τὰς ἑορτάς.

τοὺς ἀτακτοῦντας, 'those who shirk service.' Cf. ii. 31 πάντας ἐξιέναι κατὰ μέρος, ἔως ἂν ἅπαντες στρατεύσησθε ν.

12. πρὶν δὲ ταῦτα πρᾶξαι μὴ σκοπεῖτε. Cf. *infr.* 13 πρὶν δὲ ταῦτ' εὐτρεπίσαι μηδαμῶς...ἀξιοῦτε. Goodwin, *M. and T.* § 628.

τίς εἰπὼν τὰ βέλτισθ' ὑπὲρ ὑμῶν ὑφ' ὑμῶν ἀπολέσθαι βουλήσεται. Observe the juxtaposition of the prepositional phrases. 'Who will be ready to suffer ruin at your hands for urging what is best in your interests.'

ἀλλὰ καὶ εἰς τὸ λοιπὸν μᾶλλον ἔτ' ἢ νῦν τὸ τὰ βέλτιστα λέγειν φοβερώτερον ποιῆσαι. Mark the double comparative μᾶλλον...φοβερώτερον. 'Increase for the future the danger of urging what is best to a degree even greater than now.'

καὶ λύειν γ'...οἴπερ καὶ τεθήκασιν. καὶ...γε of an emphatic addition. It is common in Aristophanes in conversational retorts. Cf. ii. 10; *infr.* 34 καὶ παραχρῆμά γε τὴν αὐτὴν σύνταξιν ἀπάντων *n.* καὶ marks the correlation of the acts of abolition (λύειν) and establishment (τεθήκασιν). οἴπερ, *precise* relative.

τεθήκασιν. For the active voice cf. *infr.* 13 θεῖσιν, *de Cor.* 102 ἔθηκα νόμον.

13. τὴν μὲν χάριν, ἣ πᾶσαν ἔβλαπτε τὴν πόλιν, lit. 'the popularity which was detrimental to the whole city,' i.e. as we, in English, should rather say, 'the popularity *of the actions* which were,' etc. The popular actions were of course the diversion of public monies into the Theoric Fund, and the granting of exemption from military service. Similarly, τὴν δ' ἀπέχθειαν δι' ἧς ἂν...πράξαιμεν = 'the odium *of the action* which would improve the general position.' The unpopular action would be the repeal of what were, in Demosthenes' opinion, noxious laws.

τοῖς τότε θεῖσιν, sc. τοὺς νόμους.

εὐτρεπίσαι, 'settle,' 'arrange.' Cf. i. 13 πάνθ' ὃν ἐβούλετ' εὐτρεπίσας τρόπον.

ὥστε τοὺς νόμους τούτους παραβάντα μὴ δοῦναι δίκην, 'as to contravene these laws without suffering for it.' 'These laws' are those mentioned *supr.* 11.

14. οὐδ' ἐκεῖνό γ' ὑμᾶς ἀγνοεῖν δεῖ, 'you must not fail to recognize this *either*,' i.e. any more than the necessity for the reform of certain laws (§§ 10—13). For the use of ἐκεῖνο cf. *supr.* 3 ἀλλ' ἐκεῖν' ἀπορῶ, τίνα χρὴ τρόπον κ.τ.λ.; ii. 24 *ad init. n.* For οὐδὲ...γε cf. *supr.* 12 καὶ...γε *n.*

προθύμως, with ποιεῖν. Cf. i. 1.

ὑμᾶς. This word is considered by several editors an interpolation, and may have arisen from the latter part of the preceding adverb, προθύμως, by dittography. On the other hand its insertion in an emphatic position at the end of the sentence may have been due to a desire to add the contrast of the *people* with the *decrees* to the other contrast of the *carrying out* of decrees with the *proposal* of them.

περὶ ὧν γραφείη, sc. τὰ ψηφίσματα. γραφείη is 3rd sing. 2nd aor. pass. of γράφω, being the verb in an indefinite relative clause depending upon a principal sentence in which the predicate (ἦν) is in a secondary tense. ' If decrees were sufficient in themselves either to compel you to do what you ought to do, or to carry into effect whatever matters gave rise to their proposal.'

οὔτ' ἂν ὑμεῖς πολλὰ ψηφιζόμενοι μικρά, μᾶλλον δ' οὐδὲν ἐπράττετε τούτων, 'neither would you be passing many decrees and yet carrying into effect few, or rather none, of them.' For the use of μᾶλλον δέ cf. i. 19 προσδεῖ, μᾶλλον δ' ἅπαντος ἐνδεῖ τοῦ πόρου. τούτων refers to πολλά.

οὔτε Φίλιππος τοσοῦτον ὑβρίκει χρόνον. With ὑβρίκει supply ἄν. Mark the force of the pluperfect tense; 'nor would Philip have been maintaining all this time his attitude of insolence.'

πάλαι γὰρ ἂν ἕνεκά γε ψηφισμάτων ἐδεδώκει δίκην. Note the pluperfect tense here also. ' For as far as decrees go, he would long since be a punished man.' πάλαι is stressed by its position in the sentence. Cf. *de Cor.* 49 πάλαι ἂν ἀπωλώλειτε.

15. τὸ γὰρ πράττειν τοῦ λέγειν καὶ χειροτονεῖν ὕστερον ὂν τῇ τάξει πρότερον τῇ δυνάμει καὶ κρεῖττόν ἐστιν, 'for acting, though later in order of time than speaking and voting, is prior in effectiveness and superior.'

τοῦτ' οὖν δεῖ προσεῖναι. τοῦτο = τὸ πράττειν. For the force of πρὸς in προσεῖναι cf. i. 19 οὐδενὸς ὑμῖν προσδεῖ πόρου *n.*

ὑπάρχει, 'are provided already.'

γνῶναι, 'to judge,' 'to appraise.'

καὶ πρᾶξαι δὲ δυνήσεσθε νῦν, 'and you will now be able to act too (καί),' i.e. as well as say what ought to be said (εἰπεῖν τὰ δέοντα) and form a judgment of what you hear (γνῶναι τὰ ῥηθέντα). For καὶ...δὲ cf. *Phil.* iii. 70 ἐγὼ νὴ Δι' ἐρῶ, καὶ γράψω δέ, ὥστ' ἂν βούλησθε χειροτονήσετε. This combination of particles is employed for 'emphasis and climax.'

16. τὰ χωρί', 'positions' of strategic or mercantile importance, e.g. Amphipolis, Pydna, Poteidaea, Methone.

εἰ δὲ καὶ ταύτης κύριος τῆς χώρας γενήσεται. ταύτης τῆς χώρας, i.e. Olynthus. Cf. i. 12 εἰ δὲ προησόμεθ', ὦ ἄνδρες Ἀθηναῖοι, καὶ τούτους τοὺς ἀνθρώπους *n.*

οὐχ ἔχων τὰ ἡμέτερα; e.g. the places mentioned in the note on τὰ χωρία above.

οὐ βάρβαρος; The royal family of Macedon claimed to be descended from the Dorian princes of Argos. The claim was so far admitted that

Alexander I of Macedon was allowed to compete in the foot-race at the
Olympic games (his victory was celebrated by Pindar), a privilege never
permitted to one accounted not a Hellene. Demosthenes, however,
always speaks of Philip as 'a barbarian.' Cf. *Phil.* iii. 31 Φιλίππου...οὐ
μόνον οὐχ Ἕλληνος ὄντος οὐδὲ προσήκοντος οὐδὲν τοῖς Ἕλλησιν, ἀλλ' οὐδὲ
βαρβάρων ἐντεῦθεν, ὅθεν καλὸν εἰπεῖν, ἀλλ' ὀλέθρου Μακέδονος, ὅθεν οὐδ'
ἀνδράποδον πρίαιτό τις ἄν ποτε, *de Fals. Leg.* 305 (Aeschines, according
to Demosthenes, called Philip) βάρβαρόν τε καὶ ἀλάστορα.

17. τότε τοὺς αἰτίους οἵτινες τούτων ζητήσομεν; 'shall we *then*
enquire who are responsible for this?' After οἵτινες supply εἰσί. By
a common Greek idiom αἴτιοι, which would naturally form part of
the dependent question, is made (with the article) the object of the
verb upon which the question depends, *viz.* ζητήσομεν. Cf. i. 21 τὰ
πράγματα *n.*

οὐδὲ γάρ...κατηγορεῖ. Mark the force of οὐδέ. 'For *likewise* in
the perils of war no one of the fugitives blames himself.' Observe the
directness with which the illustration is added. Cf. *Phil.* iii. 69 ἀλλὰ
τί τούτων ὄφελος; ἕως ἄν σώζηται τὸ σκάφος...τότε χρὴ καὶ ναύτην καὶ
κυβερνήτην καὶ πάντ' ἄνδρ' ἐξῆς προθύμους εἶναι.

ἥττηνται δ' ὅμως διὰ πάντας τοὺς φυγόντας δήπου, 'yet it is owing
to the runaways as a whole, I presume, that defeat is brought about.'
For δήπου as closing word cf. *supr.* 9 σχέδον ἴσμεν ἅπαντες δήπου.

εἰ δ' ἐποίει τοῦθ' ἕκαστος, ἐνίκων ἄν. The imperfect tense (ἐποίει)
is used here to refer to *past* time, the action of standing firm (μένειν)
being extended over a period. The present tense of νικῶ often has
a *perfect* significance (='am victor,' 'have conquered'); hence the
imperfect may have, as here, a pluperfect signification, 'would have
been victorious.' Cf. *supr.* 14 ὑβρίκει and ἐδεδώκει.

18. καὶ νῦν='so now,' introducing the application of the lesson.

ταῦτα ποιεῖτ' ἀγαθῇ τύχῃ. Modal dative. 'Do this and good
luck!'

οὐκέτι τοῦθ' ὁ λέγων ἀδικεῖ, '*this* is not the fault of the speaker.'
Observe the idiomatic use of οὐκέτι. A speaker may be held to blame
for not urging what is of most advantage; but when it is a question of
urging what is not pleasant, the speaker can *no longer* (οὐκέτι) he held
in fault. Similarly below, εὔξασθαι μὲν...ῥᾴδιον...ἐλέσθαι δ'...οὐκέθ'

ὁμοίως εὔπορον. It is easy to pray, but, when it is a question of choosing, the way is *no longer* as open as before. So in Plato, e.g. *Meno* 73 A ἐμοιγέ πως δοκεῖ, ὦ Σώκρατες, τοῦτο οὐκέτι ὅμοιον εἶναι τοῖς ἄλλοις τούτοις.

δέον. Accusative absolute. Cf. *supra* 9 ἐξόν.

19. **τὰ θεωρικά.** Cf. *supr.* 11; App. B.

πόρους ἑτέρους, 'another set of ways and means.' Cf. i. 19 χρημάτων πόρου. For ἑτέρους in plural cf. i. 17 στρατιώταις ἑτέροις.

φήμ' ἔγωγε, εἴπερ ἔστιν, '*I* say yes, if it is possible.' Observe the accentuation of ἔστιν. φημί = 'yes': οὔ φημι = 'no.' For εἴπερ cf. i. 2 εἴπερ ὑπερ σωτηρίας αὐτῶν φροντίζετε *n.*

τὰ παρόντ'...τῶν ἀπόντων, 'what he has...what he has not.' τῶν ἀπόντων depends upon εὐπορῆσαι, that verb being followed by a genitive according to the rule by which words denoting 'fullness' complete their meaning by the genitive.

πρὸς ἃ μὴ δεῖ, sc. ἀναλῶσαι. The clause is a *generic* relative one; hence the negative μή.

πρὸς ἃ δεῖ, sc. εὐπορῆσαι.

μέγα τοῖς τοιούτοις ὑπάρχει λόγοις ἡ παρ' ἑκάστου βούλησις, 'the wish of the individual is to a great extent at the bottom of such speeches.'

τὰ δὲ πράγματα πολλάκις οὐχ οὕτω πέφυκεν, 'but circumstances are frequently not fashioned in this way.' οὕτω, i.e. so as to be just what we wish them to be.

20. **οὔ τοι σωφρόνων οὐδὲ γενναίων ἐστὶν ἀνθρώπων,** 'surely it is not the part of men of understanding or of generous-spirited men either.' For the genitive cf. *infr.* 21 δικαίου πολίτου, i. 16 παντός *n.*

εὐχερῶς...φέρειν, 'to endure lightly, with equanimity,' 'facile ferre.'

ἐπὶ μὲν Κορινθίους καὶ Μεγαρέας...πορεύεσθαι. Corinth was some fifty miles distant from Athens, Megara rather more than half that distance. Demosthenes must be referring to recent expeditions. In 350 B.C. the Athenians invaded Megara owing to an alleged trespass by the Megarians on land sacred to Demeter and Persephone. We are also told that the Corinthians did not invite the Athenians to attend the Isthmian games, and that in consequence an armed force was despatched from Athens to the festival.

21. τὴν ἄλλως, 'idly,' 'frivolously.' Cf. *supr.* 2 τὴν πρώτην *n.* ἀτυχής, 'ill-starred.'

δικαίου πολίτου. Cf. *supr.* 20 οὔ τοι σωφρόνων οὐδὲ γενναίων ἐστὶν ἀνθρώπων *n.*

τῆς ἐν τῷ λέγειν χάριτος. Cf. *supr.* 3 ἐκ τοῦ πρὸς χάριν δημηγορεῖν ἐνίους, *infr.* 22.

ἐπὶ τῶν προγόνων ἡμῶν, 'in the days of our forefathers.' Cf. *supr.* 2 ἐπ' ἐμοῦ.

ἀκούω, 'I am told.' This and οἶδα ἀκούων are the two expressions by which Demosthenes usually refers to historical tradition.

οἱ παριόντες, 'those who come forward to address you.' Cf. ii. 8 παρελθών *n.*

τῆς πολιτείας, 'of statesmanship.' This use of the word πολιτεία (=lit. citizenship) implies the interest and activity in the affairs of the state expected from the individual Athenian citizen.

τὸν Ἀριστείδην ἐκεῖνον, 'the renowned Aristeides.' For the use of ἐκεῖνος cf. ii. 19 Καλλίαν ἐκεῖνον τὸν δημόσιον, and ille in Latin, e.g. Verg. *Aen.* ii. 274—5 quantum mutatus ab illo | Hectore. Aristeides was an eminent statesman contemporary with Themistocles. He was ostracized in 483 B.C., but was present three years later at the battle of Salamis, where he did signal service by landing troops on the island of Psyttaleia and destroying the Persians stationed there by Xerxes. He subsequently assisted in the founding of the Delian League. The lines of Aeschylus concerning Amphiaraus (*Sept. c. Thebas* 579—81 οὐ γὰρ δοκεῖν ἄριστος ἀλλ' εἶναι θέλει, | βαθεῖαν ἄλοκα διὰ φρενὸς καρπούμενος, | ἐξ ἧς τὰ κεδνὰ βλαστάνει βουλεύματα) are said to have been understood by the audience as referring by implication to Aristeides. (Plut. *Aristeides,* c. 3.)

τὸν Νικίαν. Nicias was a leading statesman and general of Athens during the earlier half of the Peloponnesian War. He was opposed to the continuance of hostilities with Sparta, and the peace concluded in 421 B.C. is known by his name. Later he was sent in 415 B.C. against Syracuse, his colleagues being Lamachus and Alcibiades. The disaster which overtook that expedition was due in no small measure to the hesitation and superstition of Nicias, who finally surrendered to Gylippus, the Lacedaemonian ally of the Syracusans, and along with his fellow general, Demosthenes, was put to death. For the hesitation of Nicias cf. Aristoph. *Birds* 638—9 οὐχὶ νυστάζειν γ' ἔτι | ὥρα 'στὶν ἡμῖν οὐδὲ μελλονικιᾶν: for his superstitious piety cf. Aristoph. *Knights* 30—1

κράτιστα τοίνυν τῶν παρόντων ἐστὶ νῷν | θεῶν ἰόντε προσπεσεῖν τοῦ πρὸς
βρέτας, Thuc. vii. 50.

τὸν ὁμώνυμον ἐμαυτῷ, 'my own namesake,' i.e. Demosthenes, an
enterprising and brilliant general, who after being defeated in Aetolia
in 426 B.C. retrieved his position by two decisive victories. It was at
his suggestion and through his efforts that Pylos was fortified by the
Athenians in 424 B.C., an event which led to the capture of Sphacteria
and its garrison, the first serious blow of the war struck at Sparta.
Later he was despatched with reinforcements to the assistance of Nicias
in Sicily and shared that general's unhappy fate and death. The salient
characteristics of both Nicias and Demosthenes are humorously por-
trayed in the opening scene of the *Knights* of Aristophanes.

τὸν Περικλέα. This Athenian general and statesman dominated
Athenian politics during the middle of the fifth cent. B.C. to such an
extent that the result is described by Thucydides (ii. 65) as λόγῳ μὲν
δημοκρατία, ἔργῳ δὲ ὑπὸ τοῦ πρώτου ἀνδρὸς ἀρχή. He was a liberal
patron of letters, science and arts, and under his influence Athens was
adorned with beautiful buildings, graced with sculptures, and adorned
with paintings. In 430 B.C. shortly before his death, which occurred in
the following year, Pericles and the war policy which he advocated
became unpopular with the Athenians, and the statesman was charged
with peculation, convicted, and condemned to pay a fine. But the
people's indignation appears to have spent itself thus, since subsequently
Pericles was once again elected strategus. As an orator he was remark-
able for the persuasive power and incisiveness of his speech. Cf. Eupolis
(frag. 94 Kock)

> πειθώ τις ἐπεκάθιζεν ἐπὶ τοῖς χείλεσιν·
> οὕτως ἐκήλει καὶ μόνος τῶν ῥητόρων
> τὸ κέντρον ἐγκατέλειπε τοῖς ἀκροωμένοις.

22. τί ὑμῖν χαρίσωμαι; 'how shall I do your pleasure?'

**προπέποται τῆς παραυτίχ᾽ ἡδονῆς καὶ χάριτος τὰ τῆς πόλεως
πράγματα,** 'the city's interests have been sacrificed for the pleasure
and gratification of the moment.' The metaphor, from drinking a toast
accompanied by a gift of the drinking vessel, is a strong one. Cf. *de
Cor.* 296 ἄνθρωποι μιαροὶ καὶ κόλακες καὶ ἀλάστορες...τὴν ἐλευθερίαν
προπεπωκότες πρότερον μὲν Φιλίππῳ, νῦν δ᾽ Ἀλεξάνδρῳ. χάριτος is gen.
of price.

τὰ μὲν τούτων πάντα καλῶς ἔχει, τὰ δ' ὑμέτερ' αἰσχρῶς, 'their
affairs are all prosperous, while yours are a disgrace.' τούτων = τῶν
διερωτώντων ὑμᾶς ῥητόρων. Cf. *infr.* 29 ἀποβλέψατε δὴ πρὸς τοὺς ταῦτα
πολιτευομένους κ.τ.λ.

23. ἅ τις ἂν κεφάλαι' εἰπεῖν...τῶν ἐφ' ὑμῶν. The genitive τῶν
ἔργων depends upon κεφάλαια. 'What one might say in summary of
the deeds of the days of your ancestors and the deeds of your own
time.' For a similar contrast of the present with the past cf. Aeschines,
contra Ctesiphontem 178 ff.

οὐ γὰρ ἀλλοτρίοις ὑμῖν χρωμένοις παραδείγμασιν. ὑμῖν depends
upon ἔξεστιν, ἀλλοτρίοις παραδείγμασιν upon χρωμένοις.

24. οἷς οὐκ ἐχαρίζονθ' οἱ λέγοντες οὐδ' ἐφίλουν αὐτούς. Cf.
ii. 4 καὶ μεγάλ'...φαίνοιτ' ἂν ὀνείδη n.

πέντε μὲν καὶ τετταράκοντ' ἔτη τῶν Ἑλλήνων ἦρξαν ἑκόντων.
The period to which reference is made is that extending from the defeat
of the Persian invasion and the foundation of the Delian League to the
beginning of the Peloponnesian War, i.e. from 476 B.C. to 432 B.C.
Observe the emphasis thrown by its position upon ἑκόντων. It is an
exaggeration to say that Athenian rule was readily suffered by the
Greeks. Among the allies of Athens rebellion was not uncommon, for
Naxos revolted in 466 B.C., Thasos a year later, Euboea in 446 B.C.,
Samos in 440 B.C., and Poteidaea in 432 B.C.

πλείω δ' ἢ μύρια τάλαντ' εἰς τὴν ἀκρόπολιν ἀνήγαγον. The
sacred treasure of Athens, with the exception of that belonging to the
two goddesses of Eleusis, Demeter and Persephone, was stored in the
Opisthodomus, an apartment at the back of the Parthenon on the Acropolis. According to Thucydides ii. 13 the treasure in the Acropolis
reached at its highest point 9700 talents of coined silver. At the
beginning of the Peloponnesian War Pericles reckoned there were
6000 talents of coined silver as well as 500 talents of uncoined gold and
silver in private and public offerings, sacred vessels, and trophies of war.
In addition there were considerable sums of money in temples other
than the Parthenon, while the statue of Athene herself contained 40
talents weight of pure gold which was all removable.

ὑπήκουε δ' ὁ ταύτην τὴν χώραν ἔχων αὐτοῖς βασιλεύς. The king
of Macedonia (Perdiccas II) was at no time a subject of Athens. All

that can fairly be said is that Macedonia paid to Athens such respect as it was natural for a weak state to pay to a strong one.

βάρβαρον Ἕλλησι, sc. ὑπακούειν. For βάρβαρον cf. *supr.* 16 οὐ βάρβαρος; *n.* For the sentiment cf. Eurip. *Iphig. in Aul.* 1400 (quoted by Aristotle, *Politics*, i. 5) βαρβάρων δ᾽ Ἕλληνας ἄρχειν εἰκός.

πολλὰ δὲ καὶ καλά. So in Latin, multa *et* praeclara. Cf. i. 15 πολλὰ καὶ χαλεπά.

αὐτοὶ στρατευόμενοι. The pronoun strikes the familiar note. Cf. i. 24 στρατευομένους αὐτούς *n.*

μόνοι δ᾽ ἀνθρώπων...κατέλιπον. The genitive τῶν φθονούντων depends upon κρείττω (genitive of comparison). ' And alone among men have left behind them a reputation for achievement too mighty for (i.e. beyond the reach of) envy.'

25. The passage 25—31 should be compared with the similar passage in the speech *Against Aristocrates* 207—10 (Introd. p. xx).

ἐπὶ μὲν δὴ τῶν Ἑλληνικῶν ἦσαν τοιοῦτοι. The particles μὲν δή are regularly used to dismiss a topic. Cf. ii. 8, iii. 6. τοιοῦτοι refers, as it usually does, to the *preceding* description (§ 24).

ἱερῶν καὶ τῶν ἐν τούτοις ἀναθημάτων. ' In temples and the offerings in them,' the genitive describing the objects in which οἰκοδομήματα καὶ κάλλη consist. For the policy of Pericles in regard to art cf. *supr.* 21.

σφόδρ᾽ ἐν τῷ τῆς πολιτείας ἤθει μένοντες, ' steadfastly adherent to the spirit of the constitution.'

26. Ἀριστείδου. Cf. *supr.* 21 *n.*

Μιλτιάδου. By birth an Athenian, Miltiades became a tyrant in the Thracian Chersonese. He took part in the Ionian revolt in 500 B.C. and drove out the Persian garrison from the islands of Lemnos and Imbros. Subsequently, however, when the Persians re-established their power, he was compelled to fly from his kingdom to Athens. Elected strategus in 490 B.C. he was chiefly responsible for the offensive action taken by the Athenians against the Persians at Marathon, which resulted in the defeat of the invaders. In the following year he led an expedition against the island of Paros, but returned without success. He was put upon his trial and fined fifty talents, but before he could discharge the debt died from a wound received during his Parian campaign. The money was afterwards paid by his son Cimon.

εἴ τις ἄρ' οἶδεν ὑμῶν. ἄρα points to the unlikelihood of the supposition being true, and so emphasizes the inconspicuous character of these dwellings. 'If any among you happens to know.'

ἐπράττετ' αὐτοῖς. Observe the dative of the agent with the imperfect tense. The use of the dative is assisted here by the presence of the phrase εἰς περιουσίαν.

ἐκ δὲ τοῦ τὰ μὲν Ἑλληνικὰ πιστῶς...διοικεῖν, 'by dealing faithfully with the Greeks, piously with the Gods, and fairly with each other.'

27. τότε μὲν δή. Cf. supr. 25 ἐπὶ μὲν δὴ τῶν Ἑλληνικῶν ἦσαν τοιοῦτοι n.

χρωμένοις οἷς εἶπον προστάταις. The relative pronoun is attracted into the case of the antecedent (προστάταις) which is itself inserted (without article) in the relative clause. Cf. infra ὅσης ἅπαντες ὁρᾶτ' ἐρημίας ἐπειλημμένοι.

ὑπὸ τῶν χρηστῶν τῶν νῦν. The adjective is of course, as it often is in the orators, ironical.

οἷς. Owing to an anacoluthon this pronoun is left without any construction. Cf. i. 24 εἰ μηδ' ἃ πάθοιτ' ἄν...οὐ τολμήσετε; n.

πόλλ' ἂν ἔχων εἰπεῖν, 'though I could say much,' sc. if I were desirous of doing so, as I am not. The particle ἂν belongs to ἔχων (imperfect participle), not to the infinitive.

ὅσης ἅπαντες ὁρᾶτ' ἐρημίας ἐπειλημμένοι. Cf. supr. χρωμένοις οἷς εἶπον προστάταις. Observe the gen. used after ἐπιλαμβάνεσθαι = 'to lay hold of.' ἐρημία = absence of competitors, a metaphor from the public games continued in τῶν πρωτείων, βραβεύειν, ἠσκήκαμεν.

28. χώρας οἰκείας, viz. such places as Amphipolis, Poteidaea and Methone.

εἰς οὐδὲν δέον, 'to no good purpose.'

οὓς δ' ἐν τῷ πολέμῳ συμμάχους ἐκτησάμεθα κ.τ.λ. The allusion is to the second Athenian Confederacy formed in 378 B.C. to carry on war against Sparta. This league eventually came to include about seventy cities which agreed to contribute both ships and money. Its affairs were conducted by a joint board which sat at Athens, but it never attained the organization and strength of the Confederacy of Delos in the fifth cent. B.C. In 357 B.C., in consequence of the violation by Athens of the constitution of the Confederacy, the leading states revolted, and after hostilities extending over a period of two years the league broke up, Athens retaining as subjects, and not as allies, the island of Samos and certain cities on the coast of Macedonia and Thrace (e.g. Poteidaea and Methone) of which she had gained possession. At the time of this outbreak Athens was at peace with Thebes and Sparta.

οὗτοι. The political opponents of Demosthenes, Eubulus and his supporters.

παρελθών. Cf. ii. 8.

29. ἀλλ', ὥταν κ.τ.λ. A supposed objection to the depreciatory account of the results of Athens' present policy. Cf. i. 26 ἀλλ' ὥταν, οὐχὶ βουλήσεται.

καὶ τί ἂν εἰπεῖν τις ἔχοι; καί preceding an interrogative pronoun imparts to the question a contemptuous incredulity. 'Why, what could one mention?'

τὰς ἐπάλξεις ἃς κονιῶμεν κ.τ.λ. The policy of Eubulus and his party was, in Demosthenes' view, directed towards domestic improvements—the whitening of battlements, repair of roads, improvement of water supply—and not towards aggrandisement abroad. Precisely what was done with the springs is not made clear; perhaps measures were taken to prevent the possibility of pollution and pipes provided for the water, as was done by the Pisistratids in the case of the famous spring Callirrhoe (Thuc. ii. 15).

λήρους, 'tomfoolery,' 'nonsense.' Demosthenes thus summarizes the matters with which his opponents concerned themselves. Cf. Alexis (Kock 261), παροψίδες καὶ λῆρος.

ἀποβλέψατε δή. The particle increases the urgency of the imperative. 'Look, I beg you.'

ἐκ πτωχῶν πλούσιοι, 'rich men instead of beggars.' Cf. Soph. *Oed. Tyr.* 454 τυφλὸς ἐκ δεδορκότος, Xen. *Cyr.* iii. 1. 17 ἐξ ἄφρονος σώφρων γεγένηται. Politicians have always been subject to such charges. Cf. Boswell, *Life of Johnson* : 'Politicks (said he) are now nothing more than means of rising in the world. With this sole view do men engage in politicks, and their whole conduct proceeds upon it.'

σεμνοτέρας. Predicative, 'more magnificent,' 'grander.' Cf. *supr.* 26 σεμνοτέραν.

ὅσῳ δὲ τὰ τῆς πόλεως ἐλάττω γέγονεν, τοσούτῳ τὰ τούτων ηὔξηται. τοσούτῳ, dative of the amount of difference, is used with ηὔξηται, that verb implying a comparative (= μείζω γέγονεν). 'Their resources have increased in proportion as those of the city have decreased.'

30. τί δή ποθ' ἅπαντ' εἶχε καλῶς τότε, καὶ νῦν οὐκ ὀρθῶς; sc. ἔχει. Observe that the adverbs τότε and νῦν are in juxtaposition, while each occupies an emphatic placé in its clause, the whole sentence thus having a chiastic arrangement. Cf. the well-known instance of such an arrangement in Cic. *Phil.* ii. 37, 95 haec uiuus eripuit, reddit mortuus. For the force of ποτέ cf. i. 14 εἰς τί ποτ' ἐλπὶς ταῦτα τελευτῆσαι n.

πράττειν καὶ στρατεύεσθαι τολμῶν αὐτὸς ὁ δῆμος. Cf. *supr.* 24 αὐτοὶ στρατευόμενοι n.

ἀγαπητόν, 'sufficient,' 'enough.' Cf. *Phil.* iii. 74 ἀγαπητὸν γὰρ ἐὰν αὐτοὶ σώζωνται τούτων ἑκάστοις.

31. ἐκνενευρισμένοι, 'enervated,' 'emasculate,' lit. 'with *sinews* cut out.'

περιῃρημένοι χρήματα, 'stripped of money.' For the personal use of the passive of περιαιρῶ cf. *contra Aristogeit.* 5 τοὺς στεφάνους περιῄρηνται. The money, it appears, had gone into the pockets of the statesmen. Cf. *supr.* 29, *ad fin.*

συμμάχους. Cf. *supr.* 28 οὓς δ' ἐν τῷ πολέμῳ συμμάχους ἐκτησάμεθα, εἰρήνης οὔσης ἀπολωλέκασιν οὗτοι n.

ἐν ὑπηρέτου καὶ προσθήκης μέρει, 'in the position of a dependent and appendage.' Cf. ii. 18 ἐν οὐδενός...μέρει: and for προσθήκη ii. 14 ἐν μὲν προσθήκῃ μερίς ἐστί τις οὐ μικρά n.

ἐὰν μεταδιδῶσι θεωρικῶν ὑμῖν, 'if they distribute some festival money among you.' For θεωρικά cf. *supr.* iii. 11; i. 19, 20 n.

Βοηδρόμια πέμψωσιν, 'arrange a procession at the Boedromia,' a festival commemorating the aid rendered to Athens against the Amazons by Theseus (cf. βοηδρομεῖν = to haste to help). It is suggested that this festival is selected for insertion because it had recently been celebrated, possibly with the addition of a procession as a special feature, at the time when the speech was delivered.

καὶ τὸ πάντων ἀνδρειότατον, τῶν ὑμετέρων αὐτῶν χάριν προσοφείλετε, 'and, finest thing of all, you are actually grateful to them for what is your own.' τὸ πάντων ἀνδρειότατον is in apposition with the following clause τῶν ὑμετέρων...προσοφείλετε. Cf. ii. 1 καὶ τὸ μέγιστον ἁπάντων n. Mark the force of the preposition in the compound προσοφείλετε; not only do you accept just what they give you, but you add to (προς) your acceptance gratitude for what, after all, is not theirs but yours. Cf. *contra Aristocratem* 89 ὃς γάρ, ὡς ἀγαπώντων τοῦθ' ὑμῶν

καὶ προσοφειλόντων χάριν αὐτῷ, γέγραφεν καὶ πρὸς φυλάττειν ὑμᾶς ἐκεῖνον,
i. 19 προσδεῖ, 27 προσδεῖν.

οἱ δ' ἐν αὐτῇ τῇ πόλει καθείρξαντες…ποιοῦντες. Cf. ii. 30 ὑμῶν
αὐτῶν ἔτι καὶ νῦν γενομένους *n.* and Aeschines, *contra Ctesiphontem* 251.
So Plato (*Rep.* p. 493) pictures the Athenian populace as a great beast,
whose moods the sophists learn by experience and seek to gratify; and
Aristophanes in the *Wasps* represents the demagogues as cheating the
Athenians, doling out petty fees to them for service as dicasts, while
keeping the bulk of the revenue for their own enjoyment. Cf. in
particular ll. 698 ff.:

> σκέψαι τοίνυν ὡς ἐξόν σοι πλουτεῖν καὶ τοισίδ' ἅπασιν,
> ὑπὸ τῶν αἰεὶ δημιζόντων οὐκ οἶδ' ὅπη ἐγκεκύκλησαι·
> ὅστις πόλεων ἄρχων πλείστων ἀπὸ τοῦ Πόντου μέχρι Σαρδοῦς,
> οὐκ ἀπολαύεις πλὴν τοῦθ' ὃ φέρεις, ἀκαρῆ. καὶ τοῦτ' ἐρίῳ σοι
> ἐνστάζουσιν κατὰ μικρὸν ἀεὶ τοῦ ζῆν ἕνεχ' ὥσπερ ἔλαιον.
> βούλονται γάρ σε πένητ' εἶναι· καὶ τοῦθ' ὧν οὕνεκ' ἐρῶ σοι,
> ἵνα γιγνώσκῃς τὸν τιθασευτήν· κᾆθ' ὅταν οὗτός σ' ἐπισίξῃ
> ἐπὶ τῶν ἐχθρῶν τιν' ἐπιρρύξας, ἀγρίως αὐτοῖς ἐπιπηδᾷς.

32. ἔστι δ' οὐδέποτ'…πράττοντας. That character is the result
of habitual action is the doctrine of the philosophers. Cf. Plato, *Laws*,
729 Ε πᾶν ἦθος διὰ ἔθος, Aristot. *Ethics*, 1103 A, *ad fin.* οὕτω δὴ καὶ τὰ
μὲν δίκαια πράττοντες δίκαιοι γινόμεθα, τὰ δὲ σώφρονα σώφρονες, τὰ δ'
ἀνδρεῖα ἀνδρεῖοι.

ὁποῖ' ἄττα γάρ…ἔχειν, 'for whatsoever be the character of men's
practices, such must be the temper which they have also.' καὶ insists
on the parallel between τὰ ἐπιτηδεύματα and τὸ φρόνημα.

ταῦτα (with εἰπόντι) refers (as does αὐτὰ below) to the present
state of affairs at Athens as described in § 31. 'I should not be surprised if for having spoken of this state of affairs I were to be punished
more severely than those who have brought it about.'

καὶ νῦν, 'now.' Cf. *supr.* 18 καὶ νῦν *n.*

33. ἀλλὰ νῦν γ' ἔτ', 'yet even now,' 'still, late as it is.' The
phrase arises from an ellipse (e.g. εἰ μὴ πρότερον, ἀλλὰ νῦν γ' ἔτι). Cf.
Soph. *Antig.* 552 τί δῆτ' ἂν ἀλλὰ νῦν σ' ἔτ' ὠφελοῖμ' ἐγώ;

ἐθελήσητε. Cf. ii. 13; i. 6 *n.*

**ταῖς περιουσίαις ταῖς οἴκοι ταύταις ἀφορμαῖς ἐπὶ τὰ ἔξω τῶν ἀγαθῶν
χρήσησθε.** ἀφορμαῖς is predicative. 'To use these surpluses at home

as means to secure benefits abroad.' For ἀφορμή (='a beginning,' 'something to start with') cf. i. 23 τὸ γὰρ εὖ πράττειν παρὰ τὴν ἀξίαν ἀφορμὴ τοῦ κακῶς φρονεῖν τοῖς ἀνοήτοις γίγνεται.

τέλειόν τι καὶ μέγα...ἀγαθόν, 'a great and final good.' **ἀσθενοῦσι.** Cf. *infr.* 35 μηδὲν ποιοῦσι.

ἐκεῖν', sc. τὰ σιτία. Below ταῦτα=ταῦτα τὰ λήμματα. Observe that ταῦτα refers to that which is nearer *in thought,* i.e. the profits, whereas ἐκεῖνα refers to what is *logically* more remote, i.e. the diet prescribed by physicians, which is adduced only by way of illustration.

καὶ ταῦθ' ἃ νέμεσθε νῦν ὑμεῖς, '*so* these profits, which *you* now divide among yourselves.' For καί introducing a parallel cf. *supr.* 18 καὶ νῦν *n.* Mark the emphatic pronoun ὑμεῖς, which also directs attention to the parallel (*quasi,* you, *no less than the physicians,* are engaged in doling out what does no real good) and the voice of νέμεσθε.

ἔστι ταῦτα.. ἐπαυξάνοντα. The periphrasis is more insistent than ταῦτα ἐπαυξάνει. 'This it is that increases.'

34. **καὶ παραχρῆμά γε τὴν αὐτὴν σύνταξιν ἀπάντων,** sc. λέγω. καί...γε, an assent with an addition, cf. ii. 10 καὶ σφόδρα γ' ἤνθησεν. Hence it is common in conversations, e.g. Aristoph. *Acharn.* 911—4:

>   ΝΙΚ.   ἐγὼ τοίνυν ὁδὶ
>   φαίνω πολέμια ταῦτα. ΒΟΙ. τί δὲ κακὸν παθὼν
>   ὀρναπετίοισι πόλεμον ἦρα καὶ μάχαν;
> ΝΙΚ. καὶ σέ γε φανῶ πρὸς τοῖσδε.

'Yes, and therewith (I propose) the same system for everything.' For σύνταξιν cf. i. 20 ἐγὼ μὲν γὰρ ἡγοῦμαι στρατιώτας δεῖν κατασκευασθῆναι καὶ ταῦτ' εἶναι στρατιωτικὰ καὶ μίαν σύνταξιν εἶναι τὴν αὐτὴν τοῦ τε λαμβάνειν καὶ τοῦ ποιεῖν τὰ δέοντα, a passage which makes plain the meaning of Demosthenes here, *viz.* that a man should appear in the list of those receiving state pay *only if* he appeared in the list of those doing service to the state as soldiers, jurymen, or in other capacities. Cf. *infr.* 35 εἰς τάξιν ἤγαγον τὴν πόλιν τὴν αὐτὴν τοῦ λαβεῖν, τοῦ στρατεύεσθαι, τοῦ δικάζειν, τοῦ ποιεῖν τοῦθ' ὅ τι καθ' ἡλικίαν ἕκαστος ἔχοι καὶ ὅτου καιρὸς εἴη.

τὸ μέρος, 'his due share,' 'his proportion.' Cf. *infr.* ἐν ἴσῃ τάξει.

ὅτου δέοιθ' ἡ πόλις. δέοιτο is optative mood in an indefinite relative clause in secondary sequence.

ὑπάρχοι. Observe the optative mood, the purpose being referred, not to the present time in which Demosthenes is making his proposal, but to the past time in which he formed the idea embodied in it. Cf. *contra Androt.* 11 τοῦτον ἔχει τὸν τρόπον ὁ νόμος...ἵνα μηδὲ πεισθῆναι μηδ' ἐξαπατηθῆναι γένοιτ' ἐπὶ τῷ δήμῳ (the final clause goes back to the intention of the law-makers when the law was framed in the past); *contra Timocrat.* 145 οὗτος γὰρ (sc. ὁ νόμος) οὐκ ἐπὶ τοῖς κεκριμένοις καὶ ἠγωνισμένοις κεῖται...ἵνα μὴ ..χεῖρον ἀναγκάζοιντ' ἀγωνίζεσθαι ἢ καὶ παντάπασιν ἀπαράσκευοι εἶεν, *ibid.* 147 ; Aristoph. *Frogs*, 23—4 τοῦτον δ' ὀχῶ | ἵνα μὴ ταλαιπωροῖτο μηδ' ἄχθος φέροι (the final clause refers to the intention when the rider was given his mount).

ἔξεστιν ἄγειν ἡσυχίαν. This (as συμβαίνει...νῦν and ἔστι τις...ἡμῶν), represents a hypothesis.

οἴκοι μένων βελτίων κ.τ.λ. With βελτίων sc. ἐστί. The personal construction is preferred. Cf. Soph. *Ajax*, 635 κρείσσων γὰρ "Αιδα κεύθων ἢ νοσῶν μάταν. The force of the sentence falls upon τοῦ... ἀπηλλαγμένος. 'There is the advantage that while remaining at home he is free (sc. owing to the regular pay he would receive) from being forced through want to do something degrading.' The practice of arts and handicrafts was considered degrading to the free-born Greek.

συμβαίνει τι τοιοῦτον οἷον καὶ τὰ νῦν. 'There comes to pass some such situation as exists, for example, to-day.' For the force of καί with the adverb cf. *supr.* 32 ὅτι καὶ νῦν γέγονε *n.* For the addition of the article to νῦν cf. i. 12 τὸ κατ' ἀρχάς *n.*

στρατιώτης αὐτὸς ὑπάρχων, sc. βελτίων ἐστί. 'There is the advantage that he serves in the field *in person.*' The emphasis is on the pronoun. Cf. i. 6 αὐτοὺς ἐξιόντας *n.*

ἔξω τῆς ἡλικίας, 'outside the age,' *viz.* for military service. Cf. *Phil.* i. 7 ἂν τοίνυν...ἕκαστος ὑμῶν...ἕτοιμος πράττειν ὑπάρξῃ, ὁ μὲν χρήματ' ἔχων εἰσφέρειν, ὁ δ' ἐν ἡλικίᾳ στρατεύεσθαι, Thuc. viii. 75 συνώμνυσαν δὲ καὶ Σαμίων πάντες τὸν αὐτὸν ὅρκον οἱ ἐν ἡλικίᾳ, i. 28 τοὺς δ' ἐν ἡλικίᾳ. The age for military service abroad was from 20 to 60; from 18 to 20 young men served as patrols (περίπολοι) in Attica. But the age might be limited for a particular expedition, as e.g. *supr.* 4 we find service demanded only from men up to 45 years of age (τοὺς μέχρι πέντε καὶ τετταράκοντ' ἐτῶν αὐτοὺς ἐμβαίνειν).

ἀτάκτως, 'under no system' > < ἐν ἴσῃ τάξει, 'under an equitable system.'

35. ὅλως, 'in a word,' 'altogether,' summarizing the effect of the proposals. Cf. ii. 7 ὅλως *n.*

οὔτ' ἀφελὼν οὔτε προσθεὶς πλὴν μικρῶν, 'without subtraction or addition, save of what is inconsiderable.' Demosthenes means that practically his proposal neither decreases the sum distributed among citizens nor requires a larger amount than that already available. μικρῶν is the corrected reading of the Paris MS. S; the first hand in that MS. wrote μικρόν. Others adopt the reading μικρῷ (preserved by the critic Dionysius of Halicarnassus) or μικρόν ('to a slight extent'), and connect the words with those which follow, viz. τὴν ἀταξίαν ἀνελών. But τὴν ἀταξίαν ἀνελὼν seems to anticipate from a negative point of view what is stated positively in εἰς τάξιν ἤγαγον, and the balance between the two would be destroyed by joining πλὴν μικρῷ with the participial phrase.

τάξιν...τὴν αὐτὴν τοῦ λαβεῖν, τοῦ στρατεύεσθαι κ.τ.λ. Cf. supr. 34 καὶ παραχρῆμά γε τὴν αὐτὴν σύνταξιν ἁπάντων n.

ὅ τι καθ' ἡλικίαν ἕκαστος ἔχοι καὶ ὅτου καιρὸς εἴη. Cf. supr. 34 ἵνα...ἕκαστος..., ὅτου δέοιθ' ἡ πόλις, τοῦθ' ὑπάρχοι, and n. on the optative δέοιτο. Each, by Demosthenes' arrangement, is to render in return for public money received such service as his years allow (καθ' ἡλικίαν). If he is too old for military service (cf. ἔξω τῆς ἡλικίας, 34), he must do duty as a juror, or in some other capacity for which his years fit him and there is occasion.

μηδὲν...ποιοῦσι. For the negative cf. i. 11 οἱ μὴ χρησάμενοι n. For the use of the participle unaccompanied by the article cf. ii. 4 βουλομένοις ὀρθῶς δοκιμάζειν, supr. 33 ἀσθενοῦσι. The negative gains in force by its separation from the participle.

ἐγώ. The pronoun is emphatic, 'I have never proposed,' etc.

ὅ τι δ' οἱ τοῦ δεῖνος νικῶσιν ξένοι κ.τ.λ., 'be told what victories so-and-so's mercenaries have won.' For ὁ δεῖνα used to replace any particular name which the speaker is unwilling or unable to specify (='so-and-so,' 'somebody-or-other') cf. ii. 31 μὴ ἄν ὁ δεῖν' ἤ ὁ δεῖν' εἴπῃ = 'not whatsoever so-and-so or so-and-so has proposed.' For the appetite of the Athenians for news cf. Phil. i. 10 ἤ βούλεσθ', εἰπέ μοι, περιιόντες αὐτῶν πυνθάνεσθαι, λέγεταί τι καινόν; ib. 48; Ol. ii. 23 ἡμῶν μελλόντων καὶ ψηφιζομένων καὶ πυνθανομένων περιγίγνεται, and the pseudo-Demosthenic περὶ συντάξεως, 3 ἐγὼ δέ φημι δεῖν...παρασχεῖν ἕκαστον αὐτὸν μὴ μόνον ταῦτ' ἀκούειν ἐθέλοντα ἀλλὰ καὶ πράττειν βουλόμενον, ἵν', ὦ ἄνδρες Ἀθηναῖοι, τῶν ἀγαθῶν τὰς ἐλπίδας δι' ὑμῶν αὐτῶν ἔχητε καὶ μὴ τὸν δεῖνα μηδὲ τὸν δεῖνα πυνθάνησθε τί πράττει. This failing was characteristic of them alike in the fifth century B.C. (Thuc. iii. 38 (Cleon is speaking to the Athenians) οἵτινες εἰώθατε θεαταὶ μὲν τῶν λόγων γίγνεσθαι, ἀκροαταὶ δὲ τῶν ἔργων) and when St Paul visited Athens (Acts of Apostles, c. xvii. *v.* 21).

36. **τὸν ποιοῦντά τι τῶν δεόντων ὑπὲρ ὑμῶν,** i.e. the leader of mercenaries, perhaps Charidemus (iii. 5).

ὑμᾶς ὑπὲρ ὑμῶν αὐτῶν. Cf. i. 8 *ἡμεῖς ὑπὲρ ἡμῶν αὐτῶν.*

μὴ παραχωρεῖν...κατέλιπον, 'not to fall back, men of Athens, from the distinguished position which your ancestors won amid many glorious dangers and bequeathed to you.' *τῆς ἀρετῆς* is a descriptive genitive qualifying the relative *ἥν.* Its attachment to the relative pronoun, rather than to its antecedent, *τῆς τάξεως,* to which it naturally belongs, is due to a desire to avoid the awkward collocation of the double genitive. For the copula in *πολλῶν καὶ καλῶν* cf. *supr.* i. 15 *πολλὰ καὶ χαλεπά.*

σχεδὸν εἴρηχ'. The adverb modifies the positiveness of the assertion. 'I think I have stated what I believe to be of advantage.'

ὑμεῖς δ' ἕλοισθ' ὅ τι καὶ τῇ πόλει καὶ ἅπασι συνοίσειν ὑμῖν μέλλει. The indicative *μέλλει* imparts a more confident tone than the corresponding optative *μέλλοι* would do. For the happy augury of the concluding words cf. i. 28, *ad fin.*; ii. 31 *βέλτιον τῶν ὅλων πραγμάτων ὑμῖν ἐχόντων n.*; *Phil.* i. 51 *νικῴη δ' ὅτι πᾶσιν μέλλει συνοίσειν, Phil.* iii. 76 *ὅτι δ' ὑμῖν δόξει, τοῦτ', ὦ πάντες θεοί, συνενέγκοι.*

APPENDIX A

ON THE ORDER OF THE OLYNTHIAC SPEECHES

THE Olynthiac orations are printed in this edition in the order in which they have been handed down by the MSS. tradition. Dionysius of Halicarnassus (*circ.* 20 B.C.) placed them in a different order, regarding *Ol.* ii. as the first in order of delivery and *Ol.* i. as the last, the chronological sequence thus being (*a*) *Ol.* ii., (*b*) *Ol.* iii., (*c*) *Ol.* i.[1]. His view has been supported by some modern scholars, while others, notably the historian Grote, have followed him in believing *Ol.* ii. to be prior to *Ol.* i., but consider that *Ol.* i. preceded *Ol.* iii., the sequence in their opinion being (*a*) *Ol.* ii., (*b*) *Ol.* i., (*c*) *Ol.* iii. It is generally admitted that *conclusive* evidence in favour of any particular order has not been adduced.

In favour of regarding *Ol.* ii. as prior to *Ol.* i. it is argued that *Ol.* ii. contains no exposition of any urgent need of assistance in which Olynthus stands. Such assistance is indeed mentioned in § 11[2], but the body of the speech is devoted to the exhibition of Philip's weak points and the encouragement of the Athenians to prosecute the war against him with vigour. Olynthus is, for the orator, not so much an obstacle to Macedonian aggression which must at all costs be preserved, as a serviceable instrument for assisting the active operations of Athens against Philip, whose friendship the Olynthians have but lately come to mistrust[3]. In *Ol.* i., on the other hand, the tone is defensive rather than offensive ; it insists upon the danger which threatens Olynthus and the

---

[1] Dion. Hal. *Ad Ammaeum*, i. c. 4, p. 726 R.

[2] φημὶ δὴ δεῖν ἡμᾶς τοῖς μὲν Ὀλυνθίοις βοηθεῖν.

[3] *Ol.* ii. § 1 τὸ γὰρ τοὺς πολεμήσοντας Φιλίππῳ γεγενῆσθαι, καὶ χώραν ὅμορον καὶ δύναμίν τινα κεκτημένους, καὶ τὸ μέγιστον ἁπάντων, τὴν ὑπὲρ τοῦ πολέμου γνώμην τοιαύτην ἔχοντας, ὥστε τὰς πρὸς ἐκεῖνον διαλλαγὰς πρῶτον μὲν ἀπίστους, εἶτα τῆς ἑαυτῶν πατρίδος νομίζειν ἀνάστασιν, δαιμονίᾳ τινὶ καὶ θείᾳ παντάπασιν ἔοικεν εὐεργεσίᾳ.

peril in which that city's destruction will involve Athens. Hence it is concluded that *Ol.* i. was delivered at a later date than *Ol.* ii., when the situation had developed and confidence had been replaced by alarm. Had *Ol.* ii. followed in order of time upon *Ol.* i. it would have been, it is maintained, of the nature of an anti-climax[1].

To this argument, based upon the general tone of the two speeches, are added others of a more specific character. Thus it is pointed out that *Ol.* ii. makes no mention of the Theoric Fund which figures prominently in *Ol.* i. (§§ 19–20); and it is thence inferred that *Ol.* i. marks a later stage in events than *Ol.* ii., since the proposal to utilise Theoric monies for warlike purposes indicates both an advance in confidence on the part of the orator and an increased urgency in the political situation, or at least one of these. Again in *Ol.* ii. § 11 Demosthenes states that the Thessalians have passed a resolution ' to lodge a protest about Magnesia,' while in *Ol.* i. § 22 he tells us that they 'have prevented Philip from fortifying Magnesia '—the result, it is suggested, of the ' protest' mentioned in *Ol.* ii. which would thus appear to be the earlier speech.

It is important to remember that events do not always proceed, uniformly and without interruption, in one direction. In the present state of our knowledge it seems impossible to assert positively that the danger threatening Olynthus became consistently and continually more pressing; and that therefore the necessity of sending help from Athens would naturally figure more largely in a later than in an earlier speech. Apart from this consideration however, it must be borne in mind that the details of the debate in which Demosthenes delivered *Ol.* ii. are unknown to us. Previous speakers may have dealt adequately with the urgent necessity of despatching help to Olynthus. To describe *Ol.* ii., if delivered after *Ol.* i., as an 'anti-climax' merely implies a comparison of the two orations in which no account is taken of the context of their pronouncement.

On the whole it seems probable that at the time when *Ol.* ii. was spoken the peril of Olynthus had become more grave; that there was a general agreement that aid should be sent thither forthwith[2]; and that in consequence of Philip's successes a spirit of dejection had overtaken the Athenians. To dispel that dejection was now Demosthenes'

---

[1] Cf. Thirlwall, *Hist. of Greece*, Vol. v. App. iii.

[2] Cf. Demosthenes' remark in § 11 ὅπως τις λέγει κάλλιστα καὶ τάχιστα, οὕτως ἀρέσκει μοι (sc. βοηθεῖν).

first object, and the bold and cheerful tone of the speech was well calculated to attain that end[1]. The view of Grote[2]—that 'to combat the fear of Philip...he would repeat anew and more impressively than before the danger of Olynthus and the danger to Athens herself if she suffered Olynthus to fall'—seems, at least, an improbable one. Nor was it likely that, at such a moment and with such a purpose in view, he would dwell on the necessity of laying hands on that Theoric Fund so highly prized by the Athenian populace. His reference to the Thessalians having prevented Philip from fortifying Magnesia in *Ol.* i. may well be regarded as a rhetorical overstatement of what in *Ol.* ii. he more truly describes—in view, perhaps, of later and fuller knowledge now in possession of his audience—as the entering of a protest.

The argument of an increased gravity in tone is also employed to establish the posteriority in time of *Ol.* i. to *Ol.* iii. Apart from the general objection to such an argument—indicated above in the discussion of the relation of *Ol.* i. to *Ol.* ii.—the passages cited to show that in *Ol.* i. affairs have reached a more critical stage than in *Ol.* iii. are, at best, not very convincing[3]. Thus *Ol.* iii. § 3 (ὁ μὲν οὖν παρὼν καιρός, εἴπερ ποτέ, πολλῆς φροντίδος καὶ βουλῆς δεῖται) is regarded as less urgent than *Ol.* i. § 2 (ὁ μὲν οὖν παρὼν καιρός, ὦ ἄνδρες Ἀθηναῖοι, μόνον οὐχὶ λέγει φωνὴν ἀφιεὶς ὅτι τῶν πραγμάτων ὑμῖν ἐκείνων αὐτοῖς ἀντιληπτέον ἐστίν, εἴπερ ὑπὲρ σωτηρίας αὐτῶν φροντίζετε); while the menace to Attica is said to be less forcibly set forth in *Ol.* iii. § 8 (χωρὶς γὰρ τῆς περιστάσης ἂν ἡμᾶς αἰσχύνης, εἰ καθυφείμεθά τι τῶν πραγμάτων, οὐδὲ τὸν φόβον, ὦ ἄνδρες Ἀθηναῖοι, μικρὸν ὁρῶ τὸν τῶν μετὰ ταῦτα κ.τ.λ.) than in the parallel passage *Ol.* i. §§ 25-7.

On the other hand the tone in which Demosthenes speaks of the Theoric Fund in *Ol.* iii. §§ 34-5, as compared with his hesitating reference in *Ol.* i. §§ 19-20, is held by some to be in itself sufficient evidence for regarding *Ol.* iii. as subsequent in time to *Ol.* i.[4]. Yet this argument

---

[1] Demosthenes, indeed, explicitly says that he does not consider it the time to dwell on past failures. Cf. § 4 ὧν οὖν ἐκεῖνος μὲν ὀφείλει τοῖς ὑπὲρ αὐτοῦ πεπολιτευμένοις χάριν, ὑμῖν δὲ δίκην προσήκει λαβεῖν, οὐχὶ νῦν ὁρῶ τὸν καιρὸν τοῦ λέγειν.

[2] *History of Greece*, c. LXXXVIII. Appendix.

[3] Cf. Thirlwall, *loc. cit.*

[4] Butcher, *Demosthenes*, p. 64, speaks of it as 'almost decisive'; Sandys, *First Philippic and Olynthiacs*, p. lxvi, calls it '*at any rate conclusive.*'

cannot be considered conclusive. On the assumption that *Ol.* i. is later than *Ol.* iii. the diffident tone of *Ol.* i. §§ 19–20 might be explained as due to the opposition and threats, possibly acts, of reprisal which the proposal outlined in *Ol.* iii. §§ 34–5 had provoked.

Thus a consideration of the arguments advanced leads merely to the negative conclusion that no satisfactory reason has yet been put forward for disturbing the traditional order of the orations. At the same time the enquiry may well serve to exhibit the danger of considering the speeches as abstract documents, a series of essays upon Olynthus and its peril, and of taking too little into account the varying circumstances under which they were severally conceived and delivered.

I append some remarks kindly sent to me by my friend and colleague Mr M. O. B. Caspari.

'There are one or two passages which might serve to construct a Time-Table. In i. § 2 the mention of an embassy to Olynthus suggests that Athens was not yet known to have thrown in her lot with Olynthus ; an embassy subsequent to the completion of a treaty seems out of place. This would indicate that *Ol.* i. would belong to the opening stages of the war.

Ol. ii. § 24 (ὀκνεῖτ' ἐξιέναι καὶ μέλλετ' εἰσφερειν) and § 27 (μηδέν' αἰτιᾶσθαι πρὶν ἂν τῶν πραγμάτων κρατήσητε) seem to me inexplicable except as a criticism of *current* events. Demosthenes would hardly have been tactless enough to rake up the *past* failures of Athens; he must be referring to failures *during the Olynthian war.* In this case *Ol.* ii. cannot have been delivered till the war was in progress.

Ol. iii. § 33 (ἐὰν οὖν ἀλλὰ νῦν γ' ἔτι...ἐθελήσητε στρατεύεσθαι) surely means that the siege of Olynthus was drawing to a close.'

APPENDIX B

ON THE THEORIC FUND

THE distribution of money at festivals among the populace existed at Athens in the 5th cent. B.C. Pericles, we are told, sought thus to secure the support of the people, when he found himself outbidden for popularity by the lavish generosity of Cimon, against which his own comparative poverty was powerless to contend[1]. In the middle of the 4th cent. B.C. the money disbursed in this manner at festivals amounted annually to a considerable sum. The statement of Libanius (*circ.* 360 A.D.) that the Athenians 'simply divided among themselves the whole of the public funds[2]' is demonstrably exaggerated. We may also admit that Demosthenes in his zeal for reform was hardly likely to underestimate the total involved in these distributions. But his references to the Theoric Fund in the Olynthiac speeches[3] must have sounded absurd to his audience, unless the sum comprised in it had been far from a trifling or negligible one. And even Demosthenes' detractors would agree that he was much too clever to expose himself unnecessarily to refutation and ridicule.

The Theoric Fund consisted of the surplus remaining after the expenses of administration had been deducted from the revenue[4]. It was under the control of elected officials[5]. Aeschines asserts that owing to the confidence inspired in the Athenians by Eubulus certain offices in connection with the receipt and expenditure of the revenue were handed over to the Theoric officials, who had in their hands 'practically the entire administration of the city[6].' In the portion of his speech in which this passage occurs it is to Aeschines' advantage to represent the powers possessed by the Theoric officials as of a very far-reaching character. There may therefore well be some exaggeration in his statement[7].

---

[1] Plut. *Vit. Per.* ix. ἄλλοι δὲ πολλοὶ πρῶτον ὑπ' ἐκείνου (sc. τοῦ Περικλέους) φασὶ τὸν δῆμον ἐπὶ κληρουχίας καὶ θεωρικὰ καὶ μισθῶν διανομὰς προαχθῆναι......καὶ ταχὺ θεωρικοῖς καὶ δικαστικοῖς λήμμασιν (cf. λημμάτων, *Ol.* iii. §§ 33–4) ἄλλαις τε μισθοφοραῖς καὶ χορηγίαις συνδεκάσας τὸ πλῆθος κ.τ.λ.

[2] *Arg. ad Dem. Ol.* i. ἁπλῶς πάντα τὰ δημόσια χρήματα διενέμοντο.

[3] Index A s.v. Theoric Fund; and especially *Ol.* i. § 19 ἔστιν, ὦ ἄνδρες Ἀθηναῖοι, χρήμαθ' ὑμῖν, ἔστιν ὅσ' οὐδενὶ τῶν ἄλλων ἀνθρώπων στρατιωτικά.

[4] <Dem.> *contra Neaeram* § 4 τὰ περιόντα χρήματα τῆς διοικήσεως. Cf. *Ol.* iii. § 33 ταῖς περιουσίαις ταῖς οἴκοι ταύταις.

[5] Aesch. *contra Ctesiphontem* § 25 οἱ ἐπὶ τὸ θεωρικὸν κεχειροτονημένοι.

[6] Aesch. *loc. cit.* σχεδὸν τὴν ὅλην διοίκησιν εἶχον τῆς πόλεως.

[7] The whole passage runs thus: πρότερον μὲν τοίνυν, ὦ Ἀθηναῖοι, ἀντιγραφεὺς ἦν χειροτονητὸς τῇ πόλει, ὃς καθ' ἑκάστην πρυτανείαν ἀπελογίζετο τὰς προσόδους τῷ δήμῳ· διὰ δὲ τὴν πρὸς Εὔβουλον γενομένην πίστιν ὑμῖν οἱ ἐπὶ τὸ θεωρικὸν κεχειροτονημένοι ἦρχον μὲν πρὶν ἢ τὸν Ἡγήμονος νόμον γενέσθαι τὴν τοῦ ἀντιγραφέως ἀρχήν, ἦρχον δὲ τὴν τῶν ἀποδεκτῶν, καὶ νεώριον καὶ σκευοθήκην ᾠκοδόμουν, ἦσαν δὲ καὶ ὁδοποιοί, καὶ σχεδὸν τὴν ὅλην διοίκησιν εἶχον τῆς πόλεως.

As the Theoric Fund consisted in a surplus of revenue over expenditure, it does not seem unfair to conclude that the controlling officials would endeavour to reduce as far as possible the expenses of administration. Those officials who left themselves with no surplus at all, or with only a small amount for distribution at the festivals, were hardly likely to be long in favour with the Athenian public. But there does not appear to be any evidence to show that the Theoric officials absolutely starved those departments which they had to administer in order to secure a surplus[1]. On the other hand they may naturally have shown a pronounced disinclination for such warlike operations as would by the expenditure involved, and possibly in other ways[2], drain the resources of the state and diminish the surplus, even supposing the surplus itself was not, and could not legally be, directly appropriated for such purposes.

It is, however, stated in the pseudo-Demosthenic speech *Against Neaera* that 'the laws directed that, whenever there was war, the surplus funds should be devoted to military purposes[3].' But nothing further is known of these 'laws.' We learn from the same speech that a certain Apollodorus, as a member of the Council, proposed to take a vote of the people on the question whether the surplus monies should be employed for war or for distribution at festivals[4]. The proposal was in due course brought as a bill before the Assembly, and Apollo-

---

[1] On the contrary that they carried out their duties seems to be suggested by the fact that, while Aeschines tells us they were ὁδοποιοί, Demosthenes himself, contemptuously it is true, refers to the repairing of roads (*Ol.* iii. § 29 τὰς ὁδοὺς ἃς ἐπισκευάζομεν). Mr M. O. B. Caspari has directed my attention to *C.I.A.* II. 38 με(ρ)ίσαι δὲ τὸ ἀργύριον (τ)ὸ εἰρημένον τοὺς ἀποδέκτας ἐκ τῶν καταβαλλομένων χρημά(τ)ων, ἐπειδὰν τὰ ἐκ τῶν νόμων μερ(ίσωσι). The last clause proves that some, at least, of the monies received by the Apodectai, whose functions, according to Aeschines, *loc. cit.*, were taken over by the Theoric Board, were appropriated by statute and not at the free disposal of the financial officials. *C.I.A.* II. 1156 points the same way. Mr Caspari thinks that 'the discretion of the Theoric Board could only be exercised within narrow limits.'

[2] E.g. by the interruption of commerce and reduction in harbour dues (τὰ ἐλλιμένια).

[3] < Dem. > *contra Neaeram* § 4 κελευόντων μὲν τῶν νόμων, ὅταν πόλεμος ᾖ, τὰ περιόντα χρήματα τῆς διοικήσεως στρατιωτικὰ εἶναι.

[4] *Ibidem*, ἐξήνεγκε προβούλευμα εἰς τὸν δῆμον, λέγον διαχειροτονῆσαι τὸν δῆμον, εἴτε δοκεῖ τὰ περιόντα χρήματα τῆς διοικήσεως στρατιωτικὰ εἶναι εἴτε θεωρικά.

dorus was indicted for having put forward an illegal measure, the illegality apparently consisting in the suggestion that Theoric monies might be used for other than Theoric purposes. Apollodorus was convicted[1]—a result which it is difficult to reconcile with the active existence of 'laws' explicitly prescribing the application, under certain circumstances, of the surplus funds to war. Hence it has been supposed that these 'laws' are simply a rhetorical figment, designed to suggest to the jury that Apollodorus was a much-injured person, who had been made to suffer for an action which was, in reality, strictly legal[2].

That any attempt to divert the monies of the Theoric Fund to purposes other than those for which the Fund existed was fraught with serious danger to its author is sufficiently established by Demosthenes' very definite refusal to make any such proposal[3]. Libanius indeed states that there was a law prescribing death as the penalty for any one who sought to turn the Theoric into a War Fund[4]. This statement appears to rest upon too literal an interpretation of some words of Demosthenes[5]. Certainly Stephanus, the prosecutor of Apollodorus, after securing a conviction did not ask for the penalty of death to be inflicted upon the defendant, but for a fine of 15 talents, an amount which the jury in their decision reduced to a single talent[6].

Thus the information which we possess about the Theoric Fund is neither abundant nor free from difficulty and obscurity; while the authorities from whom it is derived are either of late date and doubtful value, or are pursuing rather success in debate than the exposition of truth.

---

[1] < Dem. > *contra Neaeram* § 5.

[2] If such laws continued to be valid at the time of the trial it is possible that the issue turned upon the interpretation of the clause ὅταν πόλεμος ᾖ. In ancient, as in modern, times there were different views held as to what constituted a state of war. Cf. Dem. *de Cor.* § 71; *Phil.* iii. § 17 (quoted *Introd.* p. xxxii). Libanius (*vide infra n.* 4) evidently ascribed the system of using the surplus for military purposes to an earlier date (τὴν ἀρχαίαν τάξιν).

[3] *Ol.* i. § 19 τί οὖν; ἄν τις εἴποι, σὺ γράφεις ταῦτ' εἶναι στρατιωτικά; μὰ Δί' οὐκ ἔγωγε.

[4] *Arg. ad Dem. Ol.* i. νόμον ἔθεντο περὶ τῶν θεωρικῶν τούτων χρημάτων, θάνατον ἀπειλοῦντα τῷ γράψαντι μετατεθῆναί τε ταῦτ' εἰς τὴν ἀρχαίαν τάξιν καὶ γενέσθαι στρατιωτικά.

[5] *Ol.* iii. § 12 ἀπολέσθαι, § 13 εἰς πρόῦπτον κακὸν αὐτὸν ἐμβαλεῖν

[6] < Dem. > *contra Neaeram* § 6, § 8.

INDEX A

The Arabic Figures refer to the Sections.

Accusative absolute ii. 24; iii. 9, 18, 27
— agent after verbal adjective ii. 13
— anticipatory i. 21; iii. 17
— double after ποιεῖν i. 5
— internal i. 1; ii. 17; iii. 6, 22
— after intransitive verb iii. 7
— after passive verb with transitive force ii. 5
— after passive verb, retained from active iii. 31
— respect ii. 18
Action in relation to speech ii. 12; iii. 15
Adjective in neuter as predicate i. 5
— used predicatively i. 7, 11, 28; ii. 1, 5, 8, 13; iii. 8, 11
Adverbial phrase formed with preposition i. 1
Age for military service i. 28; iii. 34
Allies of Athens iii. 28, 31
Anacoluthon i. 24; iii. 27
Antecedent attracted into case of relative ii. 2
— in relative clause i. 13; iii. 27
Aorist gnomic i. 11, 15; ii. 9, 10, 21
Aorist ingressive i. 6, 7, 13; ii. 9, 13, 19; iii. 1, 33

Aorist after ἐλπίς i. 14
Apposition ii. 1; iii. 31
Article with pronominal force i. 27
— with adverb or adverbial phrase i. 12; ii. 6; iii. 34
— omitted with antecedent placed in rel. clause i. 13, iii. 27
Asking, construction with verbs of i. 22
Asyndeton ii. 16; iii. 7, 31
Athenians' appetite for news ii. 23; iii. 35
— dislike of unpleasant truths iii. 32
— preference of words to deeds ii. 12
— subservience to statesmen ii. 30; iii. 31
Athens, embellishment of iii. 25
— favour of gods towards i. 10; ii. 1 (cf. i. 1; ii. 2)
— supreme in Greece iii. 24
— treasure of iii. 24
Attica, effect of war upon i. 27

Bacon (quoted) *Introd.* p. xiii

Character the issue of actions iii. 32
Chiasmus iii. 30
Commerce, effect of war upon ii. 16, 28
Comparative, double iii. 12

Conclusion, happy omen of i. 28; ii. 31; iii. 36

Confederacy, Second Athenian iii. 28, 31

Dancing ii. 19

Dative of agent i. 17, 28; iii. 26
— of amount of difference ii. 3; iii. 29
— modal iii. 18
— of person interested ii. 8, 13, 17; iii. 27
— of person judging i. 27; ii. 20

Directness of style iii. 17

Faction ii. 29

Farmers, losses of, through war in Attica i. 27

Fortune, power of ii. 22

Future indicative in monitory hypothetical clause i. 12, 15, 18, 19, 22, 27; ii. 13, 20; iii. 6, 16

Future perfect i. 14; iii. 6

Genitive of comparison ii. 2; iii. 24
— of description iii. 36
— of divided whole i. 26, 27; ii. 2, 8; iii. 3
— of equivalence iii. 25
— objective ii. 30
— of possessor i. 10, 16; ii. 18, 20, 30; iii. 20, 21
— of price iii. 22
— after 'desire' ii. 15
— after ἐπιλαμβάνεσθαι iii. 27
— after 'fullness' iii. 19
— after knowledge ii. 18

Government by faction ii. 29

Harbours closed by war ii. 16

Homoioteleuton ii. 16

Iambic trimeter i. 5

Infinitive consecutive after οἷος ii. 19
— epexegetic i. 3, 22; ii. 12, 20, 22; iii. 1

Johnson, Dr Samuel (quoted) iii. 29 *n.*

Lacedaemonians, overthrow of iii. 27

Licentiousness of Philip's entourage ii. 18, 19

Litotes i. 9, 27; ii. 1, 3, 17, 20; iii. 1, 30

Lucian, passages parodied by i. 1; iii. 1

Mercenaries, Macedonian i. 22; ii. 17
— in Athenian service iii. 35

Military service ii. 31; iii. 11, 34

Moral tone of Demosthenes ii. 6, 9—10; iii. 32

Neuter in predicate i. 5

News, Athenian appetite for ii. 23; iii. 35

Olynthus, embassy to Athens from ii. 6

Opponents of Demosthenes iii. 27—9

Optative mood following verb in primary tense iii. 34

Organization proposed by Demosthenes i 20; iii. 34—5

Oxymoron ii. 6

Participial phrase, emphasis on ii. 25

Participle without article ii. 4; iii. 33, 35

Past and present, contrast of iii. 23 ff.

Paul, Saint, on the Athenians iii. 35 *n.*

Periphrasis iii. 33

Personification i. 2

Philip, illness of i. 13
— secret agreement with Athens ii. 6
— success due to Athenians i. 8—9; ii. 4; iii. 5, 14, 17
— supporters at Athens ii. 4, 6

Preposition, variation of iii. 1
Prepositional phrases, juxtaposition of iii. 12
Present tense, use of ii. 25

Rapidity of style i. 11; ii. 10; iii. 17
Relative, attraction of i. 1, 7, 15, 16, 28; ii. 19, 23; iii. 3, 27
— not repeated ii. 4; iii. 24
— clause with final force ii. 26
— introducing dependent question iii. 2, 6

Simile i. 11, 15; ii. 21; iii. 33
Speech in relation to action ii. 12; iii. 15

Temple, Dorothy (quoted), i. 5 n.
Tense, variation of ii. 26; iii. 5
Thebes, attitude of i. 26; iii. 8
— preoccupation of iii. 27
Theoric Fund i. 19, 20; iii. 11, 19, 31
Tradition, appeal to Athenian iii. 36

Voice, middle i. 4
— middle, in periphrasis iii. 3
— middle (future) in passive sense i. 22, 27; iii. 9
— passive, with dependent accusative ii. 5; iii. 31

War, Sacred i. 26; ii. 7; iii. 27
Words without deeds, characteristic of Athens ii. 12; iii. 14

INDEX B

ἀεί i. 14; ii. 7
αἱρεῖσθαι ἤ ii. 22
ἀκούω iii. 21
ἀλλὰ νῦν iii. 33
ἄλλος (repeated) i. 20
ἄλλως ii. 18
ἀλλ' ὅταν i. 26; iii. 29
ἁμαρτάνειν iii. 1
Ἀμφίπολις i. 12; ii. 6
Ἀμφιπολῖται i. 8
ἄν iii. 27
ἀνάστασις i. 5; ii. 1
ἀναχαιτίζειν ii. 9
ἄνθρωπος i. 3, 23; iii. 16
ἄξιον i. 21
ἀποβλέπειν iii. 1
ἀπόρρητον, τὸ θρυλούμενόν ποτ' ii. 6
ἀποτρίβεσθαι i. 11
Ἀριστείδης iii. 21, 26
Ἀρύββαν i. 13

ἀτακτεῖν iii. 11
ἀτάκτως iii. 34
ἀταξία iii. 35
αὐτός i. 2, 6, 9; ii. 2, 22, 25, 26, 27; iii. 4, 24, 30, 34, 35
ἀφορμή ii. 22; iii. 33
βαδίζειν i. 12, 25
βάρβαρος iii. 16, 24
Βοηδρόμια iii. 31
βοηδρομιῶν iii. 5

γάρ i. 11
γίγνεσθαι iii. 1

δανείζεσθαι i. 15
δεῖνα ii. 31; iii. 35
δείξειν ii. 20
δή ii. 17; iii. 29
Δημοσθένης iii. 21
δημόσιος ii. 19
διαλέγεσθαι ii. 6

εἰ i. 24
εἴπερ i. 2; ii. 13; iii. 19
εἰς i. 9
εἶτα indignantis i. 24; ii. 26
εἶτα > < πρῶτον μέν ii. 1
εἰσφέρειν i. 6, 20; ii. 13, 24, 27;
   iii. 4
ἐκ i. 1, 27; iii. 29
ἕκαστοι ii. 7, 8, 28
ἑκατομβαιῶν iii. 5
ἐκεῖθεν i. 15
ἐκεῖνα iii. 33
ἐκεῖνο ii. 24; iii. 3, 14
ἐκεῖνος ii. 19; iii. 21
ἐν iii. 10
ἐν...μέρει ii. 18; iii. 31
ἐξιέναι ii. 13, 24, 27, 31
ἑορταί i. 20
ἐπί iii. 2; 21
ἕτεροι i. 17; iii. 19
Εὐβοεῖς i. 8
εὐήθεια ii. 6
εὔθυνα i. 28
ἐφόδια iii. 20
ἐφορμεῖν iii. 7

ἤ ii. 22
ἤδη i. 2
ἥκειν i. 8
ἡλικία i. 28; iii. 34, 35
ἡμεῖς i. 8, 9
Ἡραῖον τεῖχος iii. 4

θαυματοποιοί ii. 19
θεοί i. 10; ii. 1
Θετταλία i. 12
Θετταλοί i. 21; ii. 7, 11, 14
Θηβαῖοι i. 26; iii. 8, 27
Θρᾴκη i. 13; iii. 4

Ἱέραξ i. 8
Ἰλλύριοι i. 13, 23

καθ' ἕκαστα i. 9
καθ' ἕκαστον i. 14
καθῆσθαι ii. 23, 24
καί (with interrogative) iii. 29
καί (pointing parallel) i. 2, 4, 11,
   22, 28; ii. 5, 8, 10; iii. 32, 33

καί...γε ii. 10; iii. 12, 34
καί...δέ iii. 15
καί...μήν ii. 9
καί ταῦτα i. 7
κακοδαιμονία ii. 20
Καλλίας ii. 19
καλῶς ποιοῦντες i. 28
κατὰ καιρόν i. 4
καταστρέφεσθαι i. 12; iii. 8
κενός iii. 5
κορδακισμός ii. 18
Κορίνθιοι iii. 20
κρίνειν ii. 25, 29
κωλύειν i. 12, 25

Λάμψακος ii. 28
λόγον δοῦναι ii. 29, 31

Μαγνησία i. 13, 22; ii. 7, 11
μαιμακτηριῶν iii. 4
Μακεδονία i. 9; iii. 24
μᾶλλον δέ i. 19; ii. 8, 22; iii. 14
Μεγαρεῖς iii. 20
Μεθώνη i. 9, 12
μέν ii. 14; iii. 8
μὲν δή ii. 8; iii. 6, 10, 25, 27
μὲν...μήν i. 16
μὲν οὖν i. 2, 16, 19; ii. 3, 5; iii. 3
μεταγειτνιῶν iii. 5
μή, μηδείς (generic) i. 11; ii. 15;
   iii. 19, 35
μή, μηδείς (with hypothetical participle) i. 21, 27
μή (with subj. in cautious assertion) i. 26
μηδέ i. 25
μή τί γε ii. 23
Μιλτιάδης iii. 26
μυστήρια iii. 5

Νικίας iii. 21
νομοθέται iii. 10
νοσεῖν ii. 14 n.

ξένοι i. 22; ii. 17; iii. 35

οἰκεία ἡ i. 18, 26
οἷος ii. 19
ὅλως i. 5; ii. 7, 14; iii. 35

ὅπως ii. 2; iii. 1, 2
ὁπωσδήποτε iii. 7
ὅσῳ...τοσούτῳ ii. 3; iii. 29
ὅτε i. 1
οὐ ii. 18, 24
οὐδέ i. 5, 6
οὐδὲ...γε iii. 14
οὐκέτι iii. 18
οὐκ οἶδ᾽ ὅντινα i. 2
οὐ μὴν ἀλλά i. 4; ii. 22
οὗτος iii. 33

Παγασαί i. 9, 13, 22; ii. 11
Παίονες i. 13, 23
παρακρούεσθαι ii. 5
παρεῖναι i. 8; ii. 8
παριέναι i. 8; ii. 8, 31; iii. 21, 28
παρρησία iii. 32
Περικλῆς iii. 21
πολιτεία i. 5; iii. 21
ποτέ i. 14; iii. 30
Ποτείδαια i. 9, 12; ii. 7, 14
πράγματα i. 20; (τὰ ὅλα π.) i. 3
πρίν iii. 12, 13
προαιρεῖσθαι ii. 15
προπίνειν iii. 22
πρός (in composition) i. 19, 27;
   iii. 31
προσάγεσθαι ii. 6
πρὸς αὑτούς i. 7
προσλαμβάνειν ii. 7
πρὸς χάριν iii. 3
πταίειν ii. 20
πταῖσμα ii. 9
Πύδνα i. 9, 12

Σίγειον ii. 28
στρατηγοί ii. 28

Στρατοκλῆς i. 8
συγκεκροτημένος ii. 17
σύμμαχοι iii. 28, 31
συμμορίαι ii. 29
συμπλέκεσθαι ii. 21
συναναλίσκειν i. 11
σύνταξις i. 20; iii. 34
σφόδρα ii. 6

τάξις iii. 34, 35
τὴν ἄλλως iii. 21
τὴν πρώτην iii. 2
τὴν ταχίστην i. 2
Τιμόθεος ii. 14
τις ii. 1, 14; iii. 7
τυραννίς i. 5
τύχη i. 1; ii. 2, 22

ὑμεῖς i. 19
ὑπέρ i. 5, 7, 16; ii. 3

φαίνεσθαι (with participle) i. 15;
   ii. 2, 13
φάσκειν ii. 6
Φεραί i. 13; (Royal House of)
   ii. 14
φημί iii. 19
φιλοτιμία ii. 3, 16, 18
Φωκεῖς i. 26; iii. 8
Φωκικός (ὁ Φ. πόλεμος) i. 26; ii.
   7; iii. 27

Χαρίδημος iii. 5
χρηστός iii. 27

ὡς (causal) i. 3, 28
ὡς (with participle) i. 21
ὥστε (with participle) iii. 1

For EU product safety concerns, contact us at Calle de José Abascal, 56–1°,
28003 Madrid, Spain or eugpsr@cambridge.org.

www.ingramcontent.com/pod-product-compliance
Ingram Content Group UK Ltd.
Pitfield, Milton Keynes, MK11 3LW, UK
UKHW020314140625
459647UK00018B/1870